Praise for *Ecumenical Ventures in Ethics:*

"Most responses to the moral encyclicals of John Paul II have been both superficial and combative. But what a breath of fresh air is this volume! Here the Pope
is treated to real *engagement,* as indeed is his wish. These essays, the largest share
by Lutherans, grapple seriously and carefully at a *foundational* level with the Pope's
two moral encyclicals. And rather than being combative, the essays are fair and
sympathetic without losing their critical edge. The Roman Catholic response to
the Protestant essays is similarly nondefensive and enlightening. A profound
tribute to the work of Pope John Paul II." —ROBERT BENNE
Roanoke College

"A collection of first-rate essays. . . . This exciting volume is a sign of renewed
conversation in ethics between Catholics and Protestants, and hopefully it is
also a harbinger of things to come." —L. GREGORY JONES
Duke Divinity School

"Hütter and Dieter have done the churches a great service by assembling some
of the best minds to explore the ecumenical significance of the moral encyclicals
of John Paul II. The areas of convergence between papal moral teaching and
Reformation ethics are continually reinforced, and any fundamental themes or
moral practices that still divide the churches are presented honestly and without
acrimony. A landmark achievement that opens up a fertile research program for
the future." —THOMAS R. KOPFENSTEINER
Fordham University

"A forceful and articulate contribution to a fascinating conversation that needs to
continue. In essays that both appreciate and critique the moral teaching of John
Paul II, the authors explore topics central to Roman Catholic and Protestant
ethics. Well written, substantive, and engaging, this volume uncovers some
surprising areas of consensus between Protestants and Roman Catholics in ethics,
but also underscores ongoing differences and disagreements. A challenging and
thoughtful book that could well serve as a primer on the questions and issues that
engage and perplex Christian ethicists today." —PAUL J. WADELL
Catholic Theological Union, Chicago

"The ecumenical discussion of ethics is a dialogue far too long deferred. These
essays have finally launched this important discussion at the level of depth and
seriousness it deserves. Indispensable for those concerned with ethics, ecumenism,
or simply the integrity of Christian witness in a time of moral confusion." —DAVID S. YEAGO
Lutheran Theological Southern Seminary

Ecumenical Ventures in Ethics

Protestants Engage Pope John Paul II's
Moral Encyclicals

A Project of the Institute for Ecumenical Research, Strasbourg

Edited by

Reinhard Hütter and Theodor Dieter

WILLIAM B. EERDMANS PUBLISHING COMPANY
GRAND RAPIDS, MICHIGAN / CAMBRIDGE, U.K.

© 1998 Wm. B. Eerdmans Publishing Co.
255 Jefferson Ave. S.E., Grand Rapids, Michigan 49503 /
P.O. Box 163, Cambridge CB3 9PU U.K.

Printed in the United States of America

03 02 01 00 99 98   7 6 5 4 3 2 1

Library of Congress Cataloging-in-Publication Data

Ecumenical ventures in ethics : Protestants engage Pope John Paul II's
  moral encyclicals / edited by Reinhard Hütter and Theodor Dieter.
      p.   cm.
    "A project of the Institute for Ecumenical Studies, Strasbourg."
    Includes index.
    ISBN 0-8028-4261-5 (pbk. : alk. paper)
    1. Catholic Church.   Pope (1978– : John Paul II).   Veritatis splendor.
  2. Catholic Church.   Pope (1978– : John Paul II).   Evangelium vitae.
  3. Christian ethics — Comparative studies.   I. Hütter, Reinhard, 1958–   .
  II. Dieter, Theodor.   III. Institute for Ecumenical Research.
  BJ1249.C19183E38   1998
  241'.04 — dc21   97-30623
                                                                   CIP

Contents

v

Foreword

IF THE ECUMENICAL goal we seek is a true life together in communion, in what sense and to what degree must the churches have a common vision of the moral life? This question lies at the heart of a project of the Institute for Ecumenical Research in Strasbourg on "Koinonia in the Life of Faith." As this project was first being thought through, the Roman Catholic Church released two papal encyclicals that received extensive attention, both within and beyond the Catholic Church: *Veritatis Splendor* ("The Splendor of Truth") and *Evangelium Vitae* ("The Gospel of Life"). These two texts reassert in an intellectually forceful fashion Roman Catholic views both on ethical method and on various concrete ethical questions. As such they are of importance not just to Catholics but to all ecumenically concerned Christians who seek both the greater visible unity of the church and also the critical discussion and mutual learning that such unity should bring. The volume here presented is offered as a contribution to the ecumenical pursuit of a common understanding of the Christian life.

In editing this book and organizing the consultation it is based upon, Professor Theo Dieter of the Strasbourg Institute worked closely with Professor Reinhard Hütter of the Lutheran School of Theology in Chicago (LSTC). LSTC provided important support for the consultation, offering us hospitality and facilities that were both pleasant and conducive to work. The consultation was also financially supported by a special grant from the Council on Ecumenical and International Relations of the Church of Norway. We thank both LSTC and the Norwegian Church for their generous support.

MICHAEL ROOT, *Director*
Institute for Ecumenical Research, Strasbourg, France

The Project

REINHARD HÜTTER

What This Project Is All About

The last forty years have been characterized by intensive dialogues between various Protestant churches and the Roman Catholic Church. In many respects they resulted in the overcoming of mutual misunderstandings, a deepening of each other's understanding, and a rapprochement in some significant areas of former doctrinal dispute.[1] In comparison questions of ethics have only on rare occasions received similar attention.[2] Yet differences in these matters can be equally serious hindrances for a rapprochement between the churches. Therefore getting to know the "other's" moral tradition and praxis — in this case Roman Catholicism's — is of equal significance.

1. Cf. as one impressive example all the volumes of the American Lutheran/ Roman Catholic Dialogue and the "Joint Declaration on the Doctrine of Justification," which is before the Vatican and the churches of the Lutheran World Federation for acceptance.

2. For three fine examples of this rare occasion of dialogue in moral matters between ecclesial traditions, see Oswald Bayer and Alan Suggate, eds., *Worship and Ethics: Lutherans and Anglicans in Dialogue* (Berlin/New York: Walter de Gruyter, 1996), Michael Cromartie, ed., *A Preserving Grace: Protestants, Catholics, and Natural Law* (Grand Rapids: Eerdmans, 1997), and Oswald Bayer et al., *Zwei Kirchen — eine Moral?* (Regensburg: Pustet, 1986). For two ethicists who have addressed this issue in an explicit way, see James F. Gustafson, *Protestant and Roman Catholic Ethics: Prospects for Rapprochement* (Chicago: University of Chicago Press, 1978), and Charles E. Curran, *The Church and Morality: An Ecumenical and Catholic Approach* (Minneapolis: Fortress, 1993). For a remarkable common effort of Protestant ethicists and Roman Catholic moral theologians in response to the challenges of the modern world, see Anselm

1

Pope John Paul II's most recent moral encyclicals *Veritatis Splendor* ("The Splendor of Truth") and *Evangelium Vitae* ("The Gospel of Life") forcefully address the fundamental question of the moral life and, in addition, some of the pivotal ethical challenges all of us are faced with in the global scenery at the end of the second millennium. Thus their content, scope, and theological weight necessarily make them documents of first-order significance in any serious ecumenical dialogue. Yet to this day all the important book-length responses represent only discussions among Roman Catholics themselves.[3]

This book collects the first sustained Protestant engagement of *Veritatis Splendor* and *Evangelium Vitae* in the English-speaking world. Both the editors and all the contributors to the volume do not, however, view this enterprise as just another set of reactions. Rather, this book is meant to deepen the conversation between Protestant ethicists and Roman Catholic moral theologians in the encompassing framework of the ecumenical dialogue. Therefore two internationally recognized Roman Catholic moral theologians advance the dialogue by "engaging the Protestant engagers" and by helping a Protestant audience to appreciate better the inner complexity both of the encyclicals under discussion and of the field of contemporary Roman Catholic moral theology itself.

For us as editors and contributors the guiding aspects of an ecumenical dialogue in Christian ethics are the following: (1) to discover and learn to appreciate the other's strongest and weakest points, (2) to be challenged by the other's strengths and thereby enabled to confront one's own weaknesses, and (3) to clearly identify and honestly ques-

---

Hertz, Wilhelm Korff, Trutz Rendtorff, and Hermann Ringeling, eds., *Handbuch der christlichen Ethik*, 3 vols., rev. ed. (Freiburg: Herder, 1993).

3. Next to an innumerable number of articles published in various theological journals in response to both encyclicals, see especially four significant collections: John Wilkins, ed., *Considering "Veritatis Splendor"* (Cleveland: Pilgrim, 1994), Joseph A. Selling and Jan Jans, eds., *The Splendor of Accuracy: An Examination of the Assertions Made by "Veritatis Splendor"* (Grand Rapids: Eerdmans, 1995), Dietmar Mieth, ed., *Moral-theologie im Abseits? Antwort auf die Enzyklika "Veritatis Splendor"* (Freiburg: Herder, 1994), Michael E. Allsopp and John J. O'Keefe, eds., *Veritatis Splendor: American Responses* (Kansas City: Sheed & Ward, 1995), and Kevin Wildes, ed., *Evangelium Vitae* (Georgetown: Georgetown University Press, forthcoming). For the one remarkable exception to this rule, cf. the response of the French Protestants to *Veritatis Splendor: O. Abel et al., *Paroles de Pape, Paroles Protestantes* (Paris: Les Bergers et Les Mages, 1995).

tion the other's problems. At the same time we are highly aware of the fact that ethical conflicts and disagreements — as well as agreements — are not just phenomena occurring *between* churches but as well and at least as much *in* each church. Therefore this collection can by no means claim to be in any way representative of the variety of perspectives present in the respective church bodies. And while the framework of this project did not allow the contributors to address the diversity and complexity of moral debates in the respective church bodies, the authors hope to advance the mutual understanding *between* the various traditions in moral matters.

In the concrete case of this particular dialogue it might very well be an advantage that the participating Protestant theologians, by having no part in the internal controversy of the Roman Catholic Church and therefore being free from any tactical considerations, have the privilege of perceiving some of the core issues at the very center of the Roman Catholic controversies in a more impartial and "objective" way. In addition, because the Roman Catholic moral teaching is discussed by primarily one Protestant tradition (Lutheranism), the responses display a greater overall coherence in their theological substance than might have been the case with a broad Protestant representation.

Thus the intention of this primarily but by no means exclusively Lutheran engagement of the two most recent central Roman Catholic teaching documents on the moral life is twofold, critical and constructive: *First,* it is a critical work, one of theological and exegetical engagement of the biblical, theological, and philosophical foundations and implications of both encyclicals. Here the point is to make the particular Roman Catholic assumptions transparent to a Protestant readership — both in their strong and weak aspects. *Second,* the essays will probe, examine, and identify potential and actual points of consensus in the basic theological and ethical perspectives.

In the future more of this kind of ongoing dialogue between the churches will be necessary in order to learn how to speak "with one voice" in matters of morals and ethics, particularly in a society that is increasingly alienated from the moral orientation that the biblical witness and the churches' traditions provide.

What the Authors Are Saying

A significant first step for understanding and engaging both moral encyclicals is to see them as integral to Pope John Paul II's intellectual journey. The political theorist **Jean Bethke Elshtain** shows in her essay how and why *Veritatis Splendor* and *Evangelium Vitae* can only be isolated from the person and life of Karol Wojtyla at the danger of a serious misreading of them. She places the theme of "freedom" at the very center of Wojtyla's intellectual pilgrimage from actor and playwriter to professor of philosophy to, eventually, pope. In her first section Elshtain argues for the inherent interrelationship between his early plays, his later philosophical work, and the encyclicals: "His drama reaches toward philosophy — toward *Veritatis Splendor* and *Evangelium Vitae*. And, truly, his philosophic treatises and encyclicals play out a drama": From early on to late in his life, John Paul II develops, beyond the false alternatives of individual sovereignty and complete social determination, a rich and complex notion of freedom as the very mark of the "acting person." This freedom is the very realization of every human being's inner substance, her or his humanity. Through identity-conferring enactments of love the fullness of the person comes into being; freedom is realized. According to Elshtain, the pope intends to show in all of his works how this takes place precisely "on a stage, in full view of God, 'in front of' one's Creator."

In her second section Elshtain unfolds what all of this means for the pope's concrete anthropology, his teaching about male and female, sexuality, marriage, and family. Her major claim is that, consistent with his theological personalism, the pope embraces the absolute ontological equality, an equality on the level of being, of rights and dignity between man and woman.

In her third section Elshtain provides a reading of John Paul's catechesis on the book of Genesis. She sees it as a crucial text for understanding the pope's theology of the body, which plays a significant role especially in *Evangelium Vitae*. In a last part she shows how the pope understands Jesus of Nazareth as the revelation of a new economy of gift, a self-giving way through which we confirm each other as persons.

One of *Veritatis Splendor*'s remarkable traits is the use of numerous scriptural references in the text, first and foremost a moving exegesis of the rich young man's encounter with Jesus (Matt. 19:16-22). The New Testament scholar **Karl P. Donfried** submits this crucial exegesis in the encyclical's opening, together with all the other major scriptural references, to a critical investigation — in respect to the scriptural accounts themselves and in dialogue with the results of historical-critical exegesis. In his first section Donfried defends key elements of the pope's reading of Matthew 19:16-22 against some of his scholarly critics. In addition he points out that the hermeneutical presuppositions guiding this section are fully coherent with the Pontifical Biblical Commission's statement *The Interpretation of the Bible in the Church*. The critical concern Donfried faces in light of the use of Scripture in the encyclical's first part is the omission of any broader and more detailed discussion of Jesus' complex relationship to the Torah.

Another concern of his is the unobtrusive but extremely consequential emergence of the "natural law" in ways not warranted by the biblical texts referred to. In the rest of his essay, Donfried critically examines all the other major biblical references in the encyclical and asks whether the Bible is used as a proof text or according to the actually quite remarkable hermeneutical guidelines developed in the Pontifical Biblical Commission's statement *The Interpretation of the Bible in the Church*. The conclusion of his generally sympathetic reading is that, despite some strong exegetical moves, *Veritatis Splendor*'s central claim, namely "the reaffirmation of the universality and immutability of the moral commandments, particularly those which prohibit always and without exception intrinsically evil acts" (VS #115) lacks a convincing biblical basis.

A second remarkable characteristic of *Veritatis Splendor* is its forceful return to themes central to both the Protestant Reformation and the Council of Trent: nature and grace, law and freedom, faith and works. **Gilbert Meilaender** engages *Veritatis Splendor* regarding the most crucial of these themes and issues for the Reformation: grace, justification through faith alone, and sin. He starts out by critically comparing the pope's exegesis of Matthew 19:16-22, the young man's encounter with Jesus, with Karl Barth's reading of the same passage in *Church Dogmatics* 2/2. He shows how Barth's exposition of the story differs in a structural way, which then opens up space for the language of faith as trust *(fiducia)*, a theme Meilaender sees as virtually absent from the encyclical's first part. He then shows how this diminished significance of faith as *fiducia* bears in a highly problematic way on the encyclical's discussion and criticism of the "fundamental option" — a concept of recent Catholic moral theology Meilaender sees as bearing many similarities to the Reformation language of faith. From there he moves to a critical discussion of the encyclical's understanding of "intrinsically evil acts" in relationship to the agent's faith. He engages it in light of the Reformation emphasis on the *simul justus et peccator* with an intense reflection on the Reformers' discussion of "sin," "sins," and asks whether or not one might lose saving grace. His conversation with Luther, Melanchthon, and the *Book of Concord* leads him to the conclusion that while the encyclical grasps the importance of the *sola gratia,* it fails to enunciate clearly the *sola fide.*

Reinhard Hütter continues this engagement of *Veritatis Splendor* from the perspective of Reformation theology. He focuses on the encyclical's extensive and complex treatment of God's law: eternal law, natural law, and revealed law (both old and new). In his first section Hütter offers an account of the encyclical's impressive way of relating God's law to God's presence and activity in the person and work of Christ. But he sees the need to bring the encyclical's account into a critical discussion with Thomas Aquinas. While Hütter appreciates this forceful and fascinating return to the theme of the law, he thinks that the encyclical actually falls back behind the level of Aquinas's treatment of the law, primarily in that the encyclical fails to be sufficiently analogical in its treatment of God's law. Against its professed intention, *Veritatis Splendor* thus loses not only Aquinas's deep insight that "law" is primarily a principle of action and not a form of legislation. It also cannot do full justice to God's grace in the gospel — in its fundamental difference from the natural and the old law.

In his second section Hütter shows how this very issue has been addressed in Martin Luther's theology of law and gospel. Luther is not only able to address central concerns of the encyclical concerning the objectivity of the moral law but to maintain the fundamental difference between law and gospel. Hütter also argues that in precisely these matters there is a remarkable ecumenical convergence between Luther's theology of grace and a twentieth-century recovery of Aquinas's theology of grace and justification, in which the analogical nature of the "law" is unambiguously emphasized. Unfortunately the insights of precisely this "Thomism" are not coming to bear upon the most crucial sections regarding God's law in *Veritatis Splendor*.

Risto Saarinen critically examines one of *Veritatis Splendor*'s most crucial underlying concepts — "human nature" — which also comes to play an important role in *Evangelium Vitae*. First, he shows that the notion of nature is employed in both encyclicals in order to consolidate the absolute and immutable content of those moral precepts that prohibit harming a living human being. In other words, the notion of human nature directly undergirds both encyclicals' teaching of "intrinsically evil acts."

Second, Saarinen identifies the areas of consensus between *Veritatis Splendor*'s teaching regarding human nature and Protestantism: both reject a false dualism between soul and body, culture and nature, freedom and law. Yet, as he points out, a broad consensus regarding central convictions about natural law and human nature does not prevent marked differences in practical conclusions. For example, regarding contraception and divorce Scandinavian Lutherans draw conclusions that are consistently different from the Roman Catholic magisterium.

In a third section, therefore, Saarinen discusses those areas which remain problematic: first, the authority ascribed to the church's magisterium and, second, the philosophical question whether all human persons literally share in the *same* nature. He argues that by trying to avoid the post-Enlightenment apotheosis of individualism, *Veritatis Splendor* seems to succumb to the opposite danger of a false monism by strongly emphasizing a *common* human nature as its universal character. In this human dignity is grounded as its universal character. Although this allows the encyclical to offer a strong notion of human dignity, it makes it, according to Saarinen, virtually impossible to give an account of the human individual's significance and dignity *as* an individual. In an interesting argumentative move he presses the point that *Veritatis Splendor*'s concept of "human nature" is deficient in not paying serious attention to the problem of individuation and thereby is not sufficiently Thomistic but rather borders on Averroism.

What is ultimately binding for one's course of action: the individual agent's conscience or the magisterium's normative teaching about moral matters? **Theodor Dieter** engages *Veritatis Splendor*'s way of answering this question. In his first section Dieter describes the encyclical's understanding of conscience and magisterium, and in a second section he submits the way the encyclical relates the magisterium and conscience to a critical theological analysis. He discusses first the concept of an "erring conscience," especially with reference to Thomas Aquinas, where he shows that rather than being a modern problem, the question of reconciling the subjective and the objective aspects of conscience is an old one. As a matter of fact, "conscience" itself is to be understood, according to Dieter, as the very mediation between the subjectivity of morality and the objectivity of the moral law. And precisely here, in the very discussion of this mediation, Dieter sees a serious shortcoming of the encyclical: while it asserts a correspondence between the objectivity of the moral law and personal morality, it does not show *how* such a correspondence is possible.

Turning to the encyclical's teaching about the magisterium's role in moral matters, Dieter finds a high esteem for the agent's reason side by side with a high esteem for magisterial authority, yet again no convincing mediation between these two approaches to concrete practical truth. In light of this, Dieter argues, people will look for their own solutions without the magisterium's help and thus *Veritatis Splendor* — against its will — contributes to an individualistic approach to ethics. Dieter suggests that these problems can only be successfully overcome if human nature and the moral law are explicitly enclosed in the theological framework of sin and grace as in the theology of Martin Luther. As a result he sees Luther able to distinguish more clearly than the encyclical between a theological and a moral concept of acting and between the two dimensions of conscience.

Many strands of the previous essays are woven together by **Lois Malcolm**, who engages another of *Veritatis Splendor*'s main concerns, namely the profound modern problem of "detaching human freedom" from its "essential and constitutive relationship to truth" (VS #45). In her own reading of the pope's exposition of Matthew 19:16-22, she identifies as its central theme the concept that Christian morality finds its center and criterion in the person of Jesus Christ. She understands this passage as the pope's attempt to weave together two quite different conceptual patterns for defining freedom: one rooted in traditional concepts of natural law and magisterial authority, and the other in the encounter of call and response, dialogue, and communion between Christ and Christian believers.

First, Malcolm unfolds the encyclical's "natural law understanding of freedom," which she interprets as being primarily heteronomous. Second, she identifies another concept of freedom being operative throughout the encyclical, namely a "personalist understanding of freedom." Malcolm argues that this latter concept of freedom, one that she sees coming to the foreground in the encyclical's third part and one that is ultimately rooted in Christ's self-giving on the cross, is a more comprehensive understanding of freedom. "Personalist" freedom points to a true theonomy by giving witness against both a false autonomy and a false heteronomy.

Bernd Wannenwetsch links the discussion of *Veritatis Splendor* with that of *Evangelium Vitae* by showing how the latter's discussion of abortion and euthanasia is rooted in the first's teaching on "intrinsically evil acts." He first addresses the fundamental problem of unfolding God's commandments without justifying them on alien grounds. Rather, what is crucial is that the "nonfoundational" character of the commandments in regard to any justification extrinsic to them be understood. He illustrates this thesis by drawing upon Wittgenstein's understanding of rules. In a second part he unfolds and defends the notion of "intrinsically evil acts" as a necessary implication of a rich notion of the agent's intention. He shows what is at stake morally in the areas of abortion and euthanasia if the whole concept of human agency as inherently teleological were given up in principle.

In a further section Wannenwetsch uses the idea of "moral notions" to show the crucial importance of the communal nature of moral language as it is embedded in particular moral notions that thereby embody the community's convictions. On the basis of this insight, Wannenwetsch urges the church to resist all attempts to "neutralize" dense moral notions by replacing them with more "neutral" patterns of description, as, for example, "abortion" with "termination of pregnancy." There are no "neutral" or "objective" patterns of moral description at all. Rather, each change in the moral notion amounts precisely to a change in the moral judgment implied in its use.

In a last section Wannenwetsch identifies three areas of convergence between the papal moral teaching and Reformation ethics. Both emphasize the moral meaning of the body, both focus on the concrete neighbor, and both value suffering as an integral element of avoiding intrinsically evil acts. On the basis of these convergences and by drawing upon Luther's "Treatise on Good Works," Wannenwetsch develops a concept of "intrinsically good acts" — the "good works" of faith.

While the death penalty is not one of the central issues addressed by *Evangelium Vitae,* **Oliver O'Donovan** regards it as a central theme, next to euthanasia and abortion. In addition, precisely because he observes a serious lack of attention in the encyclical to both Christ's cross and resurrection, he regards the issue of the death penalty to be a decisive test case for the pope's "gospel of life." O'Donovan offers two readings of what *Evangelium Vitae* has to say about the death penalty: According to the first reading, the pope supports a penal system that is evolving to make capital punishment a more and more marginal possibility as the need for it disappears — although in cases of "absolute necessity" it may still be practiced. Yet, according to a second reading, the pope seems to be more convinced of the universal moral unfitness of the death penalty. Both readings of the death penalty cut, according to O'Donovan, to the very core of what the state is about. Is any form of punishment a way of the state's "legitimate defense," or does the state own an office of judgment inherent to it? O'Donovan claims that the common tradition of Christianity up to the early modern period has been that there is an office of judgment inherent to the state on the grounds of which just punishment for the breaking of the law did not need any further justification. Contrary to that, the whole concept of the state's "legitimate defense" as justification for punishment is a recent intrusion suggesting a radically weakened point of view of political authority. By seeing the ordinary operations of penal justice (including the death penalty) in an idealized light and thereby uprooting the state's office of judgment, *Evangelium Vitae* tends to undermine, according to O'Donovan, the very limits of the state and supports its ubiquitous presence. He sees the central theological failure of *Evangelium Vitae* and the cause for this tendency in the encyclical's failure to achieve a clear focus on the resurrection. The encyclical puts the cross at the center of salvation history, but the cross still remains unrelated to the phenomenology of death. While we may overcome ordinary uses of the death penalty,

O'Donovan regards it as crucial not to thereby also be rid of the symbolic role that the death penalty plays in relating death to judgment.

Eberhard Schockenhoff's response to the Protestant engagers focuses exclusively on the encyclical *Evangelium Vitae.* Because the number of responses to this very important encyclical has been sparse in comparison to *Veritatis Splendor,* it is a welcome fact for an ecumenical audience to find such a careful exposition and interpretation of this encyclical. He not only provides an introduction to contemporary Roman Catholic anthropology and its strong focus on human dignity, but also defends the encyclical's way of talking about the "sacredness of life." He then distinguishes the use of this notion clearly from similar uses in fundamentalist circles and in some strands of civil religion. Instead of misreading the encyclical's talk of "sacredness of life" as a form of vitalism or naturalism, one needs to understand it as implied in a theological ontology of creation: "sacredness of life" refers to a consequence of the creature's ineffaceable createdness, which marks that the creature belongs to God. Yet, Schockenhoff argues, as the encyclical's meditative exegesis, peaking in the Johannine depiction of Christ, unfolds, God's history with humanity, grounded in creation, is directed towards communion with the triune God. In addition, he argues that the encyclical, by focusing on a comprehensive promotion of life in the spirit of love of neighbor, both reappropriates a common ecumenical legacy of all Christian churches and makes an important contribution to the present bioethical discussion. Especially notable is his penetrating defense of the encyclical's emphasis on the human person as a spiritual-physical unity and the body's moral significance within it. As Schockenhoff shows, this clearly runs counter to utilitarianism's implied dualism between the person's free self-determination on the one side and one's own body as the first object of this determination on the other side. The essay ends with a critical discussion of the encyclical's theme of a "culture of death," appreciating it as a prophetic alert in light of the pervasive symptoms of meaninglessness and lack of orientation, failure of solidarity and growing incapacity for commitment, rampant loneliness and spiritual anxiety — manifest but unintended consequences of the modern history of freedom.

James F. Keenan responds to the Protestant engagers by situating both encyclicals in a broader Catholic context. In his first section he suggests that the disappointment which some of the contributors express about *Veritatis Splendor* not developing a Scripture-based ethics is in part due to encyclicals' inability to free themselves from the history of Catholic moral theology. Here Keenan offers a short narrative of the crucial turns in the history of Catholic moral theology, especially helpful for Protestant readers. He shows how a central strand of this tradition has grown out of the practice of confessing sins. In the "penitentials," handbooks for priests, the general classification of moral conduct was articulated in terms of particular external actions. In the service of this setting, Keenan argues, moral theology developed its primary interest in sin and identified sin as particular external acts that correspond to one of the seven deadly sins. Only in the wake of Vatican II was moral theology directed to become more integral, namely, based on the scriptural witness and centered in Christ. In an interesting historical excursus Keenan shows how in the sixteenth century Reformers established the Decalogue in place of the deadly sins as the proper text for moral instruction and thereby overcame the manualists' focus on exterior action.

In his second section Keenan adds to the recurring Lutheran complaint about *Veritatis Splendor*'s failure to recognize the absolute priority of faith in the life of sanctification. Some Roman Catholic theologians note that the moral life's rootedness in charity also has been overlooked. In close dialogue with the Protestant contributors, Keenan develops the central theological distinction between moral goodness and moral rightness, the former being a gift from God, freely given without merit and being of unconditional primacy, the latter referring to one's actions being done in accord with right reason or the law. He then shows how this theological distinction can easily be confused with a philosophical distinction between the "goodness" and the "rightness" of moral acts, and with the metaphysical notion of "goodness" as completion or perfection.

In his third section he focuses on *Evangelium Vitae* and describes the important contribution made by Pope John Paul II on the sanctity of life. Here he sees the moral tradition being advanced in a considerable way. While in its original meaning "sanctity of life" simply functioned as a euphemism for God's dominion, Pope John Paul II gives it a new meaning in the context of his magisterial teaching:

humans are in God's image, and as God's person is inviolable, so is God's image. Thus, according to Keenan, due to his "personalist" approach the pope for the first time "breathes some life" into the concept of "sanctity of life." And, in this serious expansion of the grounds for the inviolable character of human life, Keenan sees a truly innovative move in the pope's magisterial teaching.

Whom We Have to Thank

It remains the editors' privilege to thank all the contributors to this volume for making the consultation of the Institute for Ecumenical Research on the encyclicals *Veritatis Splendor* and *Evangelium Vitae,* which took place at the Lutheran School of Theology at Chicago in October 1996, a success in all respects. We also express our gratitude to Professors Oliver O'Donovan and Michael Root, the Director of the Institute for Ecumenical Research, for their help in translating some of the essays into English and in editing the English of others, and to Jon Pott from the Eerdmans Publishing House for his support of this project.[4]

---

4. Many thanks to Leslie Barnett for improving the English of this introduction.

A Pope for All Seasons?
The Many-Sidedness of John Paul II

JEAN BETHKE ELSHTAIN

Thought's resistance to words

Sometimes it happens in conversation: we stand
facing truth and lack the words,
have no gesture, no sign;
and yet — we feel — no word, no gesture
or sign would convey the whole image
that we must enter alone and face, like Jacob.

This isn't mere wrestling with images
carried in our thoughts;
we fight with the likeness of all things
that inwardly constitute man.
But when we act can our deeds surrender
the ultimate truths we presume to ponder?

From "Collected Poems" by Karol Wojtyla

VERITATIS SPLENDOR and *Evangelium Vitae* are culminations of the life's work of Karol Wojtyla, Pope John Paul II. All the themes he strikes in these powerful encyclicals are themes that have long haunted him. Haunted him "from the beginning," one might say, even before he had settled on his vocation. Themes of love and yearning and the gift of the self. A dialectic of law and grace. The unique, irreducible dignity of the human person, the "only creature God desired for himself." Freedom and responsibility and the way these are interwoven with God's free gift of life. We are created to will and to nill, to affirm or to oppose, in freedom as individuals whose very individuality is the creation — the work — of another. The nature of human freedom lies at the heart of the matter. This freedom is at odds with all subjectivist construals, doctrines in which sincerity and authenticity and our own untrammeled placing of value are the criteria deployed to assess good or bad situations or states of existence. What makes me feel comfortable? we ask. And what makes us feel good *is* good, we conclude. If that is the way we go about thinking of ourselves, we are terribly diminished. But we are likely not to know this about ourselves. Why? John Paul would suggest that the answer lies in the ways we have closed ourselves off to the loving gift of life of the Creator, and, as well, to the possibility of the gift of others to us and we, in turn, to them. Thus we spurn the workings of the Holy Spirit; we resist the call of those silent expectancies stirring within that alone would move us out of the subjectivist morass.

John Paul's freedom is so at odds with the reigning notion of freedom in late modern Western culture that even the sympathetic reader must struggle to penetrate it. In *Evangelium Vitae* he writes: "If the promotion of the self is understood in terms of absolute autonomy, people inevitably reach the point of rejecting one another. Everyone else is considered an enemy from whom one has to defend oneself. Thus society becomes a mass of individuals placed side by side, but without any mutual bonds. Each one wishes to assert himself independently of the other and in fact intends to make his own interests prevail."[1] John Paul's integral anthropology is central here and it cuts much deeper than what we mean when we say, casually, that a thinker holds to a "social theory of human nature," this by contrast to an atomistic or individualist account. Those theories or ideologies that oversocialize us, by absorbing the individual into a collective or by seeing the person as the sum total of his or her reactions to external stimuli, deny freedom and affront the dignity of persons. (Here John Paul refers to various behaviorist schools

1. EV #20.

of social science, for example.) John Paul insists that our cultures do
not exhaust our very selves; there is a surplus, a "something," which
transcends particular, relative arrangements and that is the human
person. There are others (in addition to behaviorists) that he departs
from as well, those who stress the individual as above, beyond, or
apart from social life in principle; those who make freedom an
absolute and the individual the sovereign over both means and ends;
those who worship at the idol of the self and deny the Creator's gift
of life; those who turn away from the saving presence of other
persons — parents and spouses and children and friends — persons
who quite literally make us who we are.

For John Paul II our sociality goes all the way down as the creation
over time of the person in community; it is the unfolding of that right
order that pertains when people are free to give of themselves. Human
freedom belongs to us as creatures. True freedom is "acquired in love"
and requires an appropriate relationship between Creator and creature
("participated theonomy" John Paul calls it in *Veritatis Splendor*). For
only under God's "gentle guidance" can we open up our hearts to
love; our minds to the reason that *love,* which has primacy, unlocks.
When we flatten the moral horizon and make immanence absolute,
we set up oppositions where there should be a dialectic: between
freedom and nature; freedom and the law. We see nature as something
to master and overcome rather than to *realize.* We treat our bodies and
those of others as means and, in this way, we negate the "gift of self."

This, for John Paul II, is one of the great tragedies and sins of late
modernity. The body is the bearer of meaning. We are not just spirits.
All of this adds up to the perspective of *the acting person,* not only the
title, in translation, of Karol Wojtyla's major philosophical work, but
the *cantus firmus* of his encyclicals, from *Redemptor Hominis* through
Evangelium Vitae.[2] All of John Paul's beginnings flow from the human

2. See Cardinal Karol Wojtyla, *The Acting Person,* trans. Andrej Potocki (Boston:
D. Reidel, 1979). Much controversy surrounds this particular translation and edition.
Those familiar with John Paul's writings as a teacher of Christian ethics at Lublin
University believe the English translation is clumsy and does not accurately reproduce
the fullness of his thought. They also claim that the book would be better entitled:
"Person and Act." Kenneth L. Schmitz, *At the Center of the Human Drama: The Philo-
sophical Anthropology of Karol Wojtyla/Pope John Paul II* (Washington, D.C.: Catholic
University of America Press, 1993), describes this work as deriving from Wojtyla's

person in his or her concreteness. Most often he neither affirms nor negates what is usually called "the subject." He simply begins in another place, understanding, as he does, the perils of philosophies of consciousness or many historicist accounts that, in quite different ways, construct an abstract, even reified notion of a subject. It is a complex person, a wondrous creature, that lies at the heart of the human drama. It is his or her experience that lays down the ground from which one builds.

But consider how extraordinarily different is John Paul's account of experience from that which prevails in contemporary understanding. Nowadays we talk of "my experience" or "your experience" as something we own. We sometimes even suggest incommensurability as between experiences. We are enjoined to have lots of experiences. Experience is thoroughly subjectivized and this subjectivism is then made absolute. The account of our affirmations or negations that follows is simplistic emotivism. For John Paul, however, experience is something objective; it is palpable; it signifies the primacy of being. Moral oughts are derived from that which is — a point made by a number of commentators on John Paul II's philosophy. It is the concrete person who acts; who is both subject and object of work and love and faithfulness. Faith, he tells us in *Veritatis Splendor,* is not simply a set of propositions to which one gives intellectual assent. In a conversation with André Frossard, John Paul stated: "I am convinced that never at any period of my life was my faith a purely 'sociological' phenomenon resulting from the habits or customs of my environment, in a word, from the fact that others around me 'believed and acted like that.' I have never regarded my faith as 'traditional.' "[3] Faith

---

"thoroughly modern knowledge of philosophy" and his assimilation of "one of its modern approaches — phenomenology — to his own thinking" (p. 30). In this text, deriving from lectures Wojtyla delivered in the 1970s, he "intends . . . to describe human action in such a way that it will be seen to manifest the reality of the person in and through his or her actions out of the living experience of those actions" (p. 40). See also Karol Wojtyla, *Catholic Thought from Lublin* (New York: Peter Lang, 1993), and Karol Wojtyla/Pope John Paul II, *Toward a Philosophy of Praxis* (New York: Crossroad, 1981).

3. André Frossard and Pope John Paul II, *'Be Not Afraid!' Pope John Paul II Speaks Out on His Life, His Beliefs, and His Inspiring Vision for Humanity* (New York: St. Martin's, 1984), p. 31.

is "lived knowledge of Christ . . . a truth to be lived out." For John Paul, the human person, open to giving and receiving, to surrender and affirmation, is always becoming who or what he or she *is*. And it is the concrete person who acts and realizes this lived knowledge. Only in acting is knowledge known, so to speak. It is the concrete person who yearns and seeks to be known; to give and to be given to. It is the concrete person who is both free and bound; individuated (so to speak) yet obedient. This is both the grounding of, and the frame within which, the human drama gets played out. Words must pass into action, be put into practice. Only then do we know that the word has been "truly received."[4]

The Early Drama

Karol Wojtyla's stress on work-act-self is a thread that knits together his early days as a founder of the Rhapsodic Theatre with his pontificate. Joining with a handful of other brave and talented young Poles, Wojtyla acted in, and sometimes directed, plays that were performed underground in Nazi-occupied Poland. Wojtyla "took part in all of the seven wartime productions of the Rhapsodic Theater from 1941 to 1944, that is, in twenty-two performances and over a hundred rehearsals, all clandestine."[5] The penalty, should one have been caught, was severe: immediate transportation to a death camp if not outright execution on the spot. Wojtyla was the leading actor in the Rhapsodic Theatre troop as he had been in pre–World War II days in his high school in Wadowice. Wojtyla describes this drama in exile (under occupation) as "born out of the realities of life" in a world "entirely cut off from the normal base of theatrical production." But what remained was "the living word, spoken by people in extrascenic conditions, in a room with a piano. That unheard-of-scarcity of the means of expression turned into a creative experiment" as the fundamental element of drama became "the living human word . . . a leaven through which human deeds pass, and from which they derive their

4. VS #88.
5. Karol Wojtyla, *The Collected Plays and Writings on Theater by Karol Wojtyla*, trans. Boleslaw Taborski (Berkeley: University of California Press, 1987), p. 7.

proper dynamics."[6] The word cannot remain abstract; it must appeal "not only to the mind but also to the senses and the heart." Thus Rhapsodic Theatre transmitted "to the word a powerful and quite specific burden of thought."[7]

Haunted by the power of words, Wojtyla persisted in his attunement to drama as he pursued study for the priesthood (initially underground) and moved on to dissertations in philosophy and philology. His lingering affection for theater is attested to by the fact that his best-known play, "The Jeweler's Shop," was completed in 1960 when he was already a bishop. The conventions of rhapsodic theater predominated in this "poetic drama" as they had in his earlier plays, "Job," "Jeremiah," and "Our God's Brother." These conventions, self-consciously articulated and literally enacted by Wojtyla, are explored in his essays on the theater. He writes: "The rhapsodic company has accustomed us to a theater of the word. . . . As in life, the word can appear as an integral part of action, movement, and gesture, inseparable from all human practical activity; or it can appear as 'song' — separate, independent, intended only to contain and express thought, to embrace and transmit a vision of the mind."[8] Wojtyla worries that conditions in "our nervous life today" promote an abundance of gestures, "an anxiety of movements imposed on words." The upshot is that words "lack maturity," they fail to enact the word as part of a complex, living reality. This reality was what Wojtyla hoped to convey as author, as playwright, and as translator of plays by Sophocles and Shakespeare and Molière.

In rhapsodic theater the important rhythm is that of "word and thought, in their inner tension." The actor "is a rhapsodist," meaning that he not only recites or acts but "carries the problem." He is less a character than the living articulation of a powerful tension.[9] Reverence for the word "is a moral element," and young rhapsodic actors were obliged to "subordinate themselves to the great poetic word."[10] Consider Wojtyla's "Job" — an early play, written in 1940 — in which

---

6. Ibid., p. 379. From "Drama of Word and Gesture."
7. Ibid., p. 383. From "Rhapsodies of the Millennium."
8. Ibid., p. 372. From "On the Theater of the Word."
9. Ibid., p. 274.
10. Ibid., p. 386.

Wojtyla, just twenty years old, proclaims, in the play's prologue, the nigh-inexpressible power of the Word to call a people into being. The covenant, one might say, is identity-conferring, in contrast to the contract, which is identity-recognizing: I am a juridical subject.[11] "Behold, my people, / Behold, my people — / and listen to the Word of the Lord, / you who are downtrodden, / you who are flogged, / sent to the camps, you — Jobs — Jobs. Behold, my people."[12]

A second 1940 play, "Jeremiah," articulates a central premise of *Veritatis Splendor,* written some fifty-three years later in the very different *genre* of the papal encyclical (though I am convinced John Paul II would not want to drive a wedge between the papal document and the writings of youthful Karol). "In truth are freedom and excellence — /in untruth go you to slavery./O Jerusalem! — Jerusalem!"[13] Or hear the words of the "Hetman": "At the feet of truth one must erect love; / at the foundations, low in the ground, / it will take root even in a wilderness, / will build, uplift, and transform all things. / In your speeches you call for truth."[14] The splendor of truth is, for John Paul, there from the beginning. In "Our God's Brother," a 1944 play written when he was a theology student, one is struck by Wojtyla's simultaneous commitment to realism and to mystery. In this story of a great Polish artist and priest, Adam Chmielowski, Wojtyla can encompass each because his account of moral realism is always part of a movement toward fuller integration and the articulation of a self who, while passing away, has an identity, or, perhaps better put, grows to fill out that identity through love, through making his or her self a gift to others.

Nearly forty years after this play was written, and under conditions not of Nazi occupation but of martial law imposed by the Communist regime, Brother Albert (Adam Chmielowski) was beatified before over one million people on 22 June 1983 in the Meadows of Krakow — an event I witnessed — by Pope John Paul II, who had written his play about Brother Albert as a Rhapsodist, Polish patriot, and anti-Nazi. The translator of John Paul II's plays calls this event "unique

11. This distinction I owe to my colleague, William Schweiker.
12. *Collected Plays,* p. 29. From "Job."
13. Ibid., p. 103. From "Jeremiah."
14. Ibid., p. 121.

in the history of world drama" as one playwright proclaimed the "beatification of his play's protagonist."[15] In "Our God's Brother," God knows our lives in their totality. And yet we are free. Free to tremble and free to love. As one character, simply called "Priest," declares: "These matters are too great, too important. Where love is concerned, one cannot give orders. Just think. Our Lord accomplishes so much through love, so much good. Love joins us with Him more than anything else because it transforms everything. Let yourself be molded by love."[16] Brother Albert repudiates the seduction of revolution as the culmination of rage, a rage that sees in the workings of caritas only sickly pity, mere sentiment. The problem, for Wojtyla, is that a revolutionist who proclaims that what matters is "anger alone" and the garnering of more goods (to be sure, often in the name of justice) usually cannot see that poverty that cuts "deeper than the resources of all goods."[17] The enslaved revolt only to be reenslaved. But "The Son of God is all freedom. Without a trace of slavery."[18]

Here as elsewhere Wojtyla creates word enactments that allow the force of an argument from great anger at injustice to come through, couched in the language of justice — total justice, even harsh justice. But, counterpoised, is "Brother Superior's (Albert's)" choice of a greater freedom, one receptive to God's will and power and open, thereby, to the stranger before me who needs my loving care. The power of this drama is its intense posing of alternative human routes in dealing with injustice and poverty and its deep religiosity that never becomes pious. Rather, the thoroughly unsentimentalized and sometimes dreadful way of love is here displayed; love that does not shirk when faced with the least attractive features of an often debased human condition. One might put it this way: Wojtyla's poetry strains toward or reaches toward drama. His drama reaches toward philosophy — toward *Veritatis Splendor* and *Evangelium Vitae*. And, truly, his philosophic treatises and encyclicals play out a drama. How could it be otherwise, Wojtyla might ask. All human representations, the ways

15. Ibid., p. 147.

16. Ibid., p. 210. From "Our God's Brother."

17. Ibid., p. 242.

18. Ibid., p. 263. Here, one wonders, is Wojtyla responding in part to Nietzsche's attack on Christianity as the "slave morality"?

we make ourselves known and visible to others, are word/acts and they share this much: they always take place on a stage, in full view of God, "in front of" one's Creator. We cannot see the Creator face-to-face from the standpoint of our creatureliness. But we can see the face of other persons.[19]

By all accounts his most accomplished play, "The Jeweler's Shop," is a sustained meditation on love, responsibility, marriage, and parenthood, four of Wojtyla's enduring concerns. This is a play about human love, a love that unfolds in and through the *imago Dei*. In *Veritatis Splendor,* John Paul II proclaims the human face as "reflected" in the splendor of God. The *imago Dei* is not the "will of an all-powerful externality" (this from *Veritatis Splendor*) but an always-present that helps us to realize the truth of our being. In "The Jeweler's Shop" freedom-truth-responsibility, as these cohere in marriage, are meditated upon through the characters Teresa, Andrew, Anna, Stefan, and their children, Monica and Christopher. Stefan and Anna's love has waned over time as "Life changed/into a more and more strenuous existence of two people/who occupied less and less room in each other."[20] By contrast, Teresa and Andrew help us to *see* the unfolding of the trinitarian principle of integration or interaction — here two in one but actually three as the child embodies the breaking "into" time and space of the parents' deep love.

Those who spurn the gifts of others and refuse to give themselves are all the passersby who avert their eyes and "quietly shut the door behind them or slam their garden gate. . . . Everyone carries in himself an unrealized substance called humanity."[21] It is the realization of this substance, this coming-into-being of the fullness of the person, that lies at the heart of human experience. We are born to community. But this is no thin communitarianism. It is the identity-conferring enactments of love. There is much more one could say on this theme, but I must leave it at this for now. The central point here made is to take notice of just how extraordinarily rich are the word-acts penned by Wojtyla when he was barely twenty and the fact that they revolve around those human

19. Long before he had read the work of Emmanuel Levinas, Wojtyla had seen in the face of the other a claim on us.

20. *Collected Plays,* p. 297. From "The Jeweler's Shop."

21. Ibid., p. 335. From the play "Radiations of Fatherhood."

relations and dilemmas that lie at the heart and soul of his papacy. Surely much of John Paul II's power lies in the fact that he has, throughout his life, worked a few basic themes in all their complexity and attempted to capture their shimmering intensity.

Male and Female Created He Them

John Paul II dedicated his papacy to Saint Catherine of Siena. He dedicated himself — "completely" — to Mary. Nearly all of his papal speeches and writings end with canticles, prose-poems to Mary. This, together with his reaffirmation of Church stands concerning birth control, abortion, and priestly ordination, is taken as evidence of a kind of romantic or "mystical" antifeminism, even, in some militant quarters, a narrow-minded antiwomanism. From the beginning of his pontificate, when he began to rearticulate his theology of the body in a series of homilies, but after he had already published a collection of essays on marriage and parenthood entitled *Love and Responsibility,* this pope has been a target of feminist protest.[22] This is worth trying to understand.[23] John Paul is insistent that human life, including the life

22. Published in New York by Farrar, Straus, Giroux, 1981. Originally published in Polish in 1960.

23. On one level, of course, it is quite easy to understand if one accepts the premises of Western-based liberal feminism, especially in its currently dominant juridical versions. I think it is very difficult to "read" John Paul's writings on men and women in a context in which rights are increasingly viewed as an adversarial possession of one against some other and in a situation framed by a cash, by contrast to a gift, economy. The dominant feminist project holds that equality equals identity; that there is no distinction to be marked between male and female for the purpose of distribution of any good or goods and in the creation of any good or goods. Also, what men have traditionally "had" is often construed as a "power" position, one bearing all the marks of dominance in contrast to the possibility of stewardship or service. So, of course, it is easy to understand the controversies: all one has to do is connect the dots. But it seems to me interesting to unpack an argument that sees men and women as absolutely equal in dignity, fully sharing in the *imago Dei,* yet draws from that not identity but distinction. In this paper I take no stand on the matter of priestly ordination or other internal Church matters. On this matter a recent, helpful essay is Hermann Josef Pottmeyer, "The Pope and the Women," *The Tablet* (2 November 1996): 1435-36. Pottmeyer correctly argues that for John Paul "the question of women's ordination cannot be discussed or decided in the context of the

of the church, is enriched, not impoverished, by the embodiment (in several senses) of differences between male and female, distinctions that neither imply nor require discrimination against women; indeed, to deny that women share fully in the *imago Dei* is a sin. Most contemporary Western feminists (though not all) reject this argument for equality and distinct but overlapping callings, finding in any articulation of difference an invitation to inegalitarianism.[24]

Let me begin to sort this out by meditating on John Paul's homily, "Interpreting the Concept of Concupiscence," delivered during a regular Wednesday papal audience on 8 October 1980.[25] The pope's teaching on this occasion led to John Paul being condemned for sexual priggishness and for his repudiation of open, liberated sexual attitudes. This seems to me a willful misreading. What John Paul was about instead was teasing out of the Sermon on the Mount an erotic imperative that helps to form a nonutilitarian sexual ethic for husband and wife; indeed, the pope's logic in this and many other writings pushes him in the direction of a radical egalitarianism that cuts to the

---

debate over equal rights for women. Equality of women is God's will. Whether that means that God wants women to be ordained, however, still needs to be clarified. This means we must properly understand Jesus' action in this regard, and we must decide the question in faithfulness to Jesus and in light of the 'signs of the times.' . . . I do not believe that the Pope wishes to forbid theological debate that respects these postulates." My own aim in this essay is to interpret, not to take sides in the ordination debate. As a non-Catholic, it seems rather inappropriate for me to wade in without having studied the matter thoroughly. I am, instead, to interpret John Paul's theological and philosophical arguments.

24. There are, of course, radical feminist "difference" theorists, too, but they are operating on such a different philosophical ground and their politics is, at present, so murky that I will not here take up that particular challenge. Although such feminists are found in sizeable numbers in the academy, they do not prevail in public policy and political debates, save, perhaps, in the arena of legal theory, where the difference idea now is so powerful it threatens to swamp the equality principle. This difference argument is radically opposed to John Paul's understanding of distinction, for it holds that men and women, quite literally, inhabit different epistemological universes. John Paul's egalitarianism — and his Christianity! — would find this position perplexing at best; an invitation to suspicion, enmity, and division, at worst.

25. This homily and others central to John Paul's theology of the body appear in *Blessed Are the Pure of Heart: Catechesis on the Sermon on the Mount and Writings of St. Paul* (Boston: St. Paul Editions, 1983). The pagination for this particular homily is 142-49.

bone, for he embraces absolute ontological equality — equality on the level of being — between man and woman.

John Paul assumes a scripturally based equality of rights and dignity between men and women. His concerns, in light of this equality, are the right ordering of male-female relations as these revolve around sexuality, *especially* married sexuality. He states: "The moral evaluation of lust (of 'looking lustfully') which Christ calls 'adultery committed in the heart,' seems to depend above all on the personal dignity itself of man and woman. This holds true both for those who are not united in marriage and — perhaps even more — for those who are husband and wife."[26] The pope urges Christians to "dwell on the situation described by the Master," one in which the man "commits adultery in his heart" by means of an interior act given exterior expression in a "look."[27] But the "look" is not one of longing or mutually aroused desire; it is, instead, a lust that aims to possess and to use. The look John Paul addresses springs from lustful, not sacred, Eros, and its possessing aim is divorced from authentic recognition of the humanity of the other person, thereby changing "the very intentionality of the woman's existence . . . , reducing the riches of the perennial call to the communion of persons . . . to mere satisfaction of the sexual 'need' of the body (with which the concept of 'instinct' seems to be linked more closely)."[28]

The woman, the person "lusted after" in this scenario (though certainly she, too, can lust in this way), is reduced through a possessive "look" to a thing-like status. The pope states: "The person (in this case the woman) becomes for the other person (the man) mainly the object of the potential satisfaction of his own sexual 'need.'"[29] The objectification of the other person exudes a corrosive acid that permeates the interstices, the very core, of the male-female pair. "In this way," John Paul continues, "that mutual 'for' is distorted, losing its character of communion of persons in favor of the utilitarian function."[30] A distorted "interiority" that does not usher into an explicit

26. Ibid., p. 142.
27. Ibid., p. 143.
28. Ibid., p. 144.
29. Ibid.
30. Ibid.

act is difficult, at best, to apprehend, to analyze, and to grasp in order that one might assess how and in what manner it can be transformed. This John Paul acknowledges. But he rejects as inadequate those solutions to the objectified possession of woman that concentrate solely on a "purely psychological (or 'sexological') interpretation of 'lust.'" For such reductionistic accounts provide neither a "sufficient basis to understand the text" nor a pathway for the redemption of the male and female in communion.[31] A transformation of spirit, a change so deep that vital performative consequences flow from it, including freeing the human eye from the literal short-sightedness of possession with its reduction of others to functions, is called for.

After embracing the "severity and strength" of scriptural prohibitions against adultery and covetousness and for purity of heart, John Paul resolutely celebrates "the indissolubility of marriage, in which man and woman, by virtue of the original plan of the Creator, unite in such a way that 'the two become one flesh.' Adultery, by its essence, is in conflict with this unity in the sense in which this unity corresponds to the dignity of persons. Christ not only confirms this essential ethical meaning of the commandment, but aims at strengthening it in the very depth of the human person."[32] But the pope's articulation of an egalitarian ethos suggests even more: a radical vision of the human community which, in its conceptual heart, embraces powerful imperatives toward sexual egalitarianism broadly construed. The ethos he calls for, here and elsewhere, is one that liberates the human heart *from* lust and *for* love; it is an impassioned plea for mutuality and for locating authentic human freedom within the protective constraints of a nonutilitarian community. The attitude implied in the lustful possession of the other in human intimate relations taints humanity in general. For the reduction of a human being to thing-likeness (including the woman in marriage, all too often) fuels and legitimates possession over all. That casting of a shroud over the humanity of the female is similar to the ways we have devised to sanction the excision of others, whether black, poor, Jew, or handicapped, from the fullness of communion, and it forestalls the emergence of deep communal imperatives.

31. Ibid., p. 145.
32. Ibid., p. 147.

John Paul II hints at the broader applicability of his liberatory ethos when he states (notice the way this theme later fuels *Evangelium Vitae*): "Human life, by its nature, is 'co-educative' and its dignity, its balance, depend at every moment of history and at every point of geographical longitude and latitude, on 'who' she will be for him, and he for her."[33] The requirement, then, is, first, for transformation of the basic pair: he/she. To the extent that this relationship is one of domination, possession, and consumption, predatory and possessive relations are legitimized. It follows that a transformation at this most basic level would ramify, first, throughout the little commonwealth of the family and then radiate outward, sending forth tendrils of humanity into a world that is often hostile and uncomprehending but that could not remain wholly unaltered by this permeation and per-mutation from within. John Paul insists that there are various models of human existence that are shameful or wrong-in-themselves (the possessive master/slave model, for example) or are, at best, radically incomplete. He doesn't use this language but it is apt: intimate and social relations based purely on contract are amputated relations at best and may be sinful if they legitimate possession of the other and preclude the vital "working" and co-creation of male and female in relation to one another. The moment of action, the moment when intention moves to word/act, is that moment when the male-female pair, in its coming together, transcends any contractual pairing in order to more fully embody deep ethical imperatives. That transcendence is lost if the relationship is trapped in a deadly *pas de deux* of posses-sor/possessed.

With this powerful critique of the reduction of human existence to utilitarian calculations or relations of force and lust, John Paul links himself up with vital themes embedded in what might be called *ethical* feminism. The words from John Paul's World Day of Peace Message, "Women as Teachers of Peace," 1994, are as good a place as any to bring this section to a close: "If, from the very beginning, girls are looked down upon or regarded as inferior, their sense of dignity will be gravely impaired and their healthy development in-evitably compromised. Discrimination in childhood will have lifelong effects and will prevent women from fully taking part in the

33. Ibid., p. 148.

life of society."[34] This is a strong brief against invidious comparison and ill use. This is a project that awaits further elaboration, and it is one that John Paul sees as central to the new culture of life he outlines in *Evangelium Vitae*. It has been central to his thinking for decades.

How Far Have We Fallen?

John Paul II's catechesis on the book of Genesis affords a glimpse into his complex encounter with philosophy generally and twentieth-century thought in particular. He references Scheler, Lévy-Bruhl, Eliade, Tillich, Ricoeur, Levinas, Hebrew exegetical works, semioticians and etymologists, books in analytic philosophy, anthropological texts, Plato, Freud, and on and on, in addition to the usual suspects — Augustine and Aquinas first and foremost.[35] In John Paul's account of the fall, the gravamen of the narrative is that we remain in deep ways the sorts of creatures we were from the beginning. John Paul knows, of course, that we cannot penetrate to the beginning in any historical sense, but, he argues, we can and must in an anthropological sense. Thus, in Jesus' exchange in Matthew 19:3-9, Jesus recalls the ancient truth: "Have you not read that he who made them from the beginning made them male and female?"[36] John Paul segues from this moment to the beginning Jesus has in mind, namely, Genesis 1:27: "In the beginning the Creator made them male and female." The original passage read that God created "them" in his image. What sorts of creatures were these? This is a question central to both *Veritatis Splendor* and *Evangelium Vitae*. First and foremost they are creatures

34. "World Day of Peace: Women: Teachers of Peace," *Origins* 24, no. 28 (1994): 465-69.

35. Those curious about John Paul's reading habits and impatient with his philosophical works might just consult *Crossing the Threshold of Hope* (New York: Knopf, 1994) for bibliographic hints. Although not referenced in his account of the fall, John Paul has worked through the entire corpus of works by Marx and most of the major secondary work on Marx and Marxism.

36. All cites are drawn from John Paul II, *Original Unity of Man and Woman: Catechesis on the Book of Genesis* (Boston: St. Paul Editions, 1981). The collection is drawn from a series of General Audience presentations by John Paul from 5 September 1979 to 2 April 1980.

created for communion; to be in *communio*. There is, of course, that second account of creation, from Genesis 2:24, one that "forms a conceptual and stylistic unity with the description of original innocence, man's happiness, and also his first fall." Then John Paul kicks into superscript with these words: *"From the point of view of biblical criticism,* it is necessary to mention immediately that the *first account of man's creation is chronologically* later than the second. The origin of this latter is much more remote. This more ancient text is defined as 'Yahwist' because the term 'Yahweh' is used to denominate God."[37] By comparison with this account, the first, chronologically later, "is much more mature both as regards the image of God, and as regards the formulation of the essential truths about man. This account derives from the priestly and 'elohist' tradition, from 'Elohim,' the term used in that account for God."[38]

Very interesting, no doubt, but what is the import, especially with *Veritatis Splendor* and *Evangelium Vitae* in mind? John Paul explains. The textually earlier but chronologically later account is clear that man is "male and female" — always was, always will be. The ontological equality of male and female as corporeal beings is a given. This is the "essential truth." This account, according to John Paul, is "free from any trace whatsoever of subjectivism. It contains only the objective facts and defines the objective reality, both when it speaks of man's creation, male and female, in the image of God, and when it adds a little later the words of the first blessing: 'Be fruitful and multiply, and fill the earth; subdue it and have dominion over it'" (Gen. 1:28).[39] This is critical in light of John Paul's critique of subjectivism in *Veritatis Splendor.* And it is long presaged in his prepapal writings. For example, in a series of spiritual exercises presented to Pope Paul VI, the papal household, and the cardinals and bishops of the Roman Curia during a Lenten Retreat in March 1976, Karol Cardinal Wojtyla argued that "one cannot understand either Sartre or Marx without having first read and pondered very deeply the first three chapters of Genesis. These are the key to understanding the world of today, both its roots and its extremely radical — and therefore dramatic — affirmations

37. *Original Unity,* p. 21.
38. Ibid., p. 22.
39. Ibid., p. 23.

and denials."[40] As well, attuned as he is to the subjective and to experience as a category of interpretation and philosophic and theological understanding, John Paul has always — from the beginning — stood against subjectivism. "Subjectivism is fundamentally different from subjectivity," he writes in a 1960 essay on love. "Subjectivity is in the nature of love, which involves two subjects, man and woman. Subjectivism, on the other hand, is a distortion of the true nature of love, a hypertrophy of the subjective element such that the objective value of love is partially or wholly swallowed up and lost in it."[41]

In his account of creation and fall, John Paul moves directly from scoring subjectivism to a "subjective definition of man" of the sort he finds imbedded in the first, chronologically later, account of creation. He clearly wants to put the heavy theological, philosophical, and anthropological weight on Genesis 1:27 — "created he them." So how does he deal with the second but earlier account? He speaks the language of cultural and philosophical anthropology. "The second chapter of Genesis constitutes, in a certain manner, the most ancient description and record of man's self-knowledge."[42] The narrative is archaic and manifests a primitive mythical character; thus, it "could be said that Genesis 2 presents the creation of man especially in its subjective aspect."[43] The pope brings in a bit of etymological armature at this point, telling us that the Bible calls the man *adam,* but very briefly. For from the moment of the creation of the first woman the language for man shifts to *ish* in relation to the woman *(ishshah).*

So we, *ish* and *ishshah,* are in the Garden. And there is a mysterious tree. This tree of the knowledge of good and evil "is the line of demarcation between the two original situations of which the Book of Genesis speaks." John Paul evokes the sense of a boundary or liminal divide. His Adam is innocent in a kind of primitive and not terribly interesting way. The *first* situation is one of original innocence — innocent because "man (male and female) is, as it were, outside the sphere of knowledge of good and evil." But the *second* situation is

40. Published under the title *Sign of Contradiction* (New York: Seabury, 1979), p. 24.

41. Wojtyla, *Love and Responsibility,* p. 153.

42. *Original Unity,* p. 28.

43. Ibid.

fast upon us in which man, "after having disobeyed the Creator's command . . . finds himself, in a certain way, within the sphere of the knowledge of good and evil. This second situation determines the state of human sinfulness, in contrast to the state of primitive innocence."[44] John Paul finds that the Yahwist text shows that there are "two original situations," and systematic theology must "discern in these two antithetical situations two different states of human nature: the state of integral nature and the state of fallen nature."[45] All of this is of fundamental significance for the theology of the body. There are normative conclusions "which have an essential significance not only for ethics, but especially for the theology of man and for the theology of the body."[46] This theology of the body is constituted on the basis of the Word of God: hence the importance of the Genesis accounts.

Man falls, yes, but it is remarkable in what measured tones — terms not so much of calamity as rue and regret — that John Paul addresses the fall. He sees it not as a horrific debacle, a shift to man as a destroyer, but, rather, as a kind of brokenness, a rending of the seamless garment. Man breaks the original covenant with God in his and her heart. This serves to delimit two "diametrically opposed situations and states: that of original innocence and that of original sin." What we fall into is history. With Paul Ricoeur, John Paul suggests that the ontological and the historical here part company. "But when Christ refers to the beginning, he helps us *to find* in man an essential continuity and a link between these two different states or dimensions of the human being." We are torn creatures but not debased. And it is "impossible to understand the state of 'historical' sinfulness, without referring or appealing . . . to the state of original 'prehistoric' and fundamental innocence." This boundary experience does not permit *direct* contact with what lies on the other side ("from the beginning") but points us to it and brings us closer to it. For John Paul there is something like a fading from the fullness of the *imago Dei* available to male/female once the historic threshold is crossed. Our rootedness is revealed in theological prehistory, and it is such that at every point our historical sinfulness can only be explained with reference to original innocence. "If this sin signifies, in every

44. Ibid., p. 30.
45. Ibid., p. 31.
46. Ibid.

historical man, a state of lost grace, then it also contains a reference to
that grace, which has precisely the grace of original innocence."[47] One
might say that an ontological trace remains, grazing the brow and
palpating the heart however gently of historically sinful male and female.
In Kenneth Schmitz's words: "The experience adumbrates the other
side, shadows it forth, after the manner of one of those devices that
permit us to look indirectly upon a bright eclipse without enabling us
to look directly at it."[48]

What is human history after the fall, or perhaps the slide into sin?
After breaking the original covenant with the Creator, the promise of
redemption is proffered early on, in the "so-called Proto-gospel in
Genesis 3:15," and from that moment "the creature *begins to live* in
the theological perspective of the redemption," a redemption in which
the human being participates as a historical being. Our participation
is double: as part of the history of human sinfulness and as part of the
history of salvation. We are both subjects and co-creators of that
history.[49] From the perspective of the redemption of the body, continuity is guaranteed "between the hereditary state of man's sin and
his original innocence, although this innocence was, historically, lost
by him irremediably."[50] Matters grow ever more complex as John Paul
proceeds. Concerned less with the depths of our sinfulness than with
our capacities for communion and clear understanding, John Paul lifts
up God's desire that we move out of solitude and into communion.
"It is not good that man should be alone." Standing before God,
created "man finds himself . . . in search of his own entity: it could
be said: in search of the definition of himself. A contemporary would
say: in search of his own 'identity.'" Man alone cannot find himself.
And his man, John Paul insists, is "solitary without reference to sex."
The Genesis account makes this clear, he insists. Solitariness is our
human condition as man alone.

It follows that our self-awareness is both an achievement and a gift.
We are self-conscious and self-determining in our original solitude.
After all, does God not create us in order that we might discern between

47. Ibid., p. 37.
48. Schmitz, *Center of Human Drama,* p. 106.
49. John Paul II, *Original Unity,* p. 38.
50. Ibid., p. 39.

"good and evil, between life and death" — note here that these two discernments are the basis of *Veritatis Splendor* and *Evangelium Vitae* respectively.[51] A central problem of anthropology — consciousness of the body — is here touched upon. Anthropological complexity must be addressed in a metaphysical, in fact a *radically realist,* sense,[52] for self-awareness becomes a requirement once the historic divide between solitude and innocence is affected. The heart and soul of the anthropological matter for John Paul is the original unity of man and woman. Male and female are two ways of "being a body," of the same human beings "created in the image of God."[53] John Paul makes a very interesting move in his discussion of Adam's deep sleep, the one that occasions the fashioning of Eve from his rib. Because, for John Paul, if we already *are* male and female before the deep sleep, what are we to make of Adam's recognition of an other — Eve — upon awakening? For John Paul this signifies not that some being that was *not* there before suddenly appears before Adam but, rather, that Adam has fallen into a sleep akin to nonbeing (or non-self-conscious being, at any rate) and awakened to recognition of the double unity of male and female.[54] "The rib" John Paul treats as an "archaic, metaphorical and figurative way" of expressing the thought of homogeneity of somatic structure: bone of my bones; flesh of my flesh. "Somatic homogeneity, in spite of the difference in constitution bound up with sexual difference, is so evident that the man (male), on waking up from the genetic sleep, expresses it at once."[55] The Hebrew term *adam* captures this "collective concept of

51. Ibid., p. 51.
52. Writes Stefan Swiezawski, who wrote the introduction to Wojtyla's lectures at the Catholic University of Lublin, of his former ethics colleague, "We all saw realistic metaphysics, the metaphysics of concretely existing beings, as having primacy among the philosophical disciplines. . . . I would even say [this basic . . . radical] — realism was the unshakable common denominator of our philosophical convictions." One of Wojtyla's basic concerns was to "establish a relationship between realistic metaphysics and the phenomenological method" (pp. xii, xiv).
53. Ibid., p. 62. A critique of some feminist theologians has been that woman is not fully created in the *imago Dei,* or not there fully represented, *as a body,* whatever Christian theologians said about the mind and soul. John Paul here undercuts any presupposition that the female body is not fully implicated in the *imago Dei.*
54. Ibid., p. 64.
55. Ibid., p. 66. I trust it is clear that "genetic" here means "in the beginning" and has nothing to do with RNA/DNA!

the human species" in the way many modern Indo-European languages do not, claims John Paul.

The significance of all this lies in the fact that it is the *communion* of persons *(communio personarum)* that is the authentic *imago Dei*. Communion expresses more than help or helper; it names the existence of the person *for* another; of the gift of the self to an other. It is a special reciprocity; it affords intimations of an inscrutable divine communion. "Man becomes the image of God not so much in the moment of solitude as in the moment of communion."[56] This second narrative, then, is something of a preparation for "understanding . . . the Trinitarian concept of the 'image of God.'"[57] We have arrived at the core anthropological reality, the name of which is *body,* the human body, a body that "right from the beginning" is bound up "in the image of God."[58] What are we to make, then, of our primordial human experiences, including that of shame? The human, having fallen into history, cannot consciously perceive lost ontological man but, in a certain sense, our self-awareness presupposes that beginning. Originally we were not ashamed. This experience of the body is now lost to us. All of history is colored by such "fundamental experiences . . . as the experience of shame."[59] Shame is a new situation. We failed the test connected with the tree of knowledge of good and evil. Shame is a marker, a kind of boundary experience. This cuts much deeper than the sense of sight — first seeing, then feeling shame. It is an experience of fear regarding one's second self (male or female) unknown in the state of original innocence. Shame is deeply "rooted . . . in mutual relations," and it expresses "the essential rules for the 'communion of persons' in history."[60] We lost the capacity for full

56. Ibid., pp. 73-74.

57. Ibid., p. 74.

58. Ibid., p. 75.

59. Ibid., p. 88. In a discussion of the "Metaphysics of Shame" in his collection of essays published in 1960, Karol Wojtyla argued that *"the phenomenon of shame arises when something which of its very nature or in view of its purpose ought to be private passes the bounds of a person's privacy and somehow becomes public."* As well, "The need for concealment, characteristic of shame, arises in man because it finds in him, if I may put it this way, a terrain — his inner life — which lends itself to concealment of facts or values" (from *Love and Responsibility,* pp. 173-74).

60. Ibid., p. 93.

communication; to be fully in communion as body-subjects. We communicate and we see through a glass darkly and what we see is not just an exterior perception but an "interior dimension of participation in the vision of the Creator Himself."[61] It is only through reciprocity — through processes of multiple mutual recognitions — that we come to know the meaning of our own bodies. It is only through the gift of the self that we come to understand communion. John Paul calls this "the hermeneutics of the gift."

The remainder of John Paul's account is devoted to the way the body-subject, the man (male and female) person, is at once and the same time a gift given by a loving Creator and is, in turn, himself and herself one who can make a gift of the self to others. We make ourselves a gift in the freedom of love "from the beginning." In this beginning there is "the freedom of the gift in the human body. It means that this body possesses a full 'nuptial' meaning." Men and women's mutual experience of the body involves a real communion of persons. Each, in giving, is enriched. Each grows by virtue "of the interior disposition to the exchange of the gift and to the extent to which it means with the same and even deeper acceptance and welcome, as the fruit of a more and more intense awareness of the gift itself."[62] How is any or all of this possible post-fall, in history? It is, argues John Paul, something that must be reconstructed "with great effort, the meaning of the disinterested mutual gift."[63] John Paul has no doubt — none — that this is, in fact, possible, and it helps us to understand the strenuousness of his moral injunctions and calls to reason and gift-giving in *Veritatis Splendor* and *Evangelium Vitae*.

To the skeptic, wary that he may be calling us to an impossible perfectionism, John Paul would say, by "following the trail of the historical *a posteriori* — and, above all, following the trail of human hearts — we can reproduce and, as it were, reconstruct that mutual exchange of the gift of the person, which was described in the ancient text, so rich and deep, of the Book of Genesis."[64] We all bear within ourselves the trace of that beginning. We cannot know it fully but we

61. Ibid., p. 99.
62. Ibid., p. 132.
63. Ibid., p. 164.
64. Ibid., p. 132.

can, "with great effort," in history, reconstruct it in a robust if imperfect way. That is what he calls for in the two great encyclicals under consideration.

Love and a Newborn Baby

Many see in John Paul's writings a yearning or straining toward perfectionism. Certainly he has argued for years that "the coming of Jesus of Nazareth into the world, the incarnation of the Word, is the revelation of a completely different economy."[65] Here he refers to the disinterested gift of the self.[66] He has no doubt that the human being as a person is "capable of such a gift." Only through acting in this gift-giving way do we "mutually confirm and affirm one another as persons."[67] The human being is capable of this because we have a capacity for what John Paul calls "rational community as *communio.*"[68] This emphasis means that John Paul's anthropology puts great pressure on any and all comparisons between persons, including men and women, that treat differences as invidious or as the occasion for unjustifiable discrimination. Jesus embodies the gift in its most radical form. But human beings, open to grace, are drawn to this possibility in part because it lies at the heart of our original experience, traces of which the fall did not eradicate utterly. To say that John Paul's way of understanding the self in relation to other and the mind in relation to reality is opaque to us in late modernity is to understate. We no longer appreciate the meaning of putting ourselves at the disposal of another: the donative gift of self looks like self-abnegation if not masochism. Mary's radical "yes" to God is an image that no longer computes. For the gift economy that John Paul embraces has long since been replaced by a consumer economy that sees us as most human when we are most fully in possession of our self and anything we can lay our hands on.

---

65. *Sign of Contradiction,* p. 50.
66. See, for example, the essay, "The Family as a Community of Persons," in *Person and Community,* p. 324.
67. Ibid., p. 321.
68. Ibid., p. 319.

There is no doubt in my mind that John Paul believes we have fallen much further than we should have, given the high hopes he holds forth for love and for reason. That is why I believe he is brokenhearted about human sinfulness, more brokenhearted than are those with a less optimistic reading of human prospects, those who believe that the beasts are always straining at their leashes, rattling their chains, and awaiting release upon a complacent and uncomprehending and perhaps even occasionally joyous world. And it is a joyous world that John Paul evokes over and over again. In a charming "Christmas Letter to the World's Children" of Christmas 1994, he talks about a newborn baby and claims: "I can almost see you: You are setting up the crib at home, in the parish, in every corner of the world, recreating the surroundings and the atmosphere in which the Savior was born. Yes, it is true!"[69] He tells a story of his own experience — "I am thinking of when many years ago I was a child like you" — and he calls on "dear children," remembering the baby in the crib, to pray that humanity may find the way to the paths of peace. "God loves you, dear children! . . . What joy is greater than the joy brought by love? What joy is greater than the joy which you, O Jesus, bring at Christmas to people's hearts, and especially to the hearts of children?

> Raise your tiny hand, divine child,
> And bless these young friends of yours,
> bless the children of all the earth."[70]

How easy it is to dismiss, even to be cynical, of such sentiments in our harsh time. The words I used to conclude a recent book on Saint Augustine apply with equal force to our ongoing debate about the life and work of Pope John Paul II. "This man who desired 'not only a devout reader, but also an open-minded critic,' gets too few of each, or both, in our harsh and cynical time."[71]

69. John Paul II, "Christmas Letter to the World's Children," *Origins* 24, no. 29 (1995): 481.

70. Ibid., p. 486.

71. Jean Bethke Elshtain, *Augustine and the Limits of Politics* (Notre Dame: Notre Dame University Press, 1996), p. 118. The internal quote from Saint Augustine is from *De Trinitate* (Washington, D.C.: Catholic University of America Press, 1992), Book 3, p. 96.

The Use of Scripture in *Veritatis Splendor*

KARL P. DONFRIED

Introduction: The Purpose of the Encyclical

John Paul II wishes to reflect on the whole of the Church's moral teachings because of doubts and objections that have been raised in the current cultural climate, especially among those who would detach "human freedom from its essential and constitutive relationship to truth" (*Veritatis Splendor* [VS] #4):

> In particular, the question is asked: do the commandments of God, which are written on the human heart and are part of the Covenant, really have the capacity to clarify the daily decisions of individuals and entire societies? Is it possible to obey God and thus love God and neighbour, without respecting these commandments in all circumstances? Also, an opinion is frequently heard which questions the intrinsic and unbreakable bond between faith and morality, as if membership in the Church and her internal unity were to be decided on the basis of faith alone, while in the sphere of morality a pluralism of opinions and of kinds of behavior could be tolerated, these being left to the judgment of the individual subjective conscience or to the diversity of social and cultural contexts. (VS #4)

Particularly relevant for the assignment given is this further comment by the pope: "The specific purpose of the present Encyclical is this: to set forth, with regard to the problems being discussed, *the principles of a moral teaching based on Sacred Scripture* and the living Apostolic

Tradition, and at the same time to shed light on the presuppositions and consequences of the dissent which that teaching has met" (VS #5; my italics).

Part I: The Rich Young Man

A. Matthew 19:16-22

The encounter of the rich young man with Jesus in Matthew 19:16-22 is the foundational text, the scriptural leitmotiv that runs throughout this 1993 papal encyclical. Gareth Moore, in an essay repeatedly asserting the misuse of Scripture in *Veritatis Splendor,* concludes that the encyclical ignores the central meaning of this text.[1] For Moore the point of the text is to provide an "example of the power of riches over those who own them and an occasion for the teaching of Jesus on how hard it is for the rich to enter the kingdom of heaven."[2] Given this disapproval of the central text employed by John Paul II, it would be wise to examine briefly the setting and intention of this pericope in its New Testament context.[3]

In all three synoptic versions we have an apophthegma that involves a radical call to discipleship. The young man asks about eternal life: "Teacher, what good deed must I do to have eternal life?" Jesus responds, "If you would enter life, keep the commandments" and, upon further questioning, specifies five commandments from the second part of the Decalogue and, in Matthew alone, adds, "You shall love your neighbor as yourself." In what appears to be a response to the young man's failure to really "get the point" of the commandments cited, Jesus adds, "If you would be perfect, go, sell what you possess and give to the poor, and you will have treasure in heaven;

1. Gareth Moore, "Some Remarks on the Use of Scripture in *Veritatis Splendor,*" in *The Splendor of Accuracy,* ed. Joseph A. Selling and Jan Jans (Grand Rapids: Eerdmans, 1995), pp. 71-97.

2. Moore, "Remarks," p. 74.

3. For the appropriateness of this methodological approach, see the recent publication of the Pontifical Biblical Commission, "The Interpretation of the Bible in the Church," *Origins* 23, no. 29 (1994): 497-524; also Joseph A. Fitzmyer S.J., *Scripture, The Soul of Theology* (New York: Paulist, 1994).

and come, follow me." All three Gospels contain the "come, follow me" phrase, and it lies at the heart of the tradition concerning the call to discipleship in all of its radical consequence.

As Matthew attempts to actualize this story for his audience, three modifications made by him to his *Vorlage* are particularly relevant for our purposes:

1. The Marcan "You know the commandments" (Mark 10:19) is revised to say, "If you would enter life, keep the commandments" (Matt. 19:17); anyone seeking eternal life should look to the commandments. The phrase "keep the commandments" is the "only such direct exhortation in Matthew."[4]

2. Matthew adds, as already indicated, "You shall love your neighbor as yourself" (19:19).

3. The Marcan "You lack one thing; go, sell" (Mark 10:21) reads "If you would be perfect, go, sell" in Matthew 19:21.

At the heart of Matthew's revision of Mark is the addition of the love command from Leviticus 19:18, and this addition is intended, as in 7:12 and 22:39-40, to summarize, to fulfill, to bring to their root meaning, the law and the prophets. This addition points to the deep structure that gives meaning to the Matthean form of the exhortation "If you would enter life, keep the commandments," that is, if you would be perfect, if you would be whole, if you would truly wish to be a disciple, then go and sell. Discipleship transcends obedience to the commandments; it involves participation in the kingdom (cf. Matt. 19:12, 14, 23, 24). "Loving one's neighbor as oneself (see 19:19b) is the 'perfect' fulfillment of the commandments."[5]

The young man in question is not "perfect" because he is not persuaded of the ultimate goodness of God and, as a result, of the goodness of eternal life with God.[6] And that takes us right back to the beginning of the text: "Why do you ask me about who is good? One there is who is good." This turns the original question, "Teacher, what good deed must I do?" (Matt. 16:17) upside down. The young

---

4. Donald A. Hagner, *Matthew 14–28,* Word Biblical Commentary 33B (Dallas: Word, 1995), p. 557.

5. Daniel Patte, *The Gospel According to Matthew* (Philadelphia: Fortress, 1987), p. 271.

6. Ibid., p. 272.

man is clearly unable to do this good because he does not understand that it only comes as a result of the intervention of God, from the One who issues the invitation "come, follow me" (Matt. 19:21). Thus, Ernst Haenchen, in commenting on the Marcan form of this text, comments accurately: "Wer vollkommen sein will, darf sich nicht mit der Erfüllung der Gebote des A.T. zufriedengeben!"[7]

B. The Exegesis of the Rich Young Man in Veritatis Splendor

As previously noted, Moore understands the encounter between the young man and Jesus as providing "an example of the power of riches over those who own them and an occasion for the teaching of Jesus on how hard it is for the rich to enter the kingdom of heaven (19:23ff)."[8] As a result of this exegesis he is able to conclude that the "encyclical all but ignores this central meaning of the passage. It is noted that the young man went away sorrowful (VS #22), but the fact that he is rich and the following teaching on the dangers of riches, with its vivid language designed to catch the attention . . . are passed over in silence in favor of an emphasis on Jesus's remark that with God all things are possible (19:26), which leads to an extended section on grace (VS #22-24)."[9] Thus John Paul's claim that "in the young man, whom Matthew's Gospel does not name, we can recognize every person who, consciously or not, approaches Christ the Redeemer of man and questions him about morality"[10] is in error since not all people who approach Christ are rich. "The message of this narrative is not how hard it is for those who do not keep the commandments to enter the kingdom, but how hard for those with riches."[11] A similar criticism is made by William Spohn: "The rich young man is not 'Everyman,' but a representative of the rich and their particular impediments to discipleship."[12]

---

7. Ernst Haenchen, *Der Weg Jesu* (Berlin: Töpelmann, 1966), p. 358.
8. Moore, "Remarks," p. 74.
9. Ibid.
10. Ibid.
11. Ibid., p. 77. Moore suggests that the parable of the sheep and the goats (25:31-46) would have been more appropriate — it is more generalizing.
12. William C. Spohn, "Morality on the Way of Discipleship: The Use of

But is this not too narrow a reading of the text and its intention? Nikolaus Walter, in a detailed analysis of Mark 10:17-31, persuasively shows that "Markus läßt noch erkennen, daß die nun folgenden vv. 24b-27 ein selbständiges, erst von ihm hier angeknüpftes Über- lieferungsstück waren. . . ."[13] If one agrees with Walter that πλούσιον is a latter expansion of the original apophthegma, then it follows that the emphasis of Jesus was this: "Gottes Souveränität allein ist es vorbehalten, irgend jemanden in sein Reich einzulassen; vom Men- schen aus gesehen ist das Vorhaben, in das Reich Gottes einzugehen, so unmöglich, wie es unmöglich ist, ein Kamel durch ein Nadelöhr gehen zu lassen."[14] Although John Paul II is concentrating on the Matthean version, his reading of the original intention of Jesus is remarkably close to that of Walter and, this being the case, mutes the criticism of both Moore and Spohn with regard to the particularity of the story as having relevance only to the situation of the *rich* young man and therefore only to the rich.

The pope's exegesis of the encounter of the young man with Jesus as presented by Matthew recognizes that the Gospels are functioning at different levels in the developing trajectory of the Jesus story, and it is therefore more persuasive than Moore's. From the exegesis of the rich young man presented in *Veritatis Splendor* it can be determined that:

1. All aspects of Matthew 19:16-21 are discussed and there is a clear recognition that this text has parallels in Mark and Luke.

2. The basic purpose of this text is the theme of discipleship (VS #22). Discipleship transcends knowing and obeying the command- ments. "More radically, it involves holding fast to the very person of Jesus, partaking of his life and his destiny, sharing in his free and loving obedience to the will of the Father" (VS #19). "Conscious of the young man's yearning for something greater, which would transcend a legalistic interpretation of the commandments, the Good Teacher invites him to enter upon the path of perfection" (VS #16).

Scripture in *Veritatis Splendor*," in *"Veritatis Splendor": American Responses,* ed. Michael E. Allsopp and John J. O'Keefe (Kansas City: Sheed & Ward, 1995), pp. 83-105; here p. 91.

13. Nikolaus Walter, "Zur Analyse von Mc 10, 17-31," *Zeitschrift für die neutesta- mentliche Wissenschaft und die Kunde der älteren Kirche* 53 (1962): 206-18; here 209-10.

14. Ibid., p. 210.

3. With Walter, the jump to verse 26 is appropriate and provides the opportunity to emphasize that one cannot fulfill the commandments out of one's own resources. "To imitate and live out the love of Christ is not possible for man by his own strength alone. He becomes capable of this love only by virtue of a gift received" (VS #22). Only in response to the call "follow me," that is, in discipleship, can there be new life, eternal life. "Only in this new life is it possible to carry out God's commandments. Indeed, it is through faith in Christ that we have been made righteous (cf. Rom 3:28): the righteousness which the Law demands, but is unable to give, is found by every believer to be revealed and granted by the Lord Jesus" (VS #23).

4. The call to perfection, to discipleship, does not eradicate the exhortation to "keep the commandments." The tension between these different moments in the story is captured with great insight. "But it is certain that the young man's commitment to respect all the moral demands of the commandments represents the absolutely essential ground in which the desire for perfection can take root and mature, the desire, that is, for the meaning of the commandments to be completely fulfilled in following Christ. Jesus' conversation with the young man helps us to grasp the conditions for the moral growth of man, who has been called to perfection: the young man, having observed all the commandments, shows that he is incapable of taking the next step by himself alone. To do so requires mature human freedom ('If you wish to be perfect') and God's gift of grace ('Come, follow me')" (VS #17). Based on these insights the encyclical can assert that human "freedom and God's law are not in opposition; on the contrary, they appeal one to the other" (VS #17).

5. The encyclical presents some further reflections with regard to Matthew 19:19 that are consonant with the text, namely, that this pericope upholds the singular dignity of the human person and that, with the Decalogue as a whole, safeguards the good of the human being. The commandments, it is asserted, "represent the basic condition for love of neighbor; at the same time they are the proof of that love. They are the first necessary step on the journey towards freedom, its starting point" (VS #13).

Finally, it may be useful to summarize the hermeneutical presuppositions that guide this section of the encyclical. In *Veritatis Splendor* #120 one learns that (1) God's law must be understood in light of the gospel. Further, the church "receives the gift of the New Law, which is the 'fulfillment' of God's law in Jesus Christ and in his Spirit. This is an 'interior' law (cf. Jer 31:31-33), 'written not with ink but with the Spirit of the living God, not on tablets of stone but on tablets of human hearts' (2 Cor 3:3); a law of perfection and freedom (cf. 2 Cor 3:17), 'the law of the Spirit of life in Christ Jesus' (Rom 8:2)"; (2) the Decalogue is a promise and sign of the new covenant (VS #12); (3) Christ is the key to the Scriptures and therefore it is he who brings God's commandments to fulfillment, especially the commandment of love of neighbor (VS #15); and (4) any given text, such as the invitation "if you want to be perfect," must be read and interpreted "in the context of the whole moral message of the Gospel" (VS #16).

All of these hermeneutical assertions cohere with the recent publication of the Pontifical Biblical Commission, "The Interpretation of the Bible in the Church."[15]

C. An Evaluation of the Use of Scripture in Part One of Veritatis Splendor

William Spohn has urged that no papal document "in history has concentrated to such an extent on the role of Jesus Christ in the Christian moral life or relied as much on Scripture as the source of its argument."[16] This promise of a christologically oriented ethics is further enhanced by some profoundly biblical and evangelical statements about justification and sanctification.

As a result of his keen understanding of Romans 8:2, John Paul II can proceed to urge that "if God alone is the Good, no human effort, not even the most rigorous observance of the commandments, succeeds in 'fulfilling' the Law, that is, acknowledging the Lord as God and rendering him the worship due to him alone. . . . This 'fulfillment' can come only from a gift of God: the offer of a share in the divine Goodness revealed and communicated in Jesus" (VS #11).

It is repeatedly asserted that the moral life of the Christian is a response to God's love and can only be the result of the "gratuitous

15. See note 3.
16. Spohn, "Morality," p. 83.

initiatives taken by God out of love for man" (VS #10). Yet genuine love for God can only be affirmed by the love of the neighbor. Thus there must be a close connection between the Christian life and obedience to God's commandments (VS #13). Thus, referring to Paul, it can be asserted that the "firmness with which the Apostle opposes those who believe that they are justified by the Law has nothing to do with man's 'liberation' from precepts. On the contrary, the latter are at the service of the practice of love: then follows Rom 13:8-9" (VS #17). Combining his previous reflections on Matthew 19 with Paul, the pope attempts to define the relationship of the indicative to the imperative, between justification and sanctification: "those who are impelled by love and 'walk by the Spirit' (Gal 5:16), and who desire to serve others, find in God's Law the fundamental and necessary way in which to practice love as something freely chosen and freely lived out. Indeed, they feel an interior urge — a genuine 'necessity' and no longer a form of coercion — not to stop at the minimum demands of the Law, but to live them in their 'fullness'" (VS #18).

John Paul II is keen that no "damage must be done to the *harmony between faith and life*" (VS #26), and he understands both faith and life in dynamic terms. With regard to the latter, he consciously steers away from any type of legalism. Thus the reader is repeatedly reminded that the catechesis of the apostles was always "connected to specific historical and cultural situations" (VS #26), that the New Testament shows that the Lord's precepts "are to be lived in different cultural circumstances" (VS #26), and that the commandments are to be put in practice keeping in mind "new historical and cultural situations" (VS #27). To be able to do so is a "sign and fruit of a deeper insight into Revelation" (VS #27). It is the Holy Spirit who will assist in reverently preserving, faithfully expounding, and correctly applying them "in different times and places" (VS #27).

Despite the grandeur of this first section of the encyclical, some questions need to be raised, questions that will manifest themselves as grave concerns as our exposition of the document continues. First, one should ask whether the exposition of the rich young man concentrates on the commandments that Jesus endorses in such a way that his Torah criticism as well as his other acts and deeds are excluded. The singular focus on the Matthew 19:16-22 text, with its relatively unique emphasis on the commandments, masks a far more complex situation concerning Jesus and the Torah. Not only can one speak of the ambiguity of Jesus' attitude to the Torah but also about his polemic against it and his conflict with it. Repeatedly it was annulled and breached by him. Jesus simply denied the Torah the central position it held in the judaisms of his day. Schrage summarizes the matter well: "When Jesus abrogates the letter of the law, his primary concern is not saying 'no' to the law but 'yes' to God's will, which, however, has been partially obscured and rendered innocuous by law and tradition. The Torah does indeed continue to proclaim God's will, but the two are not identical. The criteria by which even the Law must be judged are the kingdom of God and the double commandment of love."[17]

A second concern that arises in this first part of *Veritatis Splendor* is the emergence of the concept of "natural law." Unobtrusively hidden in the exposition of "if you wish to enter into life, keep the commandments" (Matt. 19:17) is a reference to Romans 2:15 and the theme of the "natural law" (VS #12). Thomas Aquinas is called upon to interpret this law as "nothing other than the light of understanding infused in us by God, whereby we understand what must be done and what must be avoided. God gave his light and this law to man at creation" (VS #12). The intention seems to be to link the "natural law" with the story of the rich young man as a way of legitimizing its elaboration in the next section of the encyclical. Neither here nor elsewhere in *Veritatis Splendor* when Romans 2:12-16 is invoked is there any attempt made to place this text in the context of Paul's overall argument in Romans 1–4.

As much as I salute the profound biblical insights that are articulated in the opening part of this encyclical and its rich promise of a christologically based ethics, I must note that both these insights and promises are blurred at times by the sections that follow. Here it is no longer a christological ethic that is pursued but a theonomous naturalism, a philosophical ethics in the natural law tradition that bases morality in the divine law. The final chapter, though not without its own problems, does make some attempts to return to the promise

17. Wolfgang Schrage, *The Ethics of the New Testament* (Philadelphia: Fortress, 1988), p. 68.

held out by the first in defining discipleship in the context of cross and resurrection and in reflecting on martyrdom as the fullest expression of such discipleship.

Part II: Present-Day Moral Theology

Many Roman Catholic theologians would agree that the sources of Christian ethics include Scripture, tradition, moral philosophy, and empirical data. In the past Catholic moral theologians tended to take biblical texts and concepts out of their original context and use them to augment natural law arguments. Thus we need to pay particular attention to the use of Scripture in the remainder of the discussion directed against moral autonomy, relativism, and the misuse of conscience and proportionalism to see whether the creative and insightful first chapter has the power to prevail over the traditional manipulation of Scripture by Catholic moral theologians.

A. Introduction: The Role of Scripture

As the encyclical moves toward the situation of moral theology today, the pope's desire to do so in the context of Scripture is evident. Not only is the reader repeatedly reminded about the relevance of the story of the rich young man but also that "sacred Scripture remains the living and fruitful source of the Church's moral doctrine" (VS #28) and that the gospel is "the source of all saving truth and moral teaching" (VS #28). Given this emphasis, it is not surprising that a biblical text is selected as the descriptor for chapter 2: "Do not be conformed to this world" (Rom. 12:2).

Since the magisterium has the responsibility of faithfully preserving and expounding Scripture as the Word of God, it is important to recognize that certain contemporary interpretations of Christian morality "are not consistent with 'sound teaching' (2 Tim 4:3)" precisely because they detach the concept of freedom from truth, thus allowing a distorted notion of freedom to become the source of values and permitting the individual conscience to be established as the criterion for good and evil (VS #32).

B. The Issues

The pope is concerned that freedom uncoupled from truth will lead to a "moral autonomy" (VS #35). Such moral autonomy, it is feared, would not only have an "absolute sovereignty" but would also deny the existence of a Divine Revelation that contains "a specific and determined moral content" which is "universally valid and permanent" (VS #37).

Between paragraphs 38 and 48 two significant shifts take place in the document: an increased reliance on natural law, which is described "as the human expression of God's eternal law," and an enhanced concern with doctrines that dissociate "the moral act from the bodily dimension of its exercise" (VS #49). What "bodily" dimensions are at stake are specified in VS #47: "contraception, direct sterilization, autoeroticism, pre-marital sexual relations, homosexual relations and artificial insemination." To support the assertion that "it is in the unity of body and soul that the person is the subject of his own moral acts" there are references, on the one hand, to 1 Corinthians 6:9 and 19 and, on the other hand, to natural law, which is defined "as the rational order whereby man is called by the Creator to direct and regulate his life and actions and in particular to make use of his own body" (VS #50).[18] What happens in this part of the encyclical is that "the immutability of the natural law" and "the objective norms of morality" (VS #53) are cloaked with the authority of Christ ("there are some things which do not change and are ultimately founded upon Christ, who is the same yesterday and today and for ever" [VS #53]) and the authority of the "Old and New Testaments" (VS #52). "Revelation . . . simply confirms the objective moral demands of nature and shows where they lead."[19] Natural law is linked with behavior prohibited by the moral commandments expressed in negative terms in the Old and New Testaments and then it is identified with the use of the term "commandments" in the story of the young man. Thus: "As we have seen, Jesus himself reaffirms that these prohibitions allow no exceptions: 'If you wish to enter into life, keep the commandments'" (VS #52).

18. Citing *Donum Vitae* and *Humanae Vitae*.
19. Spohn, "Morality," p. 95.

C. Proportionalism

Once the commandments have been so broadened as to be virtually equivalent to a particular Roman Catholic understanding of natural law, the refutation of proportionalism begins. Beginning with a faulty reference to Galatians 5:13 ("Only do not use your freedom as an opportunity for the flesh"), one finds increasingly vague references to "negative moral precepts," actions or kinds of behavior that are "intrinsically evil," disordered kinds of behavior that involve a "denial of the Catholic doctrine of mortal sin" (VS #67-70). This is an unfortunate example of biblical "proof-texting" in which the overall context of Galatians 5 is misunderstood.

The chapter heading "The Moral Act" shows how far we have moved away from the story of the rich young man. We are now involved in an imprecise morality far removed from the goodness of God revealed in Jesus Christ. No longer do we hear: "Following Christ is thus the essential and primordial foundation of Christian morality. . . . Jesus' way of acting and his words, his deeds and his precepts constitute the moral rule of Christian life" (VS #19). Rather, a very different language is now being introduced: "The morality of acts is defined by the relationship of man's freedom with the authentic good. This good is established, as the eternal law, by Divine Wisdom which orders every being towards its end: this eternal law is known by man's natural reason (hence it is 'natural law'), and — in an integral and perfect way — by God's supernatural Revelation (hence it is called 'divine law')" (VS #72). No longer is it the person in Christ[20] following the path of discipleship assisted by the Holy Spirit who is morally good, but rather that activity "is morally good when it attests to and expresses the voluntary ordering of the person to his ultimate end and the conformity of a concrete action with the human good as it is acknowledged in its truth by reason" (VS #72). The shift away from the earlier, powerful exposition of the rich young man is described by Spohn as a decision to opt for a basically "deontological ethics" that "focuses on commandments as the primary vehicle for articulating the moral content of

20. This major New Testament phrase, "in Christ," found in every Pauline letter, is essentially ignored in *Veritatis Splendor*.

Christian discipleship."[21] And he suggests, further, that "the encyclical truncates the life of Christ to make it morally normative in a deontological way."[22] This latter point is one already referred to above and one to which we will return.

The teleological ethical theories referred to as proportionalism and consequentialism are rebuked because "the negative moral precepts, those prohibiting certain concrete actions or kinds of behaviour as intrinsically evil, do not allow for any legitimate exception" (VS #67). *What precisely these negative moral precepts are is never defined.* Surely they must go well beyond the commandments cited by Jesus or Paul in Romans 13:8-10. But once the illegitimate step has been made to merge the commandments cited by Jesus with a certain understanding of natural law, then it can be stated that these ethical theories under attack "are not faithful to the Church's teaching, when they believe they can justify, as morally good, deliberate choices of kinds of behaviour contrary to the commandments of the divine and natural law. These theories cannot claim to be grounded in the Catholic moral tradition" (VS #67). To cite Paul in support of this rebuke of proportionalism is not only an illegitimate exegetical move but also one that is intellectually distorted: "When the Apostle Paul sums up the fulfillment of the law in the precept of love of neighbour as oneself (cf. Rom 13:8-10), he is not weakening the commandments but reinforcing them, since he is revealing their requirements and their gravity. Love of God and of one's neighbour cannot be separated from the observance of the commandments of the Covenant renewed in the blood of Jesus Christ and in the gift of the Spirit" (VS #76). As Jesus' Torah critique was skewed previously in this encyclical, so here is Paul's Torah critique disregarded. Complex interrelationships are simplified to the point of distortion.

D. Intrinsic Evil

Veritatis Splendor #79 begins a section entitled "'Intrinsic evil': it is not licit to do evil that good may come of it (cf. Rom 3:8)." It

---

21. Spohn, "Morality," p. 99.
22. Ibid., p. 101.

categorically rejects the thesis of the teleological and proportionalist theories that the deliberate choice of behavior must take into consideration the intention for which the choice is made. Rather, the decisive element for moral judgment is the object of the human act which must be "capable of being ordered to the good and to the ultimate end, which is God." These acts that are "incapable of being ordered" to God are "intrinsically evil" *(intrinsece malum)*. Once again no specific examples are provided. Referring to *Reconciliatio et Paenitentia,* the encyclical mentions certain acts that "are always seriously wrong by reason of their object," followed by a citation from the Second Vatican Council. Here three primary examples of acts that are "always seriously wrong"[23] are presented: "Whatever is hostile to life itself, such as . . . ; whatever violates the integrity of the human person, such as . . . ; whatever is offensive to human dignity, such as . . ." (VS #80). It is of no little importance that the Vatican II text cited actually uses neither the phrase "intrinsically evil" nor the phrase "always seriously wrong" but, rather, "all these and the like are a disgrace [*probra*]."

Two Pauline citations, Romans 3:8 and 1 Corinthians 6:9-10, are employed to support the discussion of "intrinsic evil." Are these texts properly understood within their Pauline context?

Romans 3:8. This text is linked "to contraceptive practices whereby the conjugal act is intentionally rendered infertile" (VS #80). The full verse, translated from tortured Greek, can be rendered in this way: "And why not say (as some people slander us by saying that we say), 'Let us do evil so that good may come'? Their condemnation is deserved!" This becomes a fundamental text in the attack on proportionalism (VS #78ff.) and the text is understood to mean that "no evil done with a good intention can be excused" (VS #78). On the contrary, it is asserted, the "moral quality of human acting is dependent on this fidelity to the commandments" (VS #82). This is not at all what Paul has in mind as he is attempting to defend his teaching on justification from false criticism. Rather than linking the righteousness of God with covenant law, Paul is actually breaking the link between righteousness and law; it is this "danger" that leads some to falsely accuse him of antinomianism. The redirection that the Jewish under-

---

23. *Reconciliatio et Paenitentia* does not use the phrase *intrinsece malum* at this point.

standing of righteousness takes in Romans is toward justification and
not toward some definition of "intrinsic evil."

1 Corinthians 6:9-10. This text is introduced in the following way:
"In teaching the existence of intrinsically evil acts, the Church accepts
the teaching of Sacred Scripture. The Apostle Paul emphatically
states . . ." (VS #81). Paul himself writes: "Do you not know that
wrongdoers will not inherit the kingdom of God? Do not be deceived!
Fornicators, idolaters, adulterers, male prostitutes, sodomites, thieves,
the greedy, drunkards, revilers, robbers — none of these will inherit
the kingdom of God." This is followed and brought to a conclusion
in verse 11: "And this is what some of you used to be. But you were
washed, you were sanctified, you were justified in the name of the
Lord Jesus Christ and in the Spirit of our God." What is Paul attempting to do at this point in his exhortation to the Corinthians? Is he
endeavoring to define "intrinsically evil acts"? Is he seeking to develop
a new Christian law and morality? How can one refer to 1 Corinthians
6:9-10 without reviewing the circumstances of Paul's original communication to the Corinthian Christians?[24]

The context concerns a Christian who takes another to court
"before the unrighteous [ἄδικοι], instead of taking it to the saints"
(6:1). This theme of the ἄδικοι is then explicitly taken up in 6:9. Paul
is attempting to clarify who the ἄδικοι are. Since they will not inherit
the kingdom, they should not be judging the saints. The Corinthian
Christians are no longer controlled by the ethic of the world and, as
a result, they should not allow themselves to be judged by pagan
magistrates. They are no longer in fellowship with the ἄδικοι and
their magistrates precisely because they *"were* washed, (they) *were*
sanctified, (they) *were* justified in the name of the Lord Jesus Christ
and in the Spirit of our God." It is evident that the apostle is grappling
with the tension between the indicative and the imperative. He wants
his audience to take seriously the warnings of verses 9-11 but also the
statements and rhetorical questions of verse 7. His warning is urgent,
namely, that those in the community who persist in the same behavior
as the ἄδικοι are in clear danger of not inheriting the kingdom; but
his intention is certainly not to classify lawsuits, or anything else in

24. See the literature cited in note 3; also Karl P. Donfried, *The Dynamic Word:
New Testament Insights for Contemporary Christians* (San Francisco: Harper & Row, 1981).

these lists, as "intrinsically evil." Paul's strong warning concludes with
a statement of grace; the imperative is not the last word. He does not
want to leave the impression that the Corinthian Christians are still
among the wicked; because of God's prior action in the Lord Jesus
Christ and the "Spirit of our God," they have been removed from
the realm of the ἄδικοι. As a result of this transforming work of the
Spirit present in their community and in their lives, they are now able
to live out their new life in Christ and not be influenced by the ἄδικοι.
In baptism they have been cleansed by God's action in Christ, a
cleansing that is now being effected in them by the Spirit.

In citing 1 Corinthians 6:9-10 to support the theme of "intrinsic
evil," *Veritatis Splendor* fails to understand that the "obedience God
demands cannot be subdivided or put together out of individual acts.
Like Jesus, Paul has his eye on an integral approach to life, not a
conglomerate of isolated acts of obedience to the law."[25] In Galatians
5:19-21 Paul also issues a warning about works (plural!) of the flesh
that will not lead to the kingdom. But the other side of this warning
is not that of *VS* #82 that "the moral quality of human acting is
dependent on this fidelity to the commandments, as an expression of
obedience and love." Rather, when the apostle refers to the fruit of
the Spirit as "love, joy, peace, patience . . ." he not only refers to all
of these acts in the singular — "fruit" — but also adds that there "is
no law against such things." Rather, "if we live by the Spirit, let us
also be guided by the Spirit." F. F. Bruce has got it exactly right: "Paul
does not simply mean that the nine virtues which make up the fruit
of the Spirit are not forbidden by law; he means that when these
qualities are in view we are in a sphere with which law has nothing
to do. Law may prescribe certain forms of conduct and prohibit others,
but love, joy, peace and the rest cannot be legally enforced."[26] "According to Paul," asserts Schrage, "God does not require this, that,
and the other, an endless list of details. God claims the whole self,
with all that one has and all that one is."[27] The point of the specificity

25. Schrage, *Ethics,* p. 187.
26. F. F. Bruce, *Commentary on Galatians,* New International Greek Testament
Commentary (Grand Rapids: Eerdmans, 1982), p. 255.
27. Schrage, *Ethics,* p. 188. Schrage understands well the tension / dialectic between an autonomous and hieronomous authority. Speaking of Paul, he writes on

of Paul's instructions, injunctions, and commandments was both to illustrate the concreteness of the Christian ethic and to draw attention to the totality of the new obedience. Once again the failure to explicate the Pauline understanding of "in Christ" leads to serious failures in understanding Pauline theology.

Implicit in this entire discussion of "intrinsic evil" is the story of the rich young man, which is consistently linked to the discussion of natural law. If intrinsic evil rests on the premise that the "primary and decisive element for moral judgment is the object of the human act, which establishes whether it is capable of being ordered to the good and to the ultimate end, which is God" (VS #79), and if the God who gives the commandments is good, then surely it must be correct, so the argument runs, to conclude that the "doctrine of the object as a source of morality represents an authentic explication of the Biblical morality of the Covenant and of the commandments, of charity and of the virtues" (VS #82).

Veritatis Splendor forces all Christian theologians to reach some fundamental decisions with regard to the hermeneutics of Scripture. How should one appeal to Scripture for guidance concerning the burning moral issues of the day?[28] Is the focus of our biblical herme-

---

p. 192: "The apostle does not exhort and encourage, command and admonish, in his own name but in the name of Jesus Christ; those who disregard his commands transgress against Christ and against God (1 Thess. 4:6, 8). Of course Paul never merely imposes a formal authority. He calls on his readers to judge what he writes (1 Cor. 10:15). Dialectically, it is proper to speak at once of a mature and responsible community, which is not reduced to obeying blindly apostolic decrees. Nor, however, are Paul's admonitions a more-or-less optional contribution to the dialogue or an unauthoritative personal opinion. They establish the will of God with authority and demand to be followed (2 Cor. 2:9; 7:15; Phil. 2:12; Philem. 8-11). This is also the basis on which the apostle calls on his readers to imitate his conduct (1 Cor. 4:16-17; 11:1; Phil. 4:9; 3:17)."

28. The reader may wish to consult Raymond F. Collins, *Christian Morality: Biblical Foundations* (Notre Dame, Ind.: University of Notre Dame, 1986); Richard B. Hays, *The Moral Vision of the New Testament* (San Francisco: HarperSan Francisco, 1996); Eduard Lohse, *Theological Ethics of the New Testament* (Minneapolis: Fortress, 1991); Frank J. Matera, *New Testament Ethics: The Legacies of Jesus and Paul* (Louisville: Westminster John Knox, 1996); Schrage, *Ethics* (see note 17); Jeffrey S. Siker, *Scripture and Ethics: Twentieth Century Portraits* (Oxford: Oxford University Press, 1996); William C. Spohn, *What Are They Saying About Scripture and Ethics?* (New York: Paulist, 1995).

neutic one that views Scripture primarily as a book of proof texts of individual and detailed moral commands, or will our focus be on Scripture's fundamental vision of the reality of God revealed in Jesus Christ as the generating power for a more comprehensive Christian ethic? *Veritatis Splendor* emphasizes that Scripture offers moral prescriptions. One of the many serious problems with this approach is that the New Testament writers do not consider prescriptive statements as part of a legal code that needs to be interpreted and actualized. Are the authors of the New Testament really *primarily* concerned with formulating commands and prescriptions that ought to govern the lives of Christians? *Veritatis Splendor* would have us think so.

Part III: Moral Good for the Life of the Church and the World

A. The Appeal to Scripture: 1 Corinthians 1:17 and Galatians 5:1

This final chapter begins with two Pauline texts, 1 Corinthians 1:17 and Galatians 5:1. Unfortunately they are not coherently integrated with the many other biblical texts mentioned in this part. The latter text, "For freedom Christ has set us free," is cited because it raises to the fore what is for the pope one of the most pressing issues for Christian moral thought today: the relationship between freedom and truth. According "to Christian faith and the Church's teaching," it is insisted, "only the freedom which submits to the Truth leads the human person to his true good. The good of the person is to be in the Truth and to *do* the Truth" (VS #82). But, one must ask, what exactly is the truth, especially in light of the many citations from the Johannine literature in this section of the encyclical? Does *truth* have the same meaning when it is used as a christological title in John's Gospel as it does when one is referring to the objective status of moral norms?

After citing 1 Corinthians 1:17, the encyclical states that "it is in the Crucified Christ that the Church finds the answer to the question troubling so many people today: how can obedience to universal and unchanging moral norms respect the uniqueness and individuality of the person, and not represent a threat to his freedom and dignity?"

(VS #85). Has it really been demonstrated that either Jesus or Paul desired "obedience to universal and unchanging moral norms" (VS #85)?

Once again it can be observed that natural law is equated as being synonymous with the biblical witness. It is asserted that when "it is a matter of the moral norms prohibiting intrinsic evil, there are no privileges or exceptions for anyone" (VS #96). What are these moral norms? Two sentences later the implication is made quite specific: "The commandments of the second table of the Decalogue in particular — those which Jesus quoted to the young man of the Gospel (cf. Mt 19:19) — constitute the indispensable rules of all social life" (VS #97). Although these commandments "are formulated in general terms," they can "be specified and made more explicit in a detailed code of behaviour" (VS #97). How can such a "code of behaviour" be derived from any reasonable exegesis of 1 Corinthians 1:17 or Galatians 5:1 using the guidelines proposed by the Pontifical Biblical Commission?[29]

The references to walking in the light, the repeated assertion that faith also "possesses a moral content," and the discussion of martyrdom[30] are useful discussions of the biblical witness (VS #88-90). But, quickly short-circuiting any historical exegesis, the conversation turns to the "Church's firmness in defending the universal and unchanging moral norms" (VS #96). Is this really what Jesus had in mind when he referred to the commandments in Matthew 19:16-22? The broad generalizations in this section of *Veritatis Splendor* go far beyond what is said in the Matthean pericope or what can responsibly be attributed to Paul. The assessment of William Spohn is accurate: "The encyclical promises a Christonomous ethics of discipleship but it cannot deliver because it reduces morality to a matter of rules and principles."[31]

B. The Ethical Crisis in the West

Some enormously helpful reminders are given in these final pages about

---

29. See note 3.
30. See Spohn's criticism (in "Morality," pp. 96-98) of the discussion of martyrdom in *Veritatis Splendor*.
31. Spohn, "Morality," p. 102.

"the risk of an alliance between democracy and ethical relativism" (VS #101), a relativism that is leading to an increased "dechristianization" and "defiance or obscuring of the moral sense" (VS #106). That a "new evangelization," one that includes the moral dimension, must take place, and that the question about the nature of good and evil needs to be raised (VS #111) as the church enters the third millennium, is indeed an important challenge to all Christians.

But those who understand the Pauline doctrine of justification as involving both the indicative and the imperative, the *Gabe* and *Aufgabe* dimensions of the gospel, will have difficulty with observations such as: it "is the Gospel which reveals the full truth about man and his moral journey, and thus enlightens and admonishes sinners; it proclaims to them God's mercy, which is constantly at work to preserve them both from despair at their inability fully to know and to keep God's law and from the presumption that they can be saved *without merit*. God also reminds sinners of the joy of forgiveness" (VS #112; emphasis mine). And those rooted in a New Testament ecclesiology will find problematic the assertion that it is the responsibility of the magisterium to intervene "by means of judgments normative for the conscience of believers" and in teaching "the faithful specific particular precepts and requires that they consider them in conscience as morally binding" (VS #110). *Veritatis Splendor* also asserts that dissent from such moral doctrine "is opposed to ecclesial communion and to a correct understanding of the hierarchical constitution of the People of God" (VS #114). Where many Roman Catholics and most Protestants would part company with this encyclical is in the questionable hermeneutical move made in paragraph 114, where it concludes that the pastors and bishops of the church must "teach the faithful the things which lead them to God, just as the Lord Jesus did with the young man in the Gospel." If our opening exegesis is correct, this is exactly what Jesus did not do! The call to discipleship has apparently been transformed into a "new law"[32] and the insightful exegesis of the first section has been minimized. "Christonomous ethics" in this

32. Jesus invited the "young man to follow him in poverty, humility and love: 'Come, follow me!' The truth of this teaching was sealed on the Cross in the Blood of Christ: in the Holy Spirit, it has become the new law of the Church and of every Christian" (VS #114).

concluding part of *Veritatis Splendor*, contends Spohn, "becomes not a theonomous but a 'hieronomous' ethics of the Church's magisterium."[33] In short, *Veritatis Splendor* has not demonstrated to the satisfaction of this sympathetic critic that "the reaffirmation of the universality and immutability of the moral commandments, particularly those which prohibit always and without exception intrinsically evil acts" (VS #115), a firm basis in a trinitarian, ecclesiocentric hermeneutic of Scripture.[34]

Summary Issues

1. *Veritatis Splendor* makes reference to "the principles of a moral teaching based on Sacred Scripture." Are these principles articulated with sufficient precision?

a. Especially in chapters 2 and 3, there are repeated appeals to Scripture. Most often, however, the original historical and literary settings of these texts are ignored. We concur with the judgment of Spohn that "the biblical material is cited in a timeless manner, just like the selections from patristic sources. Contrary to modern historical interpretations, the encyclical presents Paul, Augustine and Aquinas as having identical understandings of natural law, grace and freedom."[35]

b. Whereas chapter 1 subordinated a realist epistemology and the natural law to discipleship and the cross, these paradigms quickly shift to the symbols of the New Moses and martyrdom, and such symbols lead more easily to a rule-centered ethic of obedience. Thus the Christology of *Veritatis Splendor* is essentially nomistic. Note the statement in #15 that Jesus "himself became a living and personal Law, who invites people to follow him." Many interpreters would have a more paradoxical reading of the Sermon on the Mount, one in which Jesus is presented as a prophetic figure who in the name of God

---

33. Spohn, "Morality," p. 102.

34. See the discussion by Karl P. Donfried, "Alien Hermeneutics and the Misappropriation of Scripture," in *Reclaiming the Bible for the Church,* ed. Carl E. Braaten and Robert W. Jenson (Grand Rapids: Eerdmans, 1995), pp. 19-45.

35. Spohn, "Morality," p. 93.

challenges both the religious and moral attitudes of all persons. Regrettably both the eschatological and prophetic dimensions of Jesus' kingdom proclamation are muted and the Matthean emphasis on law and obedience is underscored in a way that too easily misses the tension in which these themes are held in both Matthew and the other canonical Gospels.

2. "Sacred Scripture remains the living and fruitful source of the Church's moral doctrine" (VS #106). If the encyclical had been consistent, it would have presented us with a more uniformly christonomous ethic. Instead it moves from a theonomous to a "hieronomous" ethic of the Church's magisterium.[36]

3. Divine revelation contains "a specific and determined moral content" that is "universally valid and permanent" (VS #114). "The Church affirms that underlying so many changes there are some things which do not change and are ultimately founded upon Christ who is the same yesterday and today and forever" (VS #53). But, queries Spohn, "do 'universality' and 'immutability' mean the same when predicated of Christ and of moral norms?"[37] The danger with this way of argumentation is that "certain moral practices may become sacrosanct, because criticism of them could be taken as denying the permanence of Christ."[38]

4. Much of the moral resonance of the Gospels is lost because they are read through a "deontological lens"[39] and such a reading ultimately "narrows the moral life to obedience to universal moral norms."[40]

5. The most significant flaw in *Veritatis Splendor*, however, is its failure to define with consistent clarity and through the use of concrete examples what is meant by the term "intrinsic evil."

36. Ibid., p. 102.
37. Ibid., p. 98.
38. Ibid.
39. Ibid., p. 100.
40. Ibid., p. 101.

Grace, Justification
through Faith, and Sin

GILBERT MEILAENDER

Theology is ecclesial, or it is nothing at all. And if each Church remains faithful to Revelation, "thinking its doctrines through to the end," both sides might come to agreement at some specific spot. Says Barth: "Let the Roman Catholic Church think through its doctrine on nature and grace, and the teaching on justification that was developed by Trent." And to him we say: "Let reformation theology think through its teaching on the visible Church, on obedience and law, and also its dialectic about homo simul peccator et justus. Then life will begin to flow through the Church's limbs. Questions will be posed, and the possibility of an answer will be real once again." [1]

WHEN IN AUGUST 1993 Pope John Paul II issued *Veritatis Splendor,* it was, according to the encyclical's own words, "the first time . . . that the Magisterium of the Church has set forth in detail the fundamental elements of this teaching." [2] The encyclical has generated a

1. Hans Urs von Balthasar, *The Theology of Karl Barth* (New York: Doubleday Anchor, 1972), pp. 7-8.
2. Pope John Paul II, *The Splendor of Truth* (Boston: St. Paul Books & Media, 1993), #115. Citations of the encyclical will hereafter be identified by paragraph number in parentheses within the body of the text.

considerable amount of discussion, most of it from Catholic moral theologians, and a good bit of that critical on certain points.[3]

The letter is divided into three chapters: the first offers a meditation on the story in Matthew's Gospel of the rich young ruler who comes to Jesus asking what he must do to be saved; the second treats controverted topics in moral theory (especially natural law and conscience, the meaning of a "fundamental option," and the concept of an intrinsically evil act); the third calls Christians to sacrifice even to the point of martyrdom in the service of moral truth and asserts the need for moral theologians to conform their teaching to that of the church. The encyclical's critics generally praise the first chapter as an illustration of a renewed biblical spirituality in Catholicism and an example of John Paul's own serious reflection on the Scriptures. That praise does not extend to the treatment of moral theory in chapter 2, however, nor to the discussion of the "service" of moral theologians in chapter 3. Indeed, critics sometimes suggest that, while chapter 1 grows out of the personal experience and reflection of John Paul, chapter 2 is very likely the work of other hands.[4] The encyclical is rife with references to "some authors" whose views fall short of the truth on questions of natural law, conscience, fundamental option, and intrinsically evil acts. Yet, among the candidates for likely inclusion within the class of "some authors," few seem willing to acknowledge that their views have been adequately described in chapter 2 of *Veritatis Splendor.* Thus, for example, in a strong statement but one that captures the tone of response, Richard McCormick S.J. writes of the encyclical that "its analyses [are] too frequently obscure and convoluted, and its presentation of revisionist tendencies [is] tendentious, extreme, and ultimately inaccurate."[5]

Here I offer a different angle of vision from which to think about the teaching of *Veritatis Splendor.* I seek to reopen some questions that perhaps first came to seem urgent in the Reformation. These questions involve different visions of the Christian life — differences that played a central role in the most significant split in the history of the

---

3. See, for example, Richard A. McCormick S.J., "Some Early Reactions to *Veritatis Splendor," Theological Studies* 55 (September 1994): 481-506.

4. Ibid., pp. 485ff.

5. Ibid., p. 483.

Western church, and which, if my reading of the encyclical is correct, may still constitute an unresolved problem at the heart of Christian ethics and an agenda for continuing work. From my perspective, it turns out, chapter 1 of *Veritatis Splendor* is every bit as much cause for concern as chapter 2. Indeed, the supposed gap between them — even different authorial hands, if they are present — is not terribly important. For the two chapters are of a piece on certain central issues. From my perspective the role of faith in the Christian life takes center stage.

The encyclical itself turns our attention in this direction with its stated concern for the relation of faith and life. In the letter's introduction, John Paul expresses concern about a "frequently heard" opinion "which questions the intrinsic and unbreakable bond between faith and morality, as if membership in the Church and her internal unity were to be decided on the basis of *faith alone* while in the sphere of morality a pluralism of opinions and of kinds of behavior could be tolerated" (#4, italics added). Surely anyone drawn to the questions of the Reformation might perk up at such a sentence. Again, near the close of the encyclical's first chapter, John Paul writes (and this time the italics are already in the text): "No damage must be done to the *harmony between faith and life*" (#26). Claims about "faith and morals" were important in the Council of Trent's reaction to Lutheran teaching, and the phrase's meaning continues to be discussed and disputed.[6] In order to explore this issue, I will focus on the encyclical's treatment of the story of the rich young ruler and its discussion of fundamental option.

I

The first chapter of *Veritatis Splendor* is, even as biblical exposition, a tightly knit description of the moral life.[7] The young man comes to Jesus asking about the *telos* of life, the good he should seek. This is,

6. John Mahoney, *The Making of Moral Theology* (Oxford: Clarendon, 1987), pp. 120-35.

7. I have taken this description from Oliver O'Donovan, "A Summons to Reality," in *Understanding "Veritatis Splendor,"* ed. John Wilkins (London: SPCK, 1994), pp. 41-42.

ultimately, a question about God. But his question about the good turns out to be directly related to that other important moral concept, the right. To be directed toward God, as he is by Jesus, is to be pointed toward the One who teaches us — through the natural law, the history of Israel, and the new covenant written on the heart — what it is right to do. Teleology and deontology are in themselves insufficient, however. Both must be set into the context of the hope of eschatological perfection. Hence the young man is called out on a journey toward human fulfillment. "Jesus shows that the commandments must not be understood as a minimum limit not to be gone beyond, but rather as a path involving a moral and spiritual journey towards perfection" (#15). That journey involves following Christ, being empowered by the Holy Spirit (since the new law, according to Aquinas, is finally the personal presence of the Spirit), and being guided by the church, which carries the tradition of faith and life entrusted to it by Jesus.[8]

The precise role of grace in making possible this journey is not, however, as clear as one might wish. *Veritatis Splendor* describes the moral life as a response to "the many gratuitous initiatives taken by God out of love for man" (#10). It affirms that human fulfillment of the law comes only as a gift from God (#11). Yet it appears to picture such fulfillment of the law as a necessary condition of fellowship with God. That fellowship comes at the end of a long journey toward perfection, a journey empowered by grace, which is itself characterized as "the New Law" (#23). Grace is fundamentally a power that makes possible that keeping of the law which constitutes the way back to God. "This is a still uncertain and fragile journey as long as we are on earth, but it is one made possible by grace, which enables us to possess the full freedom of the children of God" (#18).

Hence the gift of grace has the effect of increasing the demands of the law. When the disciples, taken aback at Jesus' words to the rich young man, ask who can be saved, Jesus responds: "With men this is impossible, but with God all things are possible." Drawing on a tradition of thought that goes back at least to Augustine's claim that

8. The essay by Bernd Wannenwetsch in this volume discusses in some detail the way in which moral language can be explicated and understood fully only within a particular community such as the church. This helps to explicate the manner in which the church carries the tradition of a way of life entrusted to it by Jesus.

God does not command the impossible,[9] *Veritatis Splendor* understands Jesus' answer to mean that grace is a power making possible the completion of the journey toward perfection. "Keeping God's law in particular situations can be difficult, extremely difficult, but it is never impossible" (#102). Indeed, if a redeemed person still sins, this can only be due to his unwillingness "to avail himself of the grace which flows from" Christ's redemptive act (#103).

The way back to God is, therefore, the way of growth and progress in keeping the moral law. Jesus, "the new Moses" (#12), tells the young man to keep the commandments. When he affirms that he has in fact done so, Jesus calls him in search of perfection (in the famous "if you would be perfect . . ." passage). Is grace necessary even to begin this journey toward God? Or is it necessary only for the completion of it? *Veritatis Splendor* states that "the young man's commitment to respect all the moral demands of the commandments represents the absolutely essential ground in which the desire for perfection can take root and mature" (#17). Jesus helps the young man, we are told, "to grasp *the conditions for the moral growth of man* . . . : the young man, having observed all the commandments, shows that he is incapable of taking the next step by himself alone. To do so requires mature human freedom . . . and God's gift of grace" (#17). Even if these words are not semi-Pelagian, one might worry about the use of the language of "conditions" for salvation here. At several other places similar language is used. "Jesus himself definitively confirms them [the commandments of the Decalogue] and proposes them to us as the way and condition of salvation" (#12). Or again, much later in *Veritatis Splendor:* "Jesus, in his reply, confirms the young man's conviction: the performance of good acts, commanded by the One who 'alone is good,' constitutes the indispensable condition of and path to eternal blessedness" (#72). With the Reformation disputes in mind, one may legitimately wonder whether it would not be better, even from John Paul's perspective, to say that keeping the commandments is a *description* of being on the way toward fellowship with God, not a *condition* of it. The language of "conditions" in these contexts risks undercutting the centrality of grace in the journey toward God.

Thus a reader of the first chapter of *Veritatis Splendor* may be

9. Cf. Mahoney, *Moral Theology,* pp. 48-57.

uncertain whether grace empowers the journey back to God from start to finish, or whether it only builds upon our own attempts to keep the commandments, which attempts constitute a necessary starting point for grace. Whatever the uncertainties on this point, however, a reader of chapter 1 will surely know that grace is necessary for the perfection of our fellowship with God. But the reader will also have learned to think of this grace almost entirely in one way: as a power, as "an effective means for obeying God's holy law" (#114).[10] Grace is absolutely essential, but "[i]t is precisely through his acts that man attains perfection as man" (#71). Grace makes possible growth and progress in righteous deeds; that is the picture of the Christian life at work in *Veritatis Splendor*.

II

What, if anything, does such a depiction of the Christian life lack? Taking the long way round to an answer, I will first describe another and quite different reading of the story of the rich young ruler. In a seventeen-page small-print excursus, buried deep within a discussion of "The Command as the Claim of God" in volume 2/2 of his *Church Dogmatics,* Karl Barth took up the same biblical story.[11] Stanley Hauerwas noted this "fascinating parallel" but without considering it in detail.[12] Examining Barth's exposition will position us to identify what is lacking in *Veritatis Splendor*.

Characteristically, Barth begins by emphasizing that the entire action takes place within the sphere of Jesus Christ. Even the rich man, who is disobedient, is within that sphere. Hence, Barth does not think of one who is outside Christ's rule coming to him, coming from outside to inside. Instead, he thinks of all people as inside that sphere

10. Reinhard Hütter, in his essay in this volume, discusses in some detail the way in which *Veritatis Splendor* mistakenly embeds the gospel within a more comprehensive framework of law.

11. Karl Barth, *Church Dogmatics,* vol. 2, no. 2 (Edinburgh: T. & T. Clark, 1957), pp. 613-30. Future citations will be given by page number in parentheses within the body of the text.

12. Stanley Hauerwas, *"Veritatis Splendor,"* Commonweal 120 (22 October 1993): 16.

— either in obedience or in disobedience. Although that characteristic Barthian claim is unlike anything in *Veritatis Splendor,* the initial moves in Barth's exposition are for the most part not unlike John Paul's. Barth underlines the close connection between the two love commands. Every bit as much as John Paul, he emphasizes that "it is not possible either to love one's neighbour without first loving God, or to love God without then loving one's neighbour" (p. 616). The rich man's mistake lies in supposing that he can somehow separate the two commands, and Jesus' threefold word to him (sell what you have, give to the poor, and follow me) is designed to help him see this. Just as *Veritatis Splendor* interprets this story as, ultimately, a call to follow Jesus, so does Barth. "He [the rich man] has all possessions except the one — the fulness of Jesus. And this is what condemns him" (p. 623).

Suddenly, however, Barth takes up a feature of the story almost entirely ignored in *Veritatis Splendor* — the disciples, those who are "the obedient" in contrast to the disobedient rich man. Barth notes their astonishment at Jesus' command to sell, give, and follow. The disciples have, in a sense, done this; nevertheless, they are astonished, and rightly so. For they now see clearly the lure of all they have forsaken; they understand its power; and they see that they themselves always stand "on the edge of the abyss of disobedience" (p. 624). One might have supposed that the only thing left for the disciples was greater growth in the way of life they had chosen in following Jesus. In Barth's depiction of them, however, there is no place for the language of growth and progress. Instead, even as "the obedient," the disciples learn again "how great a step obedience involves, and that even when this step has been taken once, it has to be taken again and again in all its difficulty" (p. 624). Not growth, but a continual return to the starting point characterizes the way of discipleship.

How, then, shall we depict that starting point? In the face of the disciples' astonishment, Jesus tells them that what is impossible for us is possible for God — a statement Barth describes as "obviously the hinge on which the whole narrative turns" (p. 625). It is not for Barth a promise that God does not command the impossible, or that God will surely empower us to do what he commands. Barth's is a quite different move.

[T]he impossible became possible to them. To them? No, it was never possible to them. It was still possible only to God. But in the knowledge that what is possible only to God has become possible *for* them, in this confidence, in this humility or boldness — we can now say simply in *faith* — they became obedient. They accepted it as true that Jesus was obedient for them. . . . They believed, i.e., they were pleased to have His ability attributed to them, to have their own inability covered over by His ability. . . . They undertook to live in the shade and shelter of His ability. . . . If they do not lack the one thing that is needful for the fulfillment of the divine command, it is certainly not because they themselves possess it and achieve it. It is only because it is there for them in Jesus. It is only because they are pleased to accept it by faith in him. (p. 626)

The language of faith provides Barth's starting point here. It is not, however, a starting point from which one grows and develops, no longer standing on the edge of the abyss of disobedience. Rather, it is the starting point to which one constantly returns, covering one's inability by undertaking to live within the shade and shelter of Jesus' ability — which means not so much listening to the Teacher as trusting the Savior.

The disciples are "the obedient"; the rich man, "the disobedient"; yet, "they stand with him under the judgment which is passed upon all that is possible with men, [and] he on his side is united with them under the promise of that which is possible with God" (p. 626). Hence, even for the obedient, even for the disciples, the Christian faith is not best described in terms of growth and progress, of a journey toward perfection. Unlike the rich man, the disciples have left everything to follow Jesus. When they point Jesus' attention to this fact — to the seeming difference between the obedient and the disobedient in the story — the reader suddenly realizes that they have made no progress. They still look back in sorrow at what they have left behind. "But how, then, had they really left it? . . . If they are capable of this backward look, are they even a single step in advance of the rich man who went away sorrowful?" (p. 628).

Even in the disobedience of these obedient disciples, Jesus promises them that they will have their reward in the kingdom (a promise which must, therefore, also be directed to the rich man in his disobedience). Confronted by the clear anxiety of his disciples, "[i]n face of their scarcely concealed defection, Jesus becomes and is again, and this time truly, Jesus the Saviour" (p. 629). Not a Teacher, not a new Moses, not a living and personal Law, not one to be imitated — not any of those roles which chapter 1 of *Veritatis Splendor* ascribes to Jesus. With no clear distinction remaining between the obedient and the disobedient, with both constantly standing on the edge of an abyss they cannot cross, Jesus can only be the one who is *for* both. "He steps, as it were, over that abyss for them and with them — again making them, from what they are by themselves, into what they are permitted to be by and with Him" (p. 629).

For *and* with them. They must therefore also step across that abyss to be with Jesus. They must grow in their discipleship. All that is true, yet muted in Barth's exposition. For in any moment "the obedient" may suddenly realize the depth of their disobedience, may doubt that any progress along the way of obedience has been made in their life. At such moments — which means, potentially, at any and every moment — they need to hear a promise they can trust, an invitation not to moral struggle but to take shade and shelter in the cover of Jesus' ability.

Structurally, Barth's exposition differs from John Paul's in that it focuses not just on the rich man but also on the disciples — not just the disobedient, but also the obedient. If, however, we ask ourselves whether this structural difference has any theological payoff, the answer is clear: It opens up space in Barth's exposition for the language of faith — language, we may suddenly realize, that is virtually absent from chapter 1 of *Veritatis Splendor*. It appears a few times in the sense of the "deposit of faith" or in the phrase "faith and morals," but one must look hard to find faith as *fiducia*. Perhaps we are close in a passage in which, while the full reality of the kingdom is said to be available only in eternal life, faith is described as "even now . . . an inchoate share in the full following of Christ" (#12). Closer still is paragraph 21, where discipleship is described as becoming conformed to Christ, who "dwells by faith in the heart of the believer." Yet Christ *in* us is not the same as Christ *for* us. Closest of all probably is the description in paragraph 19 of the response of faith as something more than hearing a teaching or obeying a commandment. "More radically, it involves *holding fast to the very person of Jesus,* partaking of his life and his destiny, sharing in his free and loving obedience to the will of the Father." Even in this language, however, one steps *with* Jesus across the abyss separating disobedience from obedience. We are not told that Jesus steps over the abyss *for* the disobedient, that he is obedient *for* them. And it is that *promissio* that invites *fiducia*.

Does this matter? I do not wish to underestimate the importance of John Paul's picture of the Christian life as a journey (powered by grace) toward perfection, nor the seriousness with which his invocation of the church's martyrs reckons with the fact that this journey may be difficult. At least in my view, no Christian ethic can get along without these themes.[13] Nevertheless, taken alone, as they for the most part are in *Veritatis Splendor,* they offer the *power* of grace apart from its *pardon,* a grace that does not invite us in our weakness simply to take shade and shelter in the fact that Jesus is *for* us.

> Those who live "by the flesh" experience God's law as a burden, and indeed as a denial or at least a restriction of their own freedom. On the other hand, those who are impelled by love and "walk by the Spirit" (Gal. 5:16), and who desire to serve others, find in God's law the fundamental and necessary way in which to practice love as something freely chosen and freely lived out. (#18)

But, of course, Christians are likely to experience — even simultaneously to experience — God's law in both of these ways, as both the path of true love and as a burden. If they take seriously that division within themselves, the encyclical's indicatives may be experienced as crushing rather than empowering. They do not encourage one to think of oneself as among the "disobedient" *and* the "obedient" — as disobedient yet *simultaneously* a recipient of the promise of grace. "It is precisely through his acts that man attains perfection as man" (#71), and one is either on the road toward God or one is not. Difficult to encompass within the categories of *Veritatis Splendor* is the idea that I might in my actions be journeying away from God while, at the same time, through faith taking shelter in Jesus as One who has acted on

---

13. Cf. Gilbert C. Meilaender, *The Theory and Practice of Virtue* (Notre Dame, Ind.: University of Notre Dame Press, 1984), pp. 100-26; Gilbert C. Meilaender, *Faith and Faithfulness* (Notre Dame, Ind.: University of Notre Dame Press, 1991), pp. 74-80.

my behalf.[14] Yet such a promise of shelter is the word of the gospel, and the structure of our ethic ought not to undercut our ability to speak that word.

III

How diminished the significance of faith as *fiducia* is within *Veritatis Splendor* will become clearer if we consider the treatment of fundamental option in its second chapter. This concept, with its roots in transcendental Thomism, no doubt differs in some respects from the Reformation language of faith, but it also bears many similarities. In fact, *Veritatis Splendor* describes the "decision of faith" as "a fundamental choice which qualifies the moral life and engages freedom on a radical level before God" (#66).

John Paul's concern is not so much with the concept itself as with the uses to which it can be put. He and those whom he criticizes agree, I think, in discerning a kind of two-way movement between particular acts and fundamental option. Particular actions can shape the fundamental orientation of the self, and that orientation is itself expressed in particular actions. In the categories of the Reformation, works can shape the person and the person is manifested in the works. At issue, though, is how tight the connection between these two must be. John Paul wishes to emphasize that a fundamental choice for God cannot coexist with a deliberate choice to do what one knows to be gravely wrong.

Related to this issue, of course, is the debate about the category of intrinsically evil acts, a debate that I will not attempt to elucidate here. In my judgment John Paul is correct to think there may be some acts that are intrinsically evil, and he is right to view proportionalism as the practical equivalent of consequentialism (even though it is technically different in certain respects), but the dispute between John Paul and his critics about intrinsically evil acts need not be solved to get at my concerns. We need only note that John Paul thinks it

---

14. In his essay in this volume, Theodor Dieter discusses — from a different angle — a related problem: what he calls the problem of mediating the subjectivity of morality and the objectivity of moral law.

impossible for a person to sustain a fundamental choice for God while knowingly and deliberately doing what is gravely wrong. He will allow no separation between judgment of the person and of the work. It may be that some of his critics agree with him on this point. Proportionalists' desire to demonstrate that they are not allowing the choice of moral evil (even though they may permit a choice of *pre*moral evil) suggests that they, too, may worry that such deliberate action is incompatible with a fundamental choice for God. In that case they remain essentially within John Paul's thought pattern (deliberate choice of grave evil must separate one from God), differing only on the question of whether at least some such choices can be specified as "intrinsically evil" in advance of any and all circumstances. If, however, one says with Josef Fuchs that "specific, individual moral acts as such are not the acceptance or rejection of grace," one may have adopted a different pattern of thought and set foot on a road that leads to Wittenberg.[15]

Discussing the place of norms within the Protestant tradition, Gene Outka has distinguished two questions:

> (1) Does the violation of certain moral norms always negatively affect *one's own* relation to God? Does it necessarily influence, for example, one's prospects for salvation, or define in part the content of one's disobedience to God? (2) Does such violation always conflict with the normative content of *neighbor-love?* Are there certain actions one must never do to others if one genuinely loves them?[16]

Outka suggests that the Reformers tended to answer "no" to the first question, holding that our actions could not finally have any soteriological significance. Therefore, whether there are norms defining intrinsically evil acts will, from this Reformation perspective, depend chiefly upon our answer to the second question. "Agent-performance loses some of its religious urgency and force; recipient-benefit becomes the

---

15. Josef Fuchs, "Basic Freedom and Morality," in *Introduction to Christian Ethics: A Reader,* ed. Ronald P. Hamel and Kenneth R. Himes (Mahwah, N.J.: Paulist, 1989), p. 196.

16. Gene Outka, "The Protestant Tradition and Exceptionless Moral Norms," in *Moral Theology Today: Certitudes and Doubts,* ed. Donald G. McCarthy (St. Louis: The Pope John Center, 1984), p. 137.

primary criterion for making moral judgments."[17] If there are intrinsically evil acts, they are so because they could never, under any circumstances, be done as an expression of neighbor-love. Outka's distinction
offers a useful angle of vision from which to examine *Veritatis Splendor*.

In *Veritatis Splendor* intrinsically evil acts are evil for two reasons
that are connected to the dual love command. On the one hand, such
acts violate the human dignity of the neighbor. "The different commandments of the Decalogue are really only so many reflections of
the one commandment about the good of the person, at the level of
the many different goods which characterize his identity as a spiritual
and bodily being in relationship with God, with his neighbor and with
the material world" (#13). The same point can be made with respect
not only to an individual neighbor but to the larger society. "These
[universal moral] norms . . . represent the unshakable foundation and
solid guarantee of a just and peaceful human coexistence" (#96).
Intrinsically evil acts are evil also because they "are not capable of
being ordered to God" (#81). Such *deeds,* at least if they involve grave
matter, could be undertaken deliberately and knowingly only by a
person who, by virtue of a fundamental choice, had turned against God.

When I agreed above that there may be intrinsically evil acts, I
meant that we may indeed be able to specify in advance — apart, that
is, from any particular circumstances — actions that would violate the
neighbor's dignity. The question of fundamental option remains even
after one has granted that. Could such acts involving grave matter,
undertaken knowingly and deliberately, be the acts of one who still
had saving faith, who continued to take shade and shelter in the
obedience of Jesus?[18] Could the deed be intentionally sinful and the

17. Ibid., p. 138.
18. In her essay in this volume, Lois Malcolm discusses a similar issue, though
with a somewhat different concern. My focus here is on exploring the possibility that
a deliberately sinful act might "coexist" with saving faith. Her concern is, rather,
whether any specific injunction about how we ought to act can be correlated absolutely with the call to discipleship. Her worry, I suspect, is grounded more in
epistemological considerations, and my own view is that, if one can believe in the
incarnation, one need not feel compelled to distinguish between an absolute call to
discipleship and conditioned particular injunctions as she does. Nevertheless, at least
in my view, one must still ask whether the fundamental orientation of the self can
be equated with the intention to act in any particular way on a given occasion.

person right with God through faith? If this is possible, the connection between particular actions and fundamental option cannot be as tight as John Paul says it is. He explicitly considers a view in which the connection is not tight.

> According to the logic of the positions mentioned above, an individual could, by virtue of a fundamental option, remain faithful to God independently of whether or not certain of his choices and his acts are in conformity with specific moral norms or rules. By virtue of a primordial option for charity, that individual could continue to be morally good, persevere in God's grace and attain salvation, even if certain of his specific kinds of behavior were deliberately and gravely contrary to God's commandments as set forth by the Church. (#68)

Such a position he rejects — and rejects in language that simply leaves no room for a Reformation understanding of faith as that *fiducia* which, clinging to Christ, makes us right with God even in our sin.

Human beings do not, John Paul says, "suffer perdition" only by a fundamental choice against God. On the contrary, with every deliberate and knowing choice of grave evil, one rejects God. There is no room for a divided self who chooses what is evil yet clings to God. Indeed, in what from a Reformation perspective is the most striking language in the encyclical, John Paul writes of one who freely commits mortal sin: "[E]ven if he perseveres in faith, he loses 'sanctifying grace,' 'charity' and 'eternal happiness.' As the Council of Trent teaches, 'the grace of justification once received is lost not only by apostasy, by which faith itself is lost, but also by any other mortal sin" (#68). If faith here means simply the "deposit of faith," a set of truths intellectually affirmed, it does not begin to capture the meaning of *fiducia*. If it means something more than that, if it includes the trust of the heart, then it is inconceivable that one persevering in such faith, even while knowingly and deliberately sinning, could lose eternal happiness.

At stake here, of course, is the meaning of the phrase *simul justus et peccator,* and I do not wish to overstate my claim. That any deliberate, knowing choice of evil might itself enact a rejection of God and a refusal to trust I will not deny. That is what Helmut Thielicke meant by describing prohibited acts, *prohibitiva,* as "conditions under which, in principle, the work of the Holy Spirit cannot take place."[19] In such circumstances, Thielicke writes in a striking sentence, "there is . . . no *simul*."[20] But it is one thing to know that an act is evil in the sense that it always violates the dignity of one's neighbor. It is quite another to know that the evil of any act so overcomes the division of the self that there is no longer any *simul*, no longer a "disobedient" one who still clings to the promise that in Jesus God is for us. Choosing to do what is gravely wrong one might, of course, deliberately intend to reject the claims of any objective good outside the self, intend simply to do whatever one wished. One might also, however, while deliberately and knowingly choosing evil, say, "I know this is wrong, but it is the best I can manage here and now" — deliberately choosing under the rubric of the good what one knows to be wrong. If this is possible, as I think it is, the *simul* is not destroyed in such a moment. The "disobedient" one clings to the promise, and we cannot deny that it is directed to him in all his disobedience.

Have I perhaps now pressed the Reformation position too far, driven too deep a wedge between judgment of the person and of the work? In private communications about an earlier draft of this essay, both David Yeago and Reinhard Hütter have argued as much. For Hütter, the life of faith involves "particular practices" by means of which we "again and again flee from the law's judgment to God's forgiveness in Christ . . . and this life of faith involves our very intentionality in a way that seems . . . to exclude the intentional choice of evil acts as good. . . . While each grave evil can be repented for afterwards . . . one cannot intentionally choose a grave evil and at the same time grasp Christ in faith." If the *simul* has in fact persisted through intentional evildoing, "only the eschatological 'Gericht der Werke' will bring this simultaneity to light — if it existed at all."[21] For Yeago, Luther's understanding of the *simul* did not mean that no transformation of the sinner had taken place — as if we could be "unchanged but accepted." Rather, it meant that the remaining sin which clings to a believer is sin that does not "rule" the believer's

19. Helmut Thielicke, *Theological Ethics,* vol. 1 (Philadelphia: Fortress, 1966), p. 87.

20. Ibid., p. 89.

21. Reinhard Hütter, personal communication (11 November 1995).

action. "The sin in question is located 'within' in the heart, not 'without' in the believer's 'walk.'" Serious examples of such remaining sin are Peter's denial and David's adultery and murder. These "do not negate their identity as believers" because, on the one hand, these sins "were not entered with full deliberateness," and, on the other, "were *repented of* as soon as the one who committed them became aware of what he had done." Hence "deliberate *peccatum actuale* is not really compatible with faith in Christ *at all.*"[22]

I take these claims seriously, especially because one can support them with passages from the principal Lutheran Reformers. Thus, for example, in his 1555 *Loci Communes,* Melanchthon argues that we must make a distinction between different kinds of sin.[23] Although his distinction is similar to the Roman Catholic distinction between mortal and venial sin, it does not particularly depend on any judgment of the *gravity* of the sin. Rather, *deliberateness* is the key. Granting that sin still clings to the saints in this life — and that it is truly sin — he nonetheless distinguishes between instances in which "a man acts against his conscience, that is, consciously and willingly against the command of God" and instances which "are not sins against conscience." The latter, although not insignificant, do not blot out the holiness of the believer "as long as we do not will to follow these evil tendencies with action, but painfully strive against them." But those "who consciously follow their evil tendencies with action . . . and those who are not converted again fall into eternal punishment."

Perhaps even more important, similar assumptions can be detected at work in several of the Lutheran Confessional writings. Thus, for example, the *Epitome* of the *Formula of Concord,* while maintaining that the good works that follow faith are not the ground of our justification before God, notes (3.11): "Nevertheless, we should not imagine a kind of faith in this connection that could coexist and co-persist with a wicked intention to sin and to act contrary to one's conscience. On the contrary, after a person has been justified by faith, a true living faith becomes 'active through love' (Gal. 5:6)." Even more striking, perhaps, the *Smalcald Articles,* authored by Luther himself,

22. David Yeago, personal communication (4 December 1995).
23. For the discussion that follows, see Clyde L. Manschreck, ed., *Melanchthon on Christian Doctrine* (New York: Oxford University Press, 1965), pp. 183-86.

state (3.3.43-44): "It is therefore necessary to know and to teach that when holy people, aside from the fact that they still possess and feel original sin and daily repent and strive against it, fall into open sin (as David fell into adultery, murder, and blasphemy), faith and the Spirit have departed from them. This is so because the Holy Spirit does not permit sin to rule and gain the upper hand in such a way that sin is committed, but the Holy Spirit represses and restrains it so that it does not do what it wishes. If sin does what it wishes, the Holy Spirit and faith are not present."

That these questions are neither straightforward nor uncomplicated may be seen, however, if we take note of a similar passage in Luther's 1535 Galatians commentary. Discussing Galatians 5:19, he writes:

> Nevertheless, it sometimes happens that the saints may lapse and gratify the desires of their flesh. Thus David, in a great and horrible lapse, fell into adultery and was responsible for the murder of many when he had Uriah die in battle (2 Sam. 11). . . . Peter also lapsed horribly when he denied Christ. But no matter how great these sins were, they were not committed intentionally; they were committed because of weakness. In addition, when they had been admonished, these men did not persist stubbornly in their sins but returned to their senses. . . . Those who sin because of weakness, even if they do it often, will not be denied forgiveness, provided that they rise again and do not persist in their sins; for persistence in sin is the worst of all. If they do not return to their senses but stubbornly go on gratifying the desires of their flesh, this is the surest possible sign of dishonesty in their spirit. . . . Anyone who yields to his flesh and persists in smugly gratifying its desires should know that he does not belong to Christ.[24]

In the passage cited earlier from the *Smalcald Articles,* Luther treats David's sin not simply as a sin of weakness into which a saint might fall, but as intentional sin that is incompatible with faith and the presence of the Holy Spirit. Here in the Galatians commentary he treats is as a sin of weakness that is not committed intentionally and

---

24. *Luther's Works,* vol. 27 (St. Louis: Concordia Publishing House, 1964), pp. 80-81.

that, presumably, does not involve the kind of smug persistence in sin that makes it impossible for one simultaneously to belong to Christ. This ought to warn us that even if deliberate choice of evil involves rejection of God, as Hütter and Yeago insist, and as I concede may sometimes be true, these cases are not easy to parse. The human psyche is too complicated and the human will too deeply divided to admit of any general rule here. Clearly, one who deliberately does what he believes to be wrong treads in dangerous territory; for he goes against conscience. But can one who does this out of a deeply divided self, unable to will undividedly what he knows to be right, properly be described as one who persists in "smugly gratifying" the desires of the flesh? Sin does not "rule" in one whose will is divided, precisely because it *is* divided. Nor can we always say with confidence that the believer's will is clearly on the side of God and that the sin that still clings is only the weakness of disordered affections. In this life the division always goes deeper. Augustine's analysis of his will prior to conversion depicts the truth even of the believing self: "[I]t was I who willed it, and it was I who was unwilling. It was the same 'I' throughout. But neither my will nor my unwillingness was whole and entire."[25]

To suggest, as I have, that deliberate intention to commit grave sin may sometimes coexist with saving faith is not a claim upon which to build an ethic. Whatever we conclude about the possible coexistence of *fiducia* with a deliberate intention to do wrong, it is still an intention *to do wrong*. Wrongs done by the believer are covered by the righteousness of Christ; they are not thereby made right. And to the degree that John Paul has in *Veritatis Splendor* trained his sights upon any who, in effect, claim that the subjective good of a fundamental choice for God overcomes the objective wrongness of a sinful act, he is certainly on target. Such a view loses the distinction between judgment of the person and of the work by folding the latter into the former. That would be no better — indeed, perhaps worse — than John Paul's own tendency to make judgment of the work determinative for judgment of the person. Two fundamentally different judgments are involved here, and neither can be collapsed into the other before that eschato-

---

25. Augustine, *Confessions,* trans. Rex Warner (New York: New American Library, 1963), 8.10.

logical "Gericht der Werke" in which the truth of each person will be revealed. In the meantime, however, the life of faith is precisely that in which we struggle to believe about ourselves what is not always manifest in our desires, our wills, and, even, our choices and actions — namely, that we belong to the Spirit of Christ and are therefore, in God's eyes, wholly and entirely righteous. In taking up the possibility of deliberate wrongdoing by a believer, we are not, therefore, constructing an ethic. We are situating ourselves to practice that most difficult of theological arts — the distinction of law and gospel — in the care of souls. To one whom we judge to be smugly persisting in sin, one kind of response is necessary. To one whose will we judge to be so deeply divided that he clings to Christ even in his sin, another kind of response is necessary. No general rule can be given here, for the art of theological judgment is needed. We should not, I repeat, attempt to spin an ethic out of the distinction between law and gospel, but neither should we imagine that the care of souls can be satisfactorily carried out unless and until we have loosened the tight fit that John Paul has established between judgments of the work and of the person.[26]

That this is not a problem for Christian theology alone is nicely illustrated by Jonathan Sacks, Chief Rabbi of Great Britain. Sacks discusses the problem Moroccan Jews faced in the twelfth century when political power was seized by a Muslim sect that undertook a policy of forced conversions to Islam.[27] Some Jews chose to become martyrs, but, of course, some also did not have within themselves the stuff of the martyr. Many of these "conversos" or "marranos" publicly

26. An instructive example of the difficulties Roman Catholic practice encounters here is in the pastoral care of those who are divorced and remarried. To be sure, all honor should be given to the seriousness with which the Roman Church attempts to uphold Christian teaching concerning marriage. Protestants, who have for the most part lost all such seriousness, are in no position to cast stones. But the difficulties of maintaining that the divorced remarried continue to belong to the church but are excluded from the Eucharist are profound. For an instructive discussion both of the complexity and seriousness of Catholic thought on this question and of its shortcomings, see Kenneth R. Himes O.F.M. and James A. Coriden, "Notes on Moral Theology 1995: Pastoral Care of the Divorced and Remarried," *Theological Studies* 57 (March 1996): 97-123.

27. Jonathan Sacks, "To Be a Prophet for the People," *First Things* 59 (January 1996): 27-29.

embraced Islam "though inwardly remaining Jews and practicing Judaism in secret." How were they to be judged? Some rabbis held that they were "no longer part of the house of Israel." Maimonides, however, in his "Epistle on Forced Conversion," argued otherwise. What Sacks finds so instructive in Maimonides' argument, however, and what is so appropriate to our discussion here, is that Maimonides was uncompromising in his judgment that the conversos had acted wrongly. Yet, they were not excluded from the house of Israel. "There is nothing equivocal about Maimonides' defense of those who yielded to pressure. Nor is there any ambivalence about his later analysis of what, in fact, is the right way to behave. He invests both with equal seriousness." That is, he recognizes that there can be no perfect fit between judgment of the person and judgment of the work.

Distinguishing these two judgments always opens up the possibility of abuse, of course. That is, in some measure the worry of John Paul in *Veritatis Splendor,* and it is the (quite legitimate) worry of Hütter and Yeago. I take that danger seriously, but I know of no solution except a determined commitment to make both sorts of judgments whenever they are necessary. And I would now add that a Lutheran, at least, should be willing to run some risks in order to be certain that we are theologically positioned to speak the gospel to anyone whose self is deeply divided and who seeks God's promise of grace. In his *Theology of the Lutheran Confessions* Edmund Schlink devotes two chapters to the distinction between law and gospel.[28] First he follows a way that leads from law to gospel. That is, the gospel is God's gracious promise that in Jesus he has overcome our sin and that we are justified through faith alone without the works of the law. Consciousness of the law's condemnation drives us along the way that leads from law to gospel. But there is also a way that leads from gospel to law. The gospel truly brings about renewal and transformation of the sinner, who no longer lives under the law. Yet this very announcement of the gospel's power to renew our lives may become a condemning word for us — a path that leads from gospel to law. In Schlink's words, "the doctrine of regeneration and of the new obedience can actually become a trial for faith."[29] How so? Precisely in terms of the problem

28. Philadelphia: Fortress, 1961. See chapters 3 and 4.
29. Ibid., p. 116.

we have been examining at length. "If faith cannot coexist with sin, with sinful desires, or with the intention to sin, whose faith is then still faith?"[30] That is, the confident assertion that sin will no longer rule in the life of the regenerate, since they are no longer *under* the law, becomes a word that may lead us to doubt whether we have the Spirit of Christ whenever sin seems to have us in its grip. Schlink concludes that

> the repeal of the law by the Gospel [the first way], and the establishment of the law by the Gospel [the second way] are placed in antithesis. In antithesis are the doctrine of the necessary connection between faith and the new obedience, and the attack which this doctrine launches against the harassed believer and presses on him anew each day. . . . Only when both ways — the way from the law to the Gospel . . . and the way from the Gospel to the law . . . — have been traversed to the end do the questions with which all theology is confronted by the Word of God become clear. Only then can we truly see the problem that must be called the theme of the entire Lutheran theology — the distinction between law and Gospel.[31]

That problem should by now be clear: On the one hand, we must never construct an ethic that makes it impossible for us to speak both law and gospel — in whatever way each is needed — to instruct and comfort the consciences of those for whom we are responsible. This means that we cannot permit our judgment of the person to determine our judgment of the deed — as if a believer should never be warned that his action endangers his continued membership in Christ's Body. It means that we also cannot state — as a general rule, in advance of the care of any particular individual — that an objectively wrong deed, even a gravely wrong deed, cannot coexist with saving faith. We must strive to retain the capacity to make both judgments — of the deed and the person — as best we can, in accord with the Word of God given to us in Jesus and in the Scriptures.

There is no easier or less complicated way to capture the full significance of the fact that in this life the Christian remains *simul*

30. Ibid., p. 117.
31. Ibid., pp. 123-24.

justus et peccator. This formulation must always be taken in two somewhat different ways because God's grace in Christ is both transforming power and declaration of pardon. As transforming power it enters
into the history of our lives, driving out the sin that still clings,
drawing us ever more fully into the holiness of Christ, making
possible continued growth in righteousness, giving a direction and
trajectory to the moral life, and fitting us for heaven. Yet, as Schlink
saw clearly, this very description of grace as transforming power can
be heard not as gospel but as law whenever we do not see the signs
of continued growth, whenever we seem to turn away from the
holiness to which Christ calls us. When we turn away, we need the
warning of the law, but we also need — when our wills are sorely
divided — a gospel that is not transforming power but sheer declaration of pardon, a declaration that we are pardoned precisely in our
ungodliness (Rom. 5:6). Grace must be spoken of in both ways
because our theology must do justice to both the fifth and the sixth
chapters of Romans.

   Thus, if we try to think our doctrine through to the end, we will
not be able to agree entirely with von Balthasar when he objects to
Barth's understanding of the justification of the sinner on the ground
that it does not provide "for a real happening and a real history" —
that is, for the language of gradual growth and progress in righteousness.[32] Von Balthasar insists upon a "real sanctification" of which we
can say: "in this present age the Christian, now freed from sin, participates in the divine life through grace and is under no compulsion
to sin further."[33] We need not disagree. But we must also insist that
at every moment on this journey toward God the reality of our
righteousness in Christ must be understood eschatologically — as *in
re* only insofar as it is also *in spe.* That much a Lutheran ought to say,
having thought our doctrine through to its end in both ethics and the
care of souls.

   In 2 Kings the prophet Elisha heals Naaman, commander of the
army of the king of Syria. In gratitude, Naaman tries, before returning
home, to bestow gifts upon the prophet, but Elisha will not accept
them.

---

32. Von Balthasar, *Theology of Karl Barth,* p. 254.
33. Ibid., p. 255.

Then Naaman said, "If not, I pray you, let there be given to your
servant two mules' burden of earth; for henceforth your servant will
not offer burnt offering or sacrifice to any god but the LORD. In this
matter may the LORD pardon your servant: when my master goes
into the house of Rimmon to worship there, leaning on my arm, and
I bow myself in the house of Rimmon, when I bow myself in the
house of Rimmon, the LORD pardon your servant in this matter."
He said to him, "Go in peace." (2 Kings 5:17-19)

Naaman does not yet seem to have in him the stuff of a martyr.
Perhaps that later changed in his journey toward perfection. We are
not told. But Naaman also does not, at least in this sparse account,
claim that an appreciation of his circumstances will make what he
does right. He simply asks for pardon. He stands therefore as an
instance of the truth that, short of that eschatological perfection to
which we are indeed called, judgment of the deed and judgment of
the person cannot perfectly coincide. He reminds us that, even as we
should not construct a theological ethic that is unable to call his deed
wrong, so also we should not construct a theological ethic that makes
it impossible for us to say with Elisha: "Go in peace."

IV

I have attempted to reopen some Reformation questions and direct
them to *Veritatis Splendor* in a way that other commentators have not,
to my knowledge, done. It is important, therefore, to repeat what I
said earlier: No Christian ethic can say everything that needs saying
solely through the Reformation language of "faith active in love." If
we dare never say for certain that a particular deed makes the *simul* of
faith impossible, we ought not deny that our deeds do shape our
character — and that they have the power to make of us people who
no longer trust God for our security in life and death.

Against that emphasis on the soul-making power of deeds, separated from an equally strong emphasis on an unconditional declaration
of pardon to the disobedient *in* their disobedience, the Reformers
spoke a message not just of *sola gratia* but of *sola fide*. If *Veritatis Splendor*
grasps — albeit a bit haltingly in places — the importance of *sola gratia,*

it fails to enunciate clearly the *sola fide*. It is necessary, therefore, to reassert against its pattern of thought the centrality of the language of faith for Christian life.

If *Veritatis Splendor* requires such correction, it is at least also true that it speaks a theological language serious enough to invite such a response. One is — or I, at least, am — hard pressed to imagine an equally serious statement on the nature of theological ethics issuing at this time from any major Protestant body. Those who wish to keep alive the questions of the Reformation and the centrality of the language of faith in our vision of Christian life must therefore be thankful for *Veritatis Splendor*. Ironical as such a conclusion to this essay may seem, it is in fact what we must say if, today, we attempt to think our doctrine through to the end.

"God's Law" in *Veritatis Splendor:*
Sic et Non

REINHARD HÜTTER

"Yet you are near, O LORD,
and all your commandments are true."

Ps. 119:151, NRSV

SINCE ITS PROMULGATION in 1993, the papal encyclical *Veritatis Splendor* — "The Splendor of Truth " — has enjoyed significant attention from the secular public as well as from Roman Catholic moral theologians and Protestant ethicists. The *secular public,* being increasingly concerned with the destructive effects of moral relativism and cynicism, was most interested in the encyclical's strong claims about "God" and "truth" in relationship to "freedom" and "law." In contrast, *Roman Catholics* were mainly concerned with three issues: first, the encyclical's quite specific and highly technical teaching on "intrinsically evil acts," second, the complex question of whether the issues around proportionality and teleology were rightly characterized in the encyclical's central section, and third, what the encyclical's hidden agenda might be — from undergirding *Humanae Vitae*'s condemnation of artificial contraception to the pope's claim on a normative authority in conceptual and concrete issues of moral theology, not to mention the question of the encyclical's authorship.[1] *Protestant* readers, overall, left the encyclical with the impression that they had encountered a serious theological document on the Christian moral life to whose quality and scope there simply was no match in contemporary Protestantism.[2]

The following engagement is written by someone belonging to the third category of reactions. My reading of and reaction to *Veritatis Splendor*'s teaching about God's law will be both critical and sympathetic. I hope to show that the very fact that I draw strongly upon Luther's distinction (not dichotomization!) between God's sustaining and preserving *economy of creation* and God's *salvific economy* is not simply a rehearsal of an out-worn "law and gospel"-formula, the seemingly unavoidable "shibboleth" of Lutheranism. Rather, I hope to show that it makes sense to bring some of the Reformation's central concerns into conversation with the encyclical's way of relating God's law and God's gospel.

God, the Only Good One: Foundation and Truth of the Law

The encyclical opens in a surprising as well as theologically intense way with a biblical meditation on Jesus' conversation with the rich young man in the nineteenth chapter of the Gospel of Matthew.[3] With this daring interpretive move, the encyclical draws all of humanity into an inner-Jewish dialogue between a pious observer of the Torah and Israel's Messiah. Implicitly — this is the encyclical's claim — all

1. Cf. John Wilkins, ed., *Considering "Veritatis Splendor"* (Cleveland: Pilgrim, 1994); Joseph A. Selling and Jan Jans, eds., *The Splendor of Accuracy: An Examination of the Assertions Made by "Veritatis Splendor"* (Grand Rapids: Eerdmans, 1995); Dietmar Mieth, ed., *Moraltheologie im Abseits? Antwort auf die Enzyklika "Veritatis Splendor"* (Freiburg/Basel/Vienna: Herder, 1994).

2. Cf. Gilbert Meilaender, "*Veritatis Splendor:* Reopening Some Questions of the Reformation," in *Journal of Religious Ethics* 23 (1995): 225-38; and Robert Benne, "Reflections on the *Splendor of Truth,*" in *Pro Ecclesia* 3 (1994): 271-74.

3. Cf. in this volume Professor Meilaender's excellent comparison of the encyclical's interpretation of this biblical text with Karl Barth's interpretation of it. In addition, for a biblical scholar's critical reading of the encyclical's interpretation, see Gareth Moore, "Some Remarks on the Use of Scripture in *Veritatis Splendor,*" in Selling and Jans, eds., *The Splendor of Accuracy,* pp. 71-98.

of humanity stands before God just as this young Israelite stands before Jesus in the Gospel of Matthew. By reading this story as exemplary for all humanity, the encyclical intends to illustrate that the created reality of all humanity, and also humanity's call to a moral life, is encompassed by God's salvific activity: The question of the moral life and the question of salvation are inherently linked together.[4] Humanity's integral vocation consists in responding to both questions simultaneously.

This integral vocation is mirrored precisely in the way the encyclical correlates God's law with human freedom *via* the notion of the "good." According to the encyclical, human freedom is *teleologically* structured, that is, directed toward and drawn by the good itself, which is ultimately God's own goodness. Already as creatures, human beings are ordered towards the good. This happens through the moral natural law, which is the binding norm of their humanity, since — *via* the moral natural law — humanity participates in the eternal law, in God's providential care for creation.[5] Thus, by drawing largely on the

---

4. Cf. VS #8.

5. "Only God can answer the question about the good, because he is the Good. But God has already given an answer to this question: he did so *by creating man and ordering him* with wisdom and love to his final end, through the law which is inscribed in his heart (cf. *Rom* 2:15), the 'natural law.' The latter 'is nothing other than the light of understanding infused in us by God, whereby we understand what must be done and what must be avoided. God gave this light and this law to man at creation" (VS #12). With this way of putting the matter, the encyclical seems to follow a direction of interpreting Aquinas that privileges the concept of *law* in the construal of human freedom — over against the concept of the *virtues,* which are treated in the *Summa Theologiae* 1-2 before the law, and which in many ways frame the discussion of the law. Thus, according to *Veritatis Splendor,* human freedom does not gain its genuine shape *via* the well-orderedness of the human passions and the human will on grounds of the four cardinal virtues and — in an infinitely superior way — with the help of the three infused theological virtues. Rather, the human being's participation in the eternal law *via* acting upon the first principle of the natural law seems to be the decisive point of human freedom. Yet the relationship between the "virtues" and the "law" in Aquinas's *Summa Theologiae* is hotly debated among Aquinas scholars. For two recent accounts, which seem to mutually exclude each other, see on the one hand Eberhard Schockenhoff, *Bonum hominis: Die anthropologischen und theologischen Grundlagen der Tugendethik des Thomas von Aquin* (Mainz: Grünewald Verlag, 1987), and on the other hand Martin Rhonheimer, *Natur als Grundlage der Moral. Die personale Struktur des Naturgesetzes bei Thomas von Aquin: Eine Auseinandersetzung mit autonomer und teleo-*

Thomist tradition, the encyclical is able to present an impressive and coherent vision of human life, integrating the fulfillment of the moral good, that is, the creaturely destination towards the good, with the comprehensive fulfillment of the human destination toward communion with God.[6] This one seamless arch is supported by two central pillars: *God's law* and *human freedom*.

While the concept of "law" as displayed in *Veritatis Splendor* will be the focus of the following text, it will become apparent very quickly that it is impossible to discuss the concept of "law" in *Veritatis Splendor* without making constant reference to the concept of "freedom," a circumstance which is simply reflective of the encyclical's own intention.

God's Law: Foundation and Path of Human Freedom

In an interpretation of Genesis 2:16-17[7] the encyclical determines the relationship between law and freedom. Human freedom only finds fulfillment as genuine self-conscious freedom, transparent to itself, when it knows about its limit, which makes it both possible and guarantees it. Human freedom

> must halt before the "tree of the knowledge of good and evil," for it is called to accept the moral law given by God. In fact, human

---

logischer Ethik (Innsbruck/Vienna: Styra Verlag, 1987). Already in the 1950s it was pointed out that Aquinas's teaching on human freedom has its root in the "new law" (the gospel) and is intrinsically related to the virtues. Cf. Roger Guindon, *Béatude et théologie morale chez saint Thomas d'Aquin* (Montréal: Éditions de l'Université d'Ottawa, 1956), esp. p. 326.

6. Only one is truly good, and that is God. Therefore the fact that humanity's creatureliness already is ordered toward the highest good is to be understood as an expression of God's love for humanity. For an account of the thoroughly theological character of the *lex aeterna* in Aquinas's thought, cf. Otto H. Pesch, *Theologie der Rechtfertigung bei Martin Luther und Thomas von Aquin* (Mainz: Grünewald Verlag, 1967). According to him, the *lex aeterna* "ist der Inbegriff der der Weisheit Gottes entspringenden göttlichen Weltregierung, der göttlichen Vorsehung über alle Geschöpfe, und ist damit Quelle jeglichen anderen Gesetzes. In ihm ist daher alle Gutheit des Handelns zuletzt begründet, so wie alle Sünde *per definitionem* das ewige Gesetz übertritt" (p. 414).

7. "Of the tree of the knowledge of good and evil you shall not eat."

freedom finds its authentic and complete fulfilment precisely in the acceptance of that law. . . . God's law does not reduce, much less do away with human freedom; rather, it protects and promotes that freedom. (VS #35)

On the one hand, the encyclical emphasizes the active role of human reason in the finding and application of the moral law.[8] At the same time it emphasizes that the truth and authority of human reason are rooted in the eternal law, which is identical with God's own wisdom.[9] Thus, the autonomy of this kind of human reason is not to be understood as being of a *poietic* nature, that is, being a *"creatrix"* of "values" and "norms," but of a *participatory* nature, that is, as partaker in the divine Creator's and Lawgiver's wisdom: True moral autonomy consists in the free submission under and obedience to God's moral law.[10]

Next, the encyclical unfolds two aspects of this obedience: first in regard to creation, then in regard to salvation. The reason for this is that the obedience towards the moral law has (1) an *internal* point of reference, the voice of reason distinguishing between good and evil, and (2) an *external* point of reference, the voice of God's revealed law, that is, essentially the Decalogue, the Sermon on the Mount, and the double love commandment.

God's care as loving Creator finds expression in God's call to humanity to participate *via* reason in God's providence — reason being guided into the right direction by practical reason's natural light.

8. "[T]he moral life calls for that creativity and originality typical of the person, the source and cause of his own deliberate acts" (VS #40).

9. "The rightful autonomy of the practical reason means that man possesses in himself his own law, received from the Creator" (VS #40).

10. "Nevertheless, *the autonomy of reason cannot mean* that reason itself *creates values and moral norms*. Were this autonomy to imply a denial of the participation of the practical reason in the wisdom of the divine Creator and Lawgiver, or were it to suggest a freedom which creates moral norms, on the basis of historical contingencies or the diversity of societies and cultures, this sort of alleged autonomy would contradict the Church's teaching on the truth about man" (VS #40). "Law must therefore be considered an expression of divine wisdom: by submitting to the law, freedom submits to the truth of creation" (VS #41). "Patterned on God's freedom, man's freedom is not negated by his obedience to the divine law; indeed, only through this obedience does it abide in the truth and conform to human dignity" (VS #42).

It is important to notice here that this inner law of practical reason is called *natural* law, because it is the measure which corresponds to the human nature as moral being, in which the eternal law, that is, God the Creator's own reason, finds expression. With this teaching *Veritatis Splendor* follows the classical neo-Thomist position of the last century. It strongly signals this fact by quoting a central passage from Pope Leo XIII's encylical *Libertas Praestantissimum:*

> It follows that the natural law is *itself the eternal law,* implanted in beings endowed with reason, and inclining them *towards their right action and end;* it is none other than the eternal reason of the Creator and Ruler over the universe. (VS #44)

Yet, if my impression is right, the Aquinas scholars of the twentieth century have been discussing the relationship between the eternal law and the natural law in a much more differentiated way than this quote conveys.[11]

Whose Aquinas? Which Law?

One of the crucial questions in this debate seems to be the relationship between the natural law and the "lex divina," God's revealed law in the economy of salvation.[12] Here the ways seem to part sharply between a more recent movement of Aquinas scholars and of Thomists that emphasizes the primacy of Aquinas the theologian and the overarching theological nature of all his work. This movement can be subdivided into two camps: (1) a first group that reads Aquinas simply as theologian and (2) a second group that, while acknowledging the primacy of theology in Aquinas, still maintains that one can identify and attend to his philosophical thought in distinction from his theological thought, yet inside his overall theological project. In the generation leading up to Vatican II and in the time afterwards, this movement of Aquinas-interpreters came forth with studies that sig-

---

11. Cf. for a recent example Pamela Hall's discussion of this issue in *Narrative and the Natural Law: An Interpretation of Thomistic Ethics* (Notre Dame, Ind.: University of Notre Dame Press, 1994), pp. 28-36.

12. Cf. also here ibid., pp. 45-91.

nificantly corrected the picture construed by nineteenth-century neo-Thomism.[13] Reacting against both camps of the "Aquinas-the-theologian"-movement, there is (3) a more recent reemergence of a *primarily and exclusively* philosophical interpretation of Aquinas's teaching on the natural law, which seems to reconnect with Leo XIII and the neo-Thomism of the nineteenth century.[14] While this countermovement of a strictly philosophical approach to Aquinas's teaching on law seems to have been strongly influential in the formulation of the encyclical's unquestionably central second section, one can find traces of the "Aquinas-the-theologian"-movement's interpretation regard-

13. For representatives of the first subgroup in this camp, see especially Otto H. Pesch, *Theologie der Rechtfertigung bei Martin Luther und Thomas von Aquin* (Mainz: Grünewald Verlag, 1967), 416ff. Pesch understands all of Aquinas's teaching on law as a *theology of law* and interprets it in the comprehensive framework of God's salvific intention. In Pesch's background we can see the research of French and German Thomas-scholars such as Marie-Dominique Chenu, Roger Guindon, H. M. Christmann, and Ulrich Kühn. A recent appropriation to moral theology of this way of reading Aquinas primarily as a theologian can be found in Servais Pinckaers, *The Sources of Christian Ethics* (Washington, D.C.: The Catholic University of America Press, 1995). In the English-speaking world I would count, among others, the recent work of David Burrell, Paul Wadell, Pamela Hall, Simon Harak, Romanus Cessario, Thomas S. Hibbs, and Eugene Rogers as belonging to the first camp in the "Aquinas-the theologian"-movement. The originating "spiritus rector" of the second camp — (Thomas the theologian, whose philosophical thought is nonetheless distinguishable and separable within his overall theological project) — is, of course, Étienne Gilson. Yet in his latest works he also represents an implicit transition to the first camp insofar as he regards a "Christian philosophy" as being completely framed and guided by the underlying theological convictions (cf. for this perspective his *Christian Philosophy* [Toronto: Pontifical Institute of Mediaeval Studies, 1993]). For this camp's most significant German representative, see Wolfgang Kluxen, *Philosophische Ethik bei Thomas von Aquin* (Mainz: Grünewald Verlag, 1964), and, building on from this approach, see also Alfons Auer and Eberhard Schockenhoff. In the English-speaking world I would count, among others, the recent work of Alasdair MacIntyre, Jean Porter, Russel Hittinger, and Brian Davies, but also James F. Keenan, in this camp.

14. For the German context Rhonheimer's study *Natur als Grundlage der Moral* can be read as a typical example; for the English-speaking context one needs to refer to John Finnis, *Natural Law and Natural Rights* (Oxford: Clarendon, 1980), *Fundamentals of Ethics* (Washington D.C.: Georgetown University Press, 1983), and *Moral Absolutes: Tradition, Revision, and Truth* (Washington, D.C.: The Catholic University of America Press, 1991) and Germain Grisez, Joseph Boyle, and John Finnis, "Practical Principles, Moral Truth and Ultimate Ends," *American Journal of Jurisprudence* 32 (1987): 99-151.

ing his understanding of God's law in the encyclical's first and third sections. In a rather tacit and implicit way, the encyclical thereby seems to reflect in the quite different styles and emphases of its first and third sections on the one hand, and its second section on the other hand, the ongoing discussion of Roman Catholic moral theology on the correct interpretation of Aquinas's moral teaching in general and his teaching on God's law in particular.

There are *some closely interrelated issues* which still seem to be disputed matters of both the ongoing interpretation of Aquinas and the ongoing discourse of contemporary Roman Catholic moral theology. While the encyclical has sent quite unambiguous signals in its second section as to which Aquinas-interpretation is to be followed, there seem to be enough signals for the other camp in the encyclical's first and third section in order to find its way of interpreting Aquinas still justified.

First, there is the issue of the "natural law's" participation in the "eternal law." Is it "primarily how we are directed to our end, which is ultimately God"[15] or is the natural law — in a much stronger and more normative sense — "itself the eternal law, implanted in beings endowed with reason"?[16] In other words: Does one, in order for the natural law to work well, need to assume both an overarching and framing telos (God's salvific economy) and the Holy Spirit's intervention in the form of the "new law"? *Or* is the "natural law" to be understood as the eternal law's working out in the agent's reason quite independently of God's salvific economy and without the explicit need of the Holy Spirit's intervention?

Another closely related element of this issue is the question whether a teaching of God's law — according to Aquinas — can completely stand on its own feet or whether it is essentially in need of virtues — especially the "infused virtues" of faith, hope, and love — shaping the agent's passions, will, capacity of practical judgment and overall vision.[17]

---

15. Hall, *Narrative and the Natural Law,* p. 28.

16. As Pope Leo XIII puts it in his encyclical *Libertas Praestantissimum.* Cf. VS #44.

17. Herbert McCabe provides a very thoughtful and highly convincing theological critique of the encyclical from a Thomist perspective by arguing that the omission of the centrality of the virtues for the moral life leads to a distorted emphasis on law and obedience and thus causes the encyclical to make a bad case for a good thesis, namely "that we need absolute prohibitions as well as instruction in the paths of virtue" (in Wilkins, ed., *Considering "Veritatis Splendor,"* pp. 61-68; 67).

Finally, there is the last closely related issue regarding how the "natural law" is promulgated: by the first principle of practical reason yielding specific knowledge of genuine goods — all on its own? *Or* does the natural law's promulgation require the concrete exercise of the agent's will and intellect, that is, does it require the agent to engage in practical reasoning, so that the natural law cannot "escape the impact of individual and social practice and history"?[18]

While the encyclical certainly privileges interpretations belonging to the second, neo-Thomist, camp in its middle section, it seems as if it does not give conclusive answers to any of these questions, since the encyclical's first and third parts seem to send different signals. Yet in the following we can see how these unresolved issues, which constitute the conflicts of interpretation between the various Thomisms, coalesce in the encyclical's overarching univocal use of the concept "law" in which the traces of Aquinas's analogical use are ultimately submersed.

The Economy of Salvation: Practicing Freedom as Obedience to the Divine Law

In close correlation with the creaturely reality of an incipient yet incomplete enactment of freedom in observance to the natural law, the encyclical points out the essential relevance of God's revealed law in the economy of salvation: Israel has received the Torah as a gift and as a special sign of its divine election and of the covenant. This gift of God, according to the encyclical, now plays an ongoing, albeit differentiated role in the *ekklesia*'s realm.

> The Church gratefully accepts and lovingly preserves the entire deposit of Revelation, treating it with religious respect and fulfilling her mission of authentically interpreting God's law in the light of the Gospel. (VS #45)[19]

18. Hall, *Narrative and the Natural Law,* p. 35.

19. Here the encyclical follows Aquinas's teaching very closely by using the "new law" as a hermeneutical key for the interpretation of the "old law." This move has allowed Aquinas to productively differentiate in the "old law" between judicial law, cultic law, and natural law, and to emphasize in light of salvation history the unity of

Beyond God's good Torah, which the church received from Israel, it has received the special gift which makes it the church: the "new law":

> In addition, the Church receives the gift of the New Law which is the "fulfilment" of God's law in Jesus Christ and in his Spirit. This is an "interior" law (cf. *Jer* 31:31-33), "written not with ink but with the Spirit of the living God, not on tablets of stone but on tablets of human hearts" (*2 Cor* 3:3); a law of perfection and of freedom (cf *2 Cor* 3:17); "the law of the Spirit of life in Christ Jesus" (*Rom* 8:2). Saint Thomas writes that this law "can be called law in two ways. First, the law of the spirit is the Holy Spirit . . . who, dwelling in the soul, not only teaches what it is necessary to do by enlightening the intellect on the things to be done, but also inclines the affections to act with uprightness. . . . Second, the law of the spirit can be called the proper effect of the Holy Spirit, and thus faith working through love (cf. *Gal* 5:6), which teaches inwardly about the things to be done . . . and inclines the affections to act." (VS #45)[20]

In this passage we encounter a particular way of drawing upon Aquinas's teaching of the gospel as the "new law." For Aquinas, the "new law" encompasses both justification and sanctification.[21] In its very

---

this law as God's gift to Israel. This, in turn, made it possible for him to claim the relevatory character of the whole "old law" without having to claim at the same time the binding character of the whole Torah for Christians. For a good discussion of some of these matters, cf. Hall, *Narrative and the Natural Law,* pp. 45-64.

20. The encyclical quotes from Thomas Aquinas's commentary *In Epistulam ad Romanos* chap. 8, lect. 1. Cf. also *Summa Theologiae* 1-2 q.106 a.1 ad 2: "Lex nova est indita homini, non solum indicare quid sit faciendum, sed etiam adiuvans ad implendum." See also Ulrich Kühn, *Via caritatis: Theologie des Gesetzes bei Thomas von Aquin* (Berlin: Evangelische Verlagsanstalt, 1964), 193f: "Das Naturgesetz belehrt den Menschen zwar über das, was zu tun ist, aber hilft nicht zur Erfüllung, während das neue Gesetz zugleich in der inneren Hilfe zur Erfüllung der göttlichen Erfordernisse besteht."

21. "Alio modo potest etiam intelligi inquantum hominis opera qui Spiritu Sancto agitur, magis dicuntur esse opera Spiritus Sancti quam ipsius hominis. Unde cum Spiritus Sanctus non sit sub lege, sicut nec filius, ut supra (a.4 ad 2) dictum est; sequitur quod huiusmodi opera, inquantum sunt Spiritus Sancti, non sint sub lege" (*Summa Theologiae* 1-2 q.93 a.6 ad 1; "Second, it can be understood as meaning that the works of a man, who is led by the Holy Ghost, are the works of the Holy Ghost rather than his own. Therefore, since the Holy Ghost is not under the law,

core it stands for the Holy Spirit's presence in the believer. As un-created grace it is the Holy Spirit's self-enactment in the believer's life.[22] In its last consequence *pneumatologically understood,* the notion of "new law" points for Aquinas to the radical freedom of the Christian in the Holy Spirit: *"Ubi Spiritus Domini, ibi libertas."*[23] Yet in its own way of putting the matter, *Veritatis Splendor* seems to focus one-sidedly on that specific aspect of Aquinas's notion of the "new law" that is concerned with it being the essential *help* in fulfilling God's law. Thereby in its way of rendering the "new law," the encyclical singles out its causative function in relationship to the law's fulfillment.

Yet there are good reasons for asking whether the radicality of the "novum" in Aquinas's account completely transforms the very char-acter of "law" in the "new law."[24] If one presupposes that the "new

as neither is the Son, as stated above [a.4 ad 2]; it follows that such works, in so far as they are of the Holy Ghost, are not under the law." All English quotations from the *Summa Theologiae* are taken from the translation of the Fathers of the English Dominican Province, 1911, rev. 1920.) Cf. also Hall, *Narrative and the Natural Law,* p. 69.

22. Cf. Kühn, *Via caritatis,* pp. 192-93: "One needs to emphasize first of all that the term 'new law' in the *Summa Theologiae* has primarily nothing to do with a legally posited, external precept. Rather, one must think of grace, which is being discussed by Thomas at length at a later point in the *Summa* and which essentially consists in a supernatural *habitus,* which is infused into the soul and which raises it toward God. This grace Thomas interprets as the grace of the 'Holy Spirit,' whereby its nature as rooted in God and as 'uncreated' is emphasized and, at the same time, a whole range of biblical reminiscences are evoked. Thomas himself refers especially to Romans 8, which prompts us to take the beautiful comments into account which he offers on this passage in his *Romans Commentary* regarding the term 'lex spiritus.' According to Thomas, 'lex spiritus' refers to the Holy Spirit residing in the soul, who teaches the human about right action and guides him or her to it. In addition, 'lex spiritus' refers to the closest and most genuine effects of the Holy Spirit in the human being: to faith active through love, a faith which itself again teaches inwardly about what is to be done."

23. *Summa* 1-2 q.93 a.6 ad 1 quoting 2 Corinthians 3:17.

24. In regard to this issue, the encyclical seems to be less differentiated than Aquinas, who relates eternal, old, and new law in a daring *analogical* procedure. Cf. in this matter H. M. Christmann, introduction to vol. 14 of the German edition of the *Summa Theologiae* (Heidelberg/Graz, 1955), p. 10. The very way Aquinas unfolds his discourse on "law" displays the clearly analogical character of the term: He introduces the term in the broadest sense possible: *Summa Theologiae* 1-2 q.90 a.1: "Respondeo dicendum quod lex quaedam regula est et mensura actuum, secundum

law" is for Aquinas the expression of the agent's willing and intending having been drawn — through the infused virtue of charity becoming the form of the cardinal virtues — into the Holy Spirit's willing and intending, then the "new law" cannot be *univocally* submitted to the etymological definition which Aquinas offers for "law" in the opening Quaestio of his *Treatise on Law,* namely, to have its root in the Latin *ligare* ("to bind"). Rather, in the "new law" the *analogical use* of the term *law* becomes fully transparent: the "new law" as the Holy Spirit's external principle of action in the believer is simply true freedom becoming substantive in coinciding with the divine willing and intending.

If one takes Aquinas's radically *analogical* use of the term *law* in the "new law" seriously, one has to conclude that for him — *in opposition to the encyclical* — genuine and full human freedom is grounded in the gospel as it takes hold of us and transforms us through the

---

quam inducitur aliquis ad agendum, vel ab agendo retrahitur: dicitur enim lex a *ligando,* quia obligat ad agendum. Regula autem et mensura humanorum actuum est ratio, quae est primum principium actuum humanorum." ("I answer that, Law is a rule and measure of acts, whereby man is induced to act or is restrained from acting; for lex [law] is derived from ligare [to bind], because it binds one to act. Now the rule and measure of human acts is the reason, which is the first principle of human acts.") But when he uses the term *law* in connection with the Holy Spirit ("lex spiritus"), it becomes clear that the term *law* becomes completely qualified by the fact of whose "law" — whose extrinsic principle of action — it is. Thus he can on the one hand state: "Unde cum Spiritus Sanctus non sit sub lege, sicut nec Filius, ut supra (a.4 ad 2) dictum est; sequitur quod huiusmodi opera, inquantum sunt Spiritus Sancti, non sint sub lege" (*Summa Theologiae* 1-2 q.93 a.6 ad 1). And on the other hand he can say: "Lex spiritus liberat hominem a peccato et morte; sed lex spiritus est in Jesu Christo: ergo per hoc quod aliquis est in Christo Jesu, liberatur a peccato et morte, sic probat. Lex spiritus est causa vitae: sed per vitam excluditur peccatum et mors quae est effectus peccati: nam et ipsum peccatum est spiritualis mors animae: ergo lex spiritus liberat hominem a peccato et morte" (*In Rom.* 7, lect. 1). "Nova lex generat affectum amoris, qui pertinet ad libertatem: nam qui amat ex se movetur" (*In Gal.* 4, lect. 8). "Primo habet libertatem . . . , quia Spiritus Domini ducit ad id quod rectum est" (*In Joh* 3, lect. 2,1). Thus in the case of the "lex spiritus" it is the Holy Spirit's extrinsic principle of action, in the case of the "lex fomes" it is the extrinsic principle of the root of concupiscence still active in the believer, and in the case of the "lex naturae" it is the extrinsic principle of action of the human being qua rational agent. "Law" as extrinsic principle of action needs in Aquinas's use the substantive specification as to *whose* extrinsic principle of action it is, which makes it an inherently *analogical* concept.

Spirit's work *in and through* the agent's acting according to it. Yet the
encyclical seems to follow a slightly but decisively different direction
in this matter by grounding human freedom in the obedience to and
the fulfillment of God's law — univocally understood. And it seems
to me that it cannot do it any differently, since precisely its nonanalogical use of the concept of *law* does not allow for a sufficient recognition
of the fundamental difference between the natural law and the old
law on the one hand and the "new law" on the other hand. The
following passage illustrates this problem:

> Even if moral-theological reflection usually distinguishes between
> the positive or revealed law of God and the natural law, and, within
> the economy of salvation, between the "old" and the "new" law, it
> must not be forgotten that these and other useful distinctions always
> refer to that law whose author is the one and the same God and
> which is always meant for man. (VS #45)

The very fact that *Veritatis Splendor* can, quite casually, point to certain
traditional "distinctions" which finally all refer to the one "law,"
clearly shows how the "new law" is fully subsumed under the concept
of "law," whereby the latter's whole point — at least according to
Aquinas — seems to be missed.[25] Yet before coming to a more con-

---

25. Some Protestant theologians raise the concern that even in the case of Aquinas
himself, in whose notion of the "new law" the gospel is being conceived as the Holy
Spirit's presence in the believer, the analogical use of the concept of "law" in the case of
the "new law" prohibits a full understanding of that which is utterly genuine of the
gospel in radical difference to any notion of "law," namely its character as pure gift, over
against which we can only be and always remain recipients. The Lutheran theologian
Ulrich Kühn formulated this caveat after an explicitly positive appreciation of Aquinas's
"evangelical," that is, gospel-centered, understanding of the "new law": "Nevertheless
the question needs to be raised whether the way Thomas integrates the gospel into the
general doctrine of the law does not create the danger that the genuinely decisive point
of the Gospel, which stands in opposition to all law, even to all morality, is ultimately
concealed. Undoubtedly, Thomas has put forward the new law's otherness as the
'Spirit's law' in an impressive and biblically founded way. In the use of the term 'law' we
can indeed observe an extraordinarily audacious practice of analogy. But one might still
ask whether the starting point for a Christian morality might not have looked different
if this integration [of the Gospel into an encompassing doctrine of law] and its
concomitant reductions had been avoided" ("Evangelische Anmerkungen zum Problem der Begründung der moralischen Autonomie des Menschen im Neuen Gesetz

clusive answer to this question, let us return to the encyclical itself. Does it relate God's law and human freedom in a purely abstract way?

The Path of the Commandments:
The Concrete Shape of Freedom

According to *Veritatis Splendor*, human freedom is by no means an abstract freedom. It is not simply identical with reason's right discernment and judgment. Rather, the freedom of the moral life has a concrete *creaturely shape:* it is "life with God," it is a concrete way of life in God's commandments as embodied in the Decalogue, the key of which is the first commandment:

> *The good is belonging to God, obeying him,* walking humbly with him in doing justice and in loving kindness (cf. *Mic* 6:8). *Acknowledging the Lord as God is the very core, the heart of the Law,* from which the particular precepts flow and towards which they are ordered. (VS #11)[26]

nach Thomas," *Angelicum* 51 [1974]: 235-45, quoted from Hans G. Ulrich, ed., *Freiheit im Leben mit Gott: Texte zur Tradition evangelischer Ethik* [Gütersloh: Gütersloher Verlag, 1993], pp. 78-88; 80-81). While this opens a set of complex issues, I still would maintain over against Kühn that two circumstances might help in overcoming his in and of themselves very legitimate Lutheran concerns: first, the fully analogical character of the term *law* in all its uses must be taken very seriously in Aquinas, and second, only in the *Treatise on Law* does Aquinas treat the gospel as "new law," probably to exhaust the complete analogical range of the term *law* in light of the overall theological structure of the whole *Summa Theologiae.* In its *Tertia Pars,* that is, outside of the issues dealing with human agency, Aquinas conceptualizes the gospel quite differently.

26. Unfortunately, the encyclical does not make any reference at this point to Martin Luther, according to whom all the other commandments of the Decalogue hinge on the first: from the fulfillment of the first the fulfillment of all the others follows. The fulfillment of the first commandment according to Luther is, of course, faith. Cf. Luther's remarks in his *Large Catechism* regarding the first commandment of the Decalogue: "Et haec de primo praecepto dicta sufficiant, quod verbis aliquanto fusioribus mihi explanandum fuit, quando summa et caput totius pietatis in eo vertatur, propterea quod (ut praedictum), ubi cordi cum Deo bene convenit et hoc praeceptum servatum fuerit, cetera omnia apte consequuntur" (*Die Bekenntnisschriften der evangelisch-Lutherischen Kirche,* 8th ed. [Göttingen: Vandenhoeck & Ruprecht, 1979]), 572, 14-22). ("Let this suffice for the First Commandment. We had to explain it at length since it is the most important. For, as I said before, where the heart is right with God and this

Only when we fulfill the commandments of the Decalogue do we, according to *Veritatis Splendor,* remain in the presence of the Good and — thereby — genuinely free![27] Therefore, the relationship between human freedom and God's explicit commandments *ideally* is, in a way similar to the relationship between natural law and human freedom, not one of estrangement, of heteronomy. Rather, in the very fulfill-ment of the Decalogue the human destiny in relation to God, to neighbor, and to oneself is fulfilled, because the commandments con-tain the good toward which human freedom is ordered. Human freedom comes to itself only in the fulfillment of the command-ments.[28] With its strong emphasis on the *human good,* the very foun-dation of God's commandments, the encyclical attempts to overcome the deeply modern antinomy between the autonomy of the "free" human agent and the heteronomy of any external, positive law.

In sum, the encyclical seems to operate with a comprehensive paradigm of "law" in which God's creative and salvific activities pene-trate each other in an essentially harmonious way. The origin and goal of this activity is humanity's destination "to be conformed to the image of his Son *(Rom* 8:29)" (VS #45) — on the path of observing God's law, by which also genuine human freedom is achieved. Here, by pointing to the law's origin and goal, the encyclical moves Christ's central role into the picture.

---

commandment is kept, fulfillment of all the others will follow of its own accord" [*Book of Concord,* 371].)

27. On the ground of Matthew 19:17, the encyclical understands God's com-mandments as intrinsically connected with God's promise: in the old covenant with the promise of the land, in the new covenant with the promise of eternal life (cf. VS #12). With this move the encyclical avoids the danger of isolating God's command-ments from the economy of salvation. Rather, it is able to interpret the command-ments as an integral element of God's salvific activity in the overall framework of a soteriological teleology.

28. "They are the *first necessary step on the journey towards freedom,* its starting-point. 'The beginning of freedom', Saint Augustine writes, 'is to be free from crimes . . . such as murder, adultery, fornication, theft, fraud, sacrilege and so forth. When once one is without these crimes (and every Christian should be without them), one begins to lift up one's head towards freedom. But this is only the beginning of freedom, not perfect freedom'" (VS #13). (The quote is from Augustine's *In Iohannis Evangelium tractatus,* 41, 10: *Corpus Christianorum. Series Latina* [CCL] 36, 363.)

Christ: The Law's Perfect Example

It is only consistent when the encyclical takes Christ to be "the end of the law" not in the sense of an overcoming and abolishing of the law, but as the living fulfillment of the law — along the lines of Ambrose's dictum *"Plenitudo legis in Christo est."*

> *Jesus himself is the living "fulfilment" of the Law* inasmuch as he fulfils its authentic meaning by the total gift of himself: *he himself becomes a living and personal Law,* who invites people to follow him; through the Spirit, he gives the grace to share his own life and love and provides the strength to bear witness to that love in personal choices and actions (cf. *Jn* 13:34-35). (VS #15)

In light of the above, this last sentence has to be clearly understood as an interpretation of Aquinas's notion of the "new law," which always implies the Holy Spirit's presence and work: The "new law" *is* the Spirit's life in the Christian and the Christian's life in the Spirit. While we find intimations of an analogical use of the law in this passage, it seems to be the case that also here we have an overarching univocal reality of "law," only that Jesus is the one who embodies its perfect fulfillment — and therefore he becomes, in a quite univocal sense, a living and personal law.

Here we also have the peak of the encyclical's Christology. Having fulfilled the law completely and in the very core of its intention, Christ becomes the paradigmatic *exemplum,* the most genuine witness of the law's truth. Therefore it is not at all surprising that the encyclical emphasizes Christ's universal relevance as *teacher* of morality:

> *People today need to turn to Christ once again in order to receive from him the answer to their questions about what is good and what is evil.* Christ is the Teacher, the Risen One who has life in himself and who is always present in his Church and in the world. It is he who opens up to the faithful the book of the Scriptures and, by fully revealing the Father's will, teaches the truth about moral action. At the source and summit of the economy of salvation . . . Christ sheds light on man's condition and his integral vocation. (VS #8)

Here we encounter an interesting tension between the encyclical's christological focus in its first and third parts, and its focus on human reason's participation in the "eternal law" *via* the natural law's first principle in its second part: Why is it that we are in need of Christ's example and, in addition, of the Spirit's presence in us so that through the law's fulfillment we become conformed to Christ's image? Why are we in need "to go to the heart of the Gospel's moral teaching and grasp its profound and unchanging content" (VS #8), if "[i]t follows that the natural law is *itself the eternal law,* implanted in beings endowed with reason, and inclining them *towards their right action and end;* it is none other than the eternal reason of the Creator and Ruler over the universe" (VS #44)?

God's Law as Liberation from Sin — and the Gospel?

It becomes increasingly clear that the encyclical's seemingly quite harmonic correlation of creation and redemption is torn by a deep underlying tension, since human freedom is — *post lapsum* — only inauthentic freedom. Human beings are unable to understand their freedom as gift. Rather, freedom turns into the constant temptation to turn oneself into one's own principle — in radical disobedience to the first commandment of the Decalogue. Therefore "natural" freedom of this kind constantly misses itself by failing to fulfill its destiny. Only by being liberated from itself to the truth, that is, only as freedom which is transparent in its character as gift — and thereby a freedom which fulfills itself in giving itself away — does it become authentic freedom. "Consequently, *freedom itself needs to be set free. It is Christ who sets it free:* he 'has set us free for freedom' (cf. *Gal* 5:1)" (VS #86). This aspect is — from the Reformation perspective — of course the most crucial one of our Christian existence. Yet the encyclical touches it only very briefly and does not explore the depths of this liberation to freedom through the gospel alone. But, we need to ask, to what degree must this liberation to freedom be an essential element of the path of freedom (as constituted by the obedience to God's commandments)? Is it not a daily liberation, a daily repentance, a daily reception of the gospel in faith? But how could this crucial insight come truly into view if Christ comes into the picture solely under the aspect of the "nova lex"? If the gospel is interpreted, in the last regard, inside the horizon of God's eternal law, how can it, as God's promise embodied in the self-giving gift of God's Son, come into view in its radical difference from (I did not say "contradiction to"!) God's law?

To this question the encyclical only offers a limited answer, which approximates the eschatological dialectic of "law and gospel"[29] constitutive of Reformation theology. Yet it only approximates this understanding, because the encyclical finds itself at this point strangely inhibited by its comprehensive and — in difference to Aquinas — nonanalogical use of the concept of "law."

How does the encyclical put the matter? Since liberated freedom is self-giving in love, yet this vocation to freedom constantly encounters the reality of sin, the performance of freedom does not imply a freedom *from* God's commandments. Rather, this very performance of freedom is in need of God's commandments as its path of liberation. And on this very path of liberation human beings experience something akin to the dialectic of "law and gospel," namely in the form of the eschatological tension between "flesh" and "spirit." One should, of course, not expect the encyclical to make reference to Luther here.[30] But Saint Augustine's Commentary on the Gospel of John is quoted. The encyclical states:

> St. Augustine, after speaking of the observance of the commandments as being a kind of incipient, imperfect freedom, goes on to say: "Why, someone will ask, is it not yet perfect? Because 'I see in my members another law at war with the law of my reason.' . . . In part freedom, in part slavery: not yet complete freedom, not yet pure, not yet whole, because we are not yet in eternity. In part we retain our weakness and in part we have attained freedom. . . . Therefore, since some weakness has remained in us, I dare to say that to the extent to which we serve God we are free, while to the extent that we follow the law of sin, we are still slaves." (VS #17)[31]

---

29. For a fine discussion of this topic see Albrecht Peters, *Gesetz und Evangelium* (Gütersloh: Gütersloher Verlagshaus, 1981), pp. 30-38.

30. Which the encyclical, of course, could have done, since Luther was a good Augustinian: cf. paradigmatically his treatment of "spirit" and "flesh" in *The Freedom of a Christian*.

31. The encyclical quotes from Augustine's *In Iohannis Evangelium tractatus*, 41, 10: CCL 36, 363.

Human Sin and Divine Redemption:
Through the Law and Christ, or Solo Christo?

With its reference to Augustine, the encyclical has — at least momen-
tarily — left its overarching Matthean framework and has handed itself
over to the Pauline logic. Thereby it moves into the closest possible
proximity to Luther's eschatological dialectic of "law and gospel." Yet in
light of this very proximity, the difference between the two becomes quite
clear: the unmasking and convicting aspect of God's law — in Lutheran
terminology the law's "second" or "theological" use — can only be
perceived as a "burden." Its positive *theological* point — to actively serve
the gospel by unmasking human sin and by shutting the door to wrongly
desiring acceptance before God on the ground of the law's fulfillment —
cannot come into the encyclical's view, since its comprehensive and
nonanalogical use of "law" makes the perception of the essential difference between God's law and God's gospel impossible. According to the
encyclical, the "gospel" has to play a distinctive but limited role in the
law's "ball-game." In other words, the self-communication of the only
One who is good (Matt. 19:17) along the lines of the eternal *law* —
whose binding character is expressed *via* the natural law in the economy
of creation, and *via* the "new law" in observing God's commandments
in the economy of salvation — remains the sole horizon of genuine
freedom. This freedom is not the one which the justified sinner gains
through God's self-giving love — in completely exploding the paradigm
of "law" and in being grounded in forgiveness.

The reason for this, I think, is that "sin" and "grace" do not, in
a sufficiently Augustinian way, qualify the encyclical's notion of "law."
Rather, a comprehensive, all-encompassing concept of "law" obscures
the point, that *sub conditione peccati* the law, whether natural or revealed,
is always, first and foremost, encountered by the *sinner,* by the human
being who does not live in communion with but stands in radical
opposition to God. And the encounter between humanity and God's
law is — *post lapsum* — always a conflictual encounter, in which the
experience of *heteronomy* is to be expected. Instead the encyclical envisions an overall harmonious and continuous relationship between
creation and salvation,[32] one in which the fact that all of humanity

---

32. "The different ways in which God, acting in history, cares for the world and

post lapsum stands first and foremost under God's judgment (Rom. 3:9-20) is obscured by the fact that a serious theological acknowledgment of human sin is missing as a constitutive element of the encyclical's anthropology. Yet for theologians like Augustine, Aquinas, and Luther, albeit to different degrees, it is precisely *sub conditione peccati* that the "natural law" is decisively weakened and the "old law" rendered ineffective.[33] From this perspective, the encyclical's claim that "[it] is precisely through his acts that man attains perfection as man, as one who is called to seek his Creator of his own accord and freely to arrive at full and blessed perfection by cleaving to him" (VS #71) appears as quite problematic. Isn't this claim only true if we presuppose — with Aquinas — the "new law" already being effective in the person or — with Luther — that this person already is "in faith"? And who is, we might want to ask, the referent of Saint Gregory of Nyssa's quite disconcerting claim: "Thus *we are* in a certain way our own parents, creating ourselves as we will, by our decisions" (VS #71)? Are we free to decide what kind of "parents" we are, or is it — after humanity's loss of original righteousness — precisely outside of our will's capacity to decide to be "our own parents" without sin?

At this very point, it seems to be necessary to remember one of the Reformation's crucial claims: Only on the ground of God's gift of grace — "while we were still sinners" (Rom. 5:8) — to be grasped by faith alone are we liberated for a life in communion with God. Long before Christ is an *exemplum,* he is first and foremost a *donum,* that can (and must) be grasped only by faith. Yet, *together with* this Reformation "no" to the encyclical's embedding the gospel in the comprehensive framework of the "law" and thereby seriously undercutting the fundamental difference between God's gospel and God's law, an equally strong "yes" is to be said to the encyclical's unambiguous affirmation of the law's truth. Since, without question, the law,

---

for mankind are not mutually exclusive; on the contrary, they support each other and intersect. They have their origin and goal in the eternal, wise and loving counsel whereby God predestines men and women 'to be conformed to the image of his Son' (*Rom* 8:29). God's plan poses no threat to man's genuine freedom; on the contrary, the acceptance of God's plan is the only way to affirm that freedom" (VS #45).

33. For Aquinas the point of the old law was a *training* in the natural law, which is precisely not simply available to human reason. Cf. Hall, *Narrative and the Natural Law,* pp. 45-64.

being God's law, remains God's truth — not that truth which is able to set us free into the freedom of the children of God but that truth which reflects God's will for creation and which, *sub conditione peccati,* always also unmasks our infinite distance from and fundamental opposition to God. Yet against the encyclical it needs to be maintained, *first,* that the law always encounters *sinners:* a genuine human "autonomy," on the sole ground of the "natural" and the "old" law, is — *post lapsum* — impossible; and *second,* that the gospel is not just God's handmaiden in putting the law back into its genuine place.

Despite its being teleologically directed towards the ultimate good, the law's truth, as *Veritatis Splendor* envisions it, has to remain powerless in the most essential point, has to convict or has to enforce the good in a heteronomous way *via* legal or moral norms. In its most essential regard, as the expression of the eternal law, God's providence and goodness, the law — be it natural or revealed — that encounters the sinner has to remain helpless — if the gospel is not taken away from the law's paradigm and understood as the triune God's self-giving gift, which infinitely transcends creation in its created goodness and is to be distinguished even from the eternal law, insofar as the gospel is the gift of God's triune communion, of participation in God's own triune life. In other words, there is an unbridgeable difference between participating in God's providential care for creation *via* human freedom as guided by the natural law on the one side, and the gift of participating through Christ in faith in God's own trinitarian life in an inchoate way now and eternally in the eschaton on the other side! There is no bridge long enough to reach from "this side" of creation and from God's good commandments for this creaturely life over and up to the "other side" of God's own triune life. *In this direction the distance is infinite and unbridgeable.* Thus, while the commandments of the Decalogue are unquestionably confirmed by Jesus, they never are proposed "as the way and condition of salvation" (VS #12), as the encyclical chooses to put it.

Yet there is no distance at all the other way around! Saving faith embodies itself in God's good commandments. This circumstance is reflected in the fact that while there is no "positive" connection between salvation and our obedience to God's will as reflected in the moral law, there nevertheless is a "negative" correlation. In other words, while we cannot merit salvation on grounds of the law's fulfillment, we can very well lose salvation by — as believers — blatantly disregarding or breaking the Decalogue's commandments. According to Luther and the *Book of Concord,* particular activities and acts which either cause public offense and/or are intentionally maleficent and/or become habitual as vices that are destructive of one's own life and good, the neighbor's life and good, and the common good, cause the Holy Spirit and justifying faith to depart.[34] The most crucial element in this regard is a basically unrepentant attitude that is either blind to the issues itself and/or too proud and stubborn to repent after having been reprimanded.

Christ's obedience to the Father, his own self-dedication and self-giving do become, as a matter of fact, an *exemplum,* when Christ has been and constantly is being received anew as God's *donum* for us, the forgiving and self-giving love of God that draws us into God's triune life. And this liberation *sola gratia* and *sola fide* turns us back into the realm of creation. Precisely here, being set free by the gospel's truth, the encyclical's concern comes into its full right. In its unmistakable remembrance of God's will, of the eternal law, written as natural law in our hearts, yet weakened and often almost wiped out by human sin, and of the revealed law as communicated by Scripture's witness, we encounter the encyclical's strength, *not* in its teaching that genuine human freedom is grounded in this law. Against the encyclical we have to maintain that genuine human freedom is grounded in the gospel. At the same time we have to agree with the encyclical's claim that there is no genuine human freedom *without* or *against* God's law.

While I already have referred to Reformation theology at various points of my reading of *Veritatis Splendor* on God's law, it might be helpful to draw upon some elements of Luther's theology, *first* in order to point out that any Lutheran discrediting of the encyclical's alleged "legalism" might just be another version of Lutheran antinomianism,

34. As Luther put it in the *Smalcald Articles* (3.3.43-44): "It is therefore necessary to know and to teach that when holy people, aside from the fact that they still possess and feel original sin and daily repent and strive against it, fall into open sin (as David fell into adultery, murder, and blasphemy), faith and the Spirit have departed from them. This is so because the Holy Spirit does not permit sin to rule and gain the upper hand in such a way that sin is committed, but the Holy Spirit represses and restrains it so that it does not do what it wishes. If sin does what it wishes, the Holy Spirit and faith are not present." Cf. also the *Epitome* of the *Formula of Concord* (3.11).

which — unfortunately — cannot be called a rare phenomenon in twentieth-century Lutheranism,[35] and *second,* in order to put into stronger relief the points of agreement and disagreement between the encyclical's teaching on law and Lutheran ethics.

The Freedom of a Christian: Being "Back in Paradise"

Luther's *magna charta* of the Christian life, his treatise "The Freedom of a Christian" (1520), is still one of the most decisive and foundational texts for Christian ethics done in the Reformation tradition. After having laid out the dynamic of salvation (focusing on the image of the "happy exchange" between Christ and the sinner), Luther zeros in on his main concern, the telos of it all, namely the Christian life, in which this faith is embodied in love. How is this life of evangelical freedom in Christ to be understood and grasped? Luther makes two very telling biblical references at this point.

One is Philippians 2:4-11,[36] the christological hymn. Here, Luther, with Saint Paul, points to Christ's, and in the most radical sense, God's own humility in the very economy of salvation. This is the embodiment of God's freedom in love, which we are called to emulate in our own life of faith. Here is our evangelical paradigm, the overarching model of our Christian freedom. In this model, love, God's self-giving love, is the effective and the final cause, and service the very shape of this freedom in humility. Thus, "in faith," in union with Christ, the Christian participates in God's own freedom,[37] the inner dynamic of God's triune love, which — through Christ and the Spirit's mission — aims at drawing all of creation into communion with the triune God. Christian freedom *is* our participation in this very mission through our loving service to the neighbor.

35. Here I am referring as well to the general Lutheran "ethos," insofar as such exists, as well as to Lutheran ethics. For an excellent account of this problem, see David Yeago, "Gnosticism, Antinomianism and Reformation Theology: Reflections on the Cost of a Construal," in *Pro Ecclesia* 2 (1993): 37-49.

36. *Weimarer Ausgabe* 7:64f.

37. For a fascinating elaboration of this thought from a Lutheran perspective, see Robert W. Jenson, "An Ontology of Freedom in the *De servo arbitrio* of Luther," in *Modern Theology* 10 (1994): 247-52.

Yet at precisely this point we need to turn to Luther's other biblical reference.[38] "In faith," that is, "in union with Christ," the Christian is restored to the original righteousness of prelapsarian life with God. In other words, "in faith" Christians are "back in paradise." In order to fully understand what Luther has in mind with this astounding theological claim we need to turn to the second chapter of his *Lectures on Genesis,* an enterprise that occupied him during the last ten years of his life.

The Law's Original Use; or, God's Commandment as Way of Life for Adam and Eve

Here Luther states in regard to chapter 2 of the book of Genesis:

> And so when Adam had been created in such a way that he was, as it were, intoxicated with rejoicing toward God and was delighted also with all the other creatures, there is now created a new tree for the distinguishing of good and evil, so that Adam might have a definite way to express his worship and reverence toward God. After everything had been entrusted to him to make use of it according to his will, whether he wished to do so for necessity or for pleasure, God finally demands from Adam that at this tree of the knowledge of good and evil he demonstrate his reverence and obedience toward God and that he maintain this practice, as it were, of worshiping God by not eating anything from it.[39]

David Yeago draws the following consequence, with which I fully agree:

> The commandment is not given to Adam so that he might *become* a lover of God by keeping it; Adam already *is* a lover of God, "drunk with joy towards God," by virtue of his creation in the image of God, by the grace of original righteousness. The commandment is given, rather, in order to allow Adam's love for God to *take form* in a

38. *Weimarer Ausgabe* 7:61.
39. *Luther's Works,* vol. 1 (*Lectures on Genesis 1–5*), ed. Jaroslav Pelikan (St. Louis: Concordia, 1958), p. 94. (*Weimarer Ausgabe* 42:71)

historically concrete way of life. Through the commandment, Adam's joy takes form as *cultus Dei,* the concrete social practice of worship. . . . The importance of this cannot be overstated, particularly in view of conventional Lutheran assumptions: here Luther is describing a function of divine law, divine commandment, which is neither correlative with sin nor antithetical to grace; indeed, it presupposes the presence of grace and not sin. This function of the divine commandment is, moreover, its original and proper function, its function at the beginning. The fundamental significance of the law is thus neither to enable human beings to attain righteousness nor to accuse their sin, but to give concrete, historical form to the "divine life" of the human creature deified by grace. . . . The commandment is given originally to a subject deified by the grace of original righteousness, a subject living as the image of God; it calls for specific behaviors as the concrete historical realization of the spiritual life of the deified, God-drunken human being. What happens after sin comes on the scene is simply that this *subject* presupposed by the commandment is no longer there; the commandment no longer finds an Adam living an "entirely divine life," "drunk with joy towards God," but rather an Adam who has withdrawn from God, who believes the devil's lies about God and therefore flees and avoids God. It is precisely the anomaly of this situation that causes the commandment to become, in Luther's terms, "a different law" *(alia lex).*[40]

According to Luther, God's commandments are nothing else than the concrete guidance, the concrete social practices which allow us as believers to embody — in concrete creaturely ways — our communion with God, which always includes God's other creatures. Or, to reclaim a fashionable term of contemporary Western culture: God's commandments shape and guide that "lifestyle" of "God-drunkenness" for which human beings, created in God's image, are destined.

Now we are in a much better position to understand the radical perspective behind Luther's rather innocent-sounding claim that "in faith" human beings are "back in paradise": they are back in commu-

---

40. David Yeago, "Grace and the Moral Life: Martin Luther's Theology of Divine Law Reconsidered, as Prolegomenon to an Ecumenical Discussion of *Veritatis Splendor,*" *The Thomist* (forthcoming). I am indebted to Professor Yeago's Luther-research as he unfolds it in his forthcoming book on Luther's theology.

nion with God, back — *sola gratia* and *sola fide* — in that righteousness that God's commandment presupposes and to which God's commandment gives creaturely form and shape! And this is precisely why for Luther the "freedom of a Christian" never contradicts God's commandments and never comes without them, but rather rejoices in them and welcomes them as ways of creaturely embodying our love of God and of neighbor. In contrast, receiving the law as an *external code* is typical of *sinful* humanity.

Thus, if the referent of the encyclical's claim would either be the human being in original righteousness — "drunk with joy towards God" — or the restored human being "in faith," Luther would fully agree with the encyclical's claim in regard to Genesis 2:17 that "[i]n fact, human freedom finds its authentic and complete fulfilment precisely in the acceptance of that law. God, who is good, knows perfectly what is good for man, and by virtue of his very love proposes this good to man in the commandments" (VS #35).

Yet both the law of Moses and the natural law are subject to serious distortions *sub conditione peccati,* humanity having lost the original grace of being created in the image of God. The experience of the law's "otherness" — its *hetero*-nomy — is to be expected due to our "otherness" in relationship to God's will. God's grace received in faith rectifies this distortion by restoring the believers to those who are "drunk with joy towards God," humanity in their paradisical condition. Now the original, *spiritual understanding* of the law is accessible again. As David Yeago puts it:

> This means that the spiritual understanding of the law does remember that all God's commandments presuppose a subject deified by grace, a human being who is drunk with joy toward God and rejoices in all God's creatures. This is, after all, precisely what Jesus teaches: the law and the prophets hang on the double commandment of love, the commandment to love God with all our heart, soul, mind and strength and our neighbor as ourselves.[41]

Thus, according to Luther's eschatological understanding of faith, when Christ himself, the new Adam, is present in the believer, there

41. Yeago, "Grace and the Moral Life."

is no difference anymore between, on the one hand, God's gospel, God's forgiving, restoring, and sanctifying activity in Christ, and, on the other hand, God's commandments as its creaturely form of freedom. Faith is, Luther says,

> that living and spiritual flame inscribed by the Spirit in human hearts, which wills, does, and indeed *is* that which the law of Moses commands and requires verbally. . . . And so the law of Christ is properly not teaching but living, not word but reality, not sign but fulfillment. And it is the word of the gospel which is the ministry of this life, reality, and fulfillment and the means by which it is brought to our hearts.[42]

The freedom of a Christian is embodied in the fulfillment of God's commandments, the core and summary of which is the double love commandment.[43] Yet this way of life can never acquire the easiness of an infused (or well-acquired) habitus, since, according to Luther *and* the encyclical, the Christian's eschatological existence is one in the tension between "spirit" and "flesh."[44] The Holy Spirit's work is an *opus inchoatum;* it has begun. There is a "new person," who calls herself or himself "I." But this work is not yet completed. The "flesh," namely our not yet extinguished concupiscence, and other "external" tribulations remain powerful forces.[45]

42. *Weimarer Ausgabe* 8:458 (David Yeago's translation).
43. While letter and spirit are never to be severed from each other, they need to be distinguished lest God's commandment be received again as a purely external code and not be spiritually understood as that which gives Christian freedom its concrete creaturely form when the Christian is — like humanity in paradise — "drunk with joy towards God."
44. Here *Veritatis Splendor* and Luther have a common ground in the long tradition of interpreting Romans 7:7-25 as reflective of the ongoing earthly life of Christians. Saint Augustine's interpretation, as it is well reflected in VS #17, was of crucial importance for the Western tradition's ongoing consensus in this matter up to the days of historical-critical research.
45. It is of crucial importance to note that for Luther there is no personal identity transcending the struggle between "spirit" and "flesh." Rather, "in faith" the Christian experiences concupiscence — what we as moderns would call "inner" temptations — as a form of *external* tribulation, since the self is identical with the new person in faith. Luther has found a drastic picture for this state of affairs in his third disputation against the Antinomians. The person who believes in Christ already is in heaven

Remembering God's Commandments —
A Training in the Original Sense of God's Good Law

"Yet you are near, O LORD,
and all your commandments are true." (Ps. 119:151, NRSV)

Thus, for theological ethics in the Reformation tradition, *Veritatis Splendor*'s insistence on the centrality of God's law represents a welcome catalyst for rethinking God's commandments and, thereby, being reclaimed by them. Despite a whole range of problematic issues, the encyclical reminds us to understand in a renewed way God's closeness in the goodness of his will, whether communicated *via* the natural or the revealed law. The encyclical's theological ambiguity sets in when it teaches an *integral unity between salvation and God's commandments* in which the fulfillment of God's commandments seems to play a crucially *effective* role.[46] In order not to fall into old mutual misunderstandings or substantive conflicts, an ecumenical conversation about God's good commandments will have to make clear whether as well as a negative relation to salvation[47] there also is a "positive"

---

dressed with the nicest heavenly gown. Yet her feet still are hanging out from the gown, and the devil bites into them as much as he can. Thus the person feels that she still has flesh and blood and that the devil still is present. The exact passage reads: "Homo credens in Christum est reputatione divina iustus et sanctus, versatur estque iam in coelo, circumdatus coelo misericordiae. Sed dum hic ferimur in sinu patris vestiti veste optima, pedes nostri mihi extra pallium descendunt, quos quantum potest mordet sathan, dar zappelt das Kindelein et clamat et sentit, se adhuc et sanguinem habere et diabolum adhuc adesse" (*Weimarer Ausgabe* 39:1, 521, 5-10).

46. "God's commandments show man the path of life and they lead to it. From the very lips of Jesus, the new Moses, man is once again given the commandments of the Decalogue. Jesus himself definitely confirms them and proposes them to us as the way and *condition* of salvation" (VS #12; my emphasis).

47. The "intrinsically evil acts" in *Veritatis Splendor* and the habitual, intentional, publicly insisted-upon and nonrepented breaking of the Decalogue's commandments spoken of by Lutherans are not the same thing but seem to point to some overlapping concerns. For some crucial questions which still need to be asked even in this respect, see Gilbert Meilaender's and Bernd Wannenwetsch's essays in this volume.

For a defense and constructive interpretation of the encyclical's teaching on this matter, see Martin Rhonheimer, "Intrinsically Evil Acts and the Moral Viewpoint: Clarifying a Central Teaching of *Veritatis Splendor*," *The Thomist* 58 (1994): 1-39; for one. The *sola gratia* and *sola fide* of the Christian faith, according to the Reformation tradition, allow for one kind of "positive" relationship between God's commandments and salvation: by reading God's commandments in their "original sense" as God's good gift for those who are "drunk with joy towards God." These commanded practices, which enable us to be ordered towards God in worship and towards the neighbor in service, are *intrinsically good* and satisfying in themselves. Thus, while persons "in faith" take training in them willingly as their grateful response to faith in love, others will experience the result of this training as intrinsically satisfying.[48]

---

more critically engaging contributions see Louis Janssens's and Bernard Hoose's contributions in *The Splendor of Accuracy,* ed. Selling and Jans.

The basic agreement from all sides, including Protestants, includes the concepts that (a) there are *specific acts* (depending on circumstances and intention) that are unambiguously evil and to be unambiguously condemned and that (b) there are *kinds of activities* that are, under most circumstances, to be unambiguously condemned. The more complex issues set in with questions regarding (a) the nature and scope of the "object" of "intrinsically evil acts" — i.e. whether there exist specific acts that — irrespective of all circumstances and any intention — are "intrinsece" evil, (b) the status of the lists which *Veritatis Splendor* presents as examples for "intrinsically evil acts," and (c) the magisterium's role in the concrete definition of "intrinsically evil acts" — that is, whether certain *kinds of activities* can — irrespective of any circumstances and intentions — be identified as "intrisically evil kinds of acts." Since the promulgation of *Humanae Vitae,* the use of artificial contraception has been the most hotly debated "kind of activity" of this sort.

48. It is the Luther of the *Small Catechism* and the *Large Catechism,* who in his interpretation of the Decalogue implied this understanding of a training in God's commandments, a training that is good for everyone, and neither identical with a "first" or "civil" use of the law or with a "third" use (the "usus in renatis"). The Luther-scholar and ecumenical theologian George Lindbeck once put it very well: "As Luther perceived it, Christian tradition had confused two fundamentally different senses of the concepts of 'precept' (his usual word for 'commandment') and therefore also of 'obedience.' . . . His innovative method of unmasking the confusions was to call precepts 'doctrine' or instruction and confine the term 'law' exclusively to the sphere of legally enacted norms enforced by punishment and rewards. Luther described God's precepts as instructions in the performance of practices, which, when well learned, are intrinsically satisfying. As fallen creatures, to be sure, we do not spontaneously experience the practices in which the commandments instruct us as intrinsically good, but God's goodness gives us the confidence that that is what they are. We thus need not hesitate to train ourselves in them, even without faith or desire. . . . The practices God commands can to some degree be satisfying in them-

When we take into account that for Aquinas the practical knowledge of the "natural law" was gradually and increasingly lost *post lapsum* and was only to be regained through experience,[49] and that according to him the precepts of the old law — especially its moral precepts — were "functioning . . . as a kind of communal law ordering the Jews to God . . . to conduce towards social habits and forms in new consonance with the natural law,"[50] there might be some common ground between Aquinas and Luther to understand the "positive" element of God's commandments in relation to salvation that avoids the encyclical's ambiguity at this crucial point: While God's commandments have no constructive role whatsoever in the coming about of salvation, they are reflective of God's good will and intention for human life, and a training in them will be wholesome and constructive for human life together.

Thus, with both Thomas Aquinas *and* Martin Luther we can again take up the task of remembering God's commandments by submitting to their practices and thereby — to say it with Aquinas — to slowly relearn the practical knowledge of the "natural law" or — to say it with Luther — to receive an ongoing training in God's good "orders of creation."[51]

Yet there is no "organic" or "intrinsic" transition from this training in God's commandments to salvation. Only the other way around. This is the very "economy of salvation": "In faith," life according to God's commandments, having its very center in the first commandment of the Decalogue, *is* genuine freedom. It is life with God and, as such, the way in which we are drawn into the very freedom of God's own inner-trinitarian life of love, which is life for the other.

---

selves, quite apart from rewards and punishments, even when performance is as inadequate as it always is for human beings, and even when true faith and love of God and neighbor is lacking" (George Lindbeck, "Martin Luther and the Rabbinic Mind," in Peter Ochs, ed., *Understanding the Rabbinic Mind: Essays on the Hermeneutics of Max Kadushin* [Atlanta: Scholars, 1990], pp. 141-64; 156-57).

49. Cf. Hall, *Narrative and the Natural Law,* p. 52.

50. Ibid., p. 54.

51. As Lindbeck puts it ("Martin Luther and the Rabbinic Mind," p. 158): "Because the commandments provide instruction in the 'natural law' inscribed in the heart — 'orders of creation,' as Lutherans would prefer to say — deontology coincides with an ethics of virtue."

Participating in God's very freedom, we walk the walk that God has walked for us already, for — according to Ephesians 2:10 — "we are what he has made us, created in Christ Jesus for good works, which God prepared beforehand to be our way of life" (NRSV). Good works, according to the Reformers, are thus nothing else than the shape of Christian freedom as in-formed by God's commandments. By embodying them as particular practices, in obedience to them we participate in the freedom of the One who already has prepared in triune love all of these good works for us. And this *is* the law's fulfillment.[52]

52. I am grateful to the following people for their criticisms of and suggestions for an earlier draft of this essay: Theodor Dieter, L. Gregory Jones, James F. Keenan, Jean Porter, Risto Saarinen, Eberhard Schockenhoff, and Paul Wadell.

Protestant Undertones, Averroist Overtones? The Concept of Nature in *Veritatis Splendor*

RISTO SAARINEN

IN CHAPTERS 46-50 of his encyclical letter *Veritatis Splendor* (VS), Pope John Paul II outlines the magisterium's view of "nature" as related to "freedom" and the "human person." In the following I will first describe the pope's argumentation in *Veritatis Splendor* 46-50 and then pay attention to other places in this encyclical (especially #51-53) and in the encyclical letter *Evangelium Vitae* (EV #22) in which the concept of nature is employed.

Commentators have rightly pointed out that John Paul II in *Veritatis Splendor* 46-50 follows Martin Rhonheimer's book *Natur als Grundlage der Moral*.[1] Relevant passages of that study are quoted in the footnotes. With the help of quotations the wider context of the encyclical letter should become transparent.

In the second part of this article I will discuss the pope's position

---

1. Walter Schöpsdau, "Rekonfessionalisierung der Moral? Beobachtungen aus evangelischer Sicht zur nachkonziliaren Entwicklung und zur Enzyklika 'Veritatis Splendor,'" in S. Pfürtner et al., *Abschottung statt Dialog? Das Lehramt der Kirche und die Moral* (Luzern: Exodus, 1994), esp. pp. 163-64. Many of the criticized authors are identified in J. Selling, "The Context and the Arguments of *Veritatis Splendor*," in *The Splendor of Accuracy: An Examination of the Assertions Made by "Veritatis Splendor,"* ed. Joseph A. Selling and Jan Jans (Grand Rapids: Eerdmans, 1995), pp. 22-26. For the background of German discussion, see, e.g., *Der umstrittene Naturbegriff*, ed. F. Böckle (Düsseldorf: Patmos, 1987).

from the perspective of Protestant theology, especially Lutheranism. This discussion leads to a special problem, which I consider to be a major difficulty, in *Veritatis Splendor* 46-53. The third and last part of my paper is devoted to this problem.

1. The Concept of Nature in *Veritatis Splendor* and *Evangelium Vitae*

1.1. *Veritatis Splendor 46-50*

According to *Veritatis Splendor* 46, two different positions have emerged in modern debates concerning the relation between nature and freedom: whereas "some ethicists" follow a philosophy that reduces the study of human realities to a statistical behaviorism,[2] "other moralists" affirm the importance of values and the dignity of freedom. Although the second view avoids many errors of the first view, it is nevertheless also problematic. The pope aims at showing its weak points, which result from "overlooking the created dimension of nature" and "misunderstanding its integrity."[3]

The "other moralists" strongly connect the human body with "nature" and separate both from the realm of "freedom." In their view, culture and values essentially belong to the realm of freedom, whereas human nature and the human body are treated as mere biological material. The pope remarks that if this view is consistently followed, man ceases to have a "nature," since his "personal life-project" takes place within the realm of freedom. Such freedom would be "creative of itself and its values" (VS #46).[4]

Since the view of "other moralists" separates the concepts of person and freedom from those of nature and body, a resemblance to

2. Martin Rhonheimer, *Natur als Grundlage der Moral. Eine Auseinandersetzung mit autonomer und teleologischer Ethik* (Innsbruck: Tyrolia, 1987), p. 262: "Karl Rahner hat dieser Auffassung vorgearbeitet, mit seiner, wie mir scheint, unzutreffenden Meinung, philosophische Anthropologie (d.h. die Kenntnis der menschlichen Natur) beruhe auf einer Verallgemeinerung empirischer Daten."
3. Cf. ibid., p. 409.
4. Ibid., pp. 181-85. (A linguistic note: when "man" is used instead of "human being/person," the usage of source texts is being followed.)

Immanuel Kant's moral philosophy can be observed.[5] The pope does not, however, mention Kant in this context.

The "other moralists" further criticize adherents of natural law theory for having physicalist or naturalist presuppositions, since laws which refer to nature are not moral, but only biological laws (VS #47). Moreover, "certain theologians," who obviously belong to the group of "other moralists," claim that such a problematic "biologistic or naturalistic" assumption colors positions taken by the church's magisterium.[6] According to those theologians, the human person as a rational agent must freely determine the meaning of his own behavior. Although they admit that natural inclinations[7] and other behavioral patterns can in some way provide moral orientation, they nevertheless claim that judgments concerning individual human acts can only be determined by means of free rational decisions.

Contrary to this view, the church's magisterium teaches the unity of the human person as soul and body. A moral theory that adopts any of the following claims is not in accordance with the church's teaching:

1. The human body does not have any moral significance apart from the shaping power of freedom.[8]

5. Ibid., p. 69: "Eine metaphysische Disjunktion von Natur und Vernunft, wie auch von freiem Willen und Natur besitzt ja in einem thomistischen Kontext keinen Sinn — man müßte sich dazu eher auf Kant berufen. Eine solche dualistische Anthropologie . . . entspringt letztlich dem Versuch, einer weiterhin naturalistisch — 'physizistisch' — interpretierten 'Naturordnung' eine Vernunft gegenüberzustellen, die den Charakter einer gegenüber dem Natürlichen ungebundenen Freiheit beansprucht."

6. Cf. ibid., p. 124 (with reference to J. Fuchs and L. Janssens concerning the discussion around *Humanae Vitae*). According to Selling, "Context and Arguments," p. 65, "certain theologians" here refers to Charles Curran.

7. *Inclinatio naturalis* occurs often both in VS #47-50 and in Rhonheimer, *Natur als Grundlage der Moral,* esp. pp. 89-91. For natural inclinations in VS, see also Selling, "Context and Arguments," pp. 67-68.

8. Rhonheimer, *Natur als Grundlage der Moral,* p. 107: "Geht diese ganzheitliche Sicht verloren, die allein eine *Ethik des Leibes* und der *Sinnlichkeit* ermöglicht, dann befindet man sich auf den Wegen einer auf dualistischen Argumentationsbasis beruhenden spiritualistischen Fehldeutung des Menschen, — wobei mit 'Spiritualismus' hier eine Anthropologie und Ethik gemeint sind, in der Leiblichkeit und Sinnlichkeit im Kontext menschlichen Handelns keine im sittlichen Sinne konstitutive Bedeutung zugesprochen wird, sondern — aufgrund einer dualistischen Gegen-

2. The human body, although materially necessary for the person's freedom, is finally extrinsic to the person.[9]

3. The functions of human nature or body only incline toward physical goods and therefore do not give reference points for moral decisions.[10]

These false claims resolve the tension between freedom and nature by creating a division within man.

But the church teaches that the human person consists of a unity of both soul and body. The human person is the subject of his own moral acts "in the unity of body and soul."[11] Moreover, this unity reminds us that reason and free will are linked with all the bodily and sense faculties. Since the human person has a "particular spiritual and bodily structure," his freedom cannot be reduced to a self-designing capacity but it must "respect certain fundamental goods" given by this structure (VS #48).

The pope further condemns

4. the "doctrine which dissociates the moral act from the bodily dimensions of its exercise"[12]

as being contrary to the teaching of Scripture and tradition. This doctrine is similar to some "ancient errors" that conceive the human freedom as a purely spiritual or formal notion and, consequently, misunderstand the moral meaning of the body and of the kinds of

überstellung von 'Person' und 'Natur' — *alle* menschlichen Akte als *ursprünglich* geistige Phänomene angesehen werden."

9. Ibid., p. 408: "Die Leiblichkeit des Menschen ist ebenso konstitutiv für das Verständnis der menschlichen Person, das menschliche Ich oder Selbstbewußtsein; sie darf nicht als 'untermenschlich' (Rahner) bezeichnet werden."

10. Ibid., p. 93 (criticizing the position of L. Janssens).

11. Ibid., p. 408: "Der Mensch nimmt am ewigen Gesetz gemäß seinem *ganzen* Sein teil. Die menschliche Person ist Leib und Geist, die in unverbrüchlicher Einheit menschliche Güter und sinnhaftes menschliches Seinkönnen definieren."

12. Ibid., p. 409: "Die menschliche Leiblichkeit ist nicht ein, wenn auch 'sittlich bedeutsamer,' zugleich jedoch 'neutraler,' in sich 'untermenschlicher' oder 'unterpersonaler' Bereich. Sie formuliert für spezifisch menschliches Sein-Können vielmehr grundlegende *menschliche Güter* (oder Ziele), die für *personales* Handeln konstitutiv sind."

external behavior condemned by Saint Paul in 1 Corinthians 6:9 and 10 (VS #49).

What are these ancient errors? Since the criticized positions resemble Kantian ethics, one could think of Kant's principle of a good will as the only absolute good. Another point of reference could be Peter Abelard's view that external works are morally indifferent.[13] Somewhat surprisingly, however, the pope here quotes the Council of Trent's *Decree on Justification,* which lists the mortal sins mentioned in 1 Corinthians 6:9-10. More importantly, however, the *Decree on Justification* is quoted throughout *Veritatis Splendor* against those who downplay the importance of external manifestation of moral life.[14] In this way the theology of the Reformation becomes connected with the condemned views of "certain theologians," who themselves are not Lutherans but liberal Roman Catholics.

Finally, *Veritatis Splendor* 50 connects the human nature with the natural law: this law refers to the nature of the human person in the unity of soul and body. Although the biological inclinations of the body thus belong to the realm of nature, the natural law is not merely on the biological level, but it comprises the rational order whereby man is called to direct and regulate his life.

As we have seen, the pope on the one hand emphasizes the unity of soul and body in order to affirm the view that the body has an important moral significance. On the other hand, however, the unity argument in *Veritatis Splendor* 50 qualifies and limits the importance earlier ascribed to the body. Therefore the pope can conclude by saying that the natural inclinations have moral significance "only insofar as they refer to the human person and his authentic fulfill-

13. See *Enchiridion Symbolorum Definitionum et Declarationum de Rebus Fidei et Morum,* ed. H. Denzinger and P. Hünermann (Freiburg: Herder, 1991), p. 733. Risto Saarinen, *Weakness of the Will in Medieval Thought: From Augustine to Buridan* (Leiden: Brill, 1994), pp. 51-60, discusses Abelard's position in detail. Rhonheimer, *Natur als Grundlage der Moral,* p. 97, connects the false position of L. Janssens with Abelard. As to Kant, Rhonheimer (p. 173) thinks that "[die] Leistung und Tiefe Kants vermag in der 'autonomen Moral' [A. Auer] nur einen indirekten Einfluß auszuüben, und zwar in der Gestalt einer Art 'transzendentalphilosophischen' Thomas-Exegese, die dem Anliegen Kants selbst nicht gerecht zu werden vermag."

In neo-Thomist contexts the notion of transcendentalism is often ascribed to Karl Rahner and his coworkers.

14. See footnotes 63, 85, 88, 125, and 162 of VS.

ment."[15] But in spite of this qualification the main point of the passage remains valid, that since the natural law does not allow division between freedom and nature, the "authentic fulfillment" takes place in the human nature as a whole and not only in the soul.[16]

1.2. Veritatis Splendor 51-53 and Other Passages

Veritatis Splendor 46-50 has not been in the primary focus of the reception of the encyclical letter.[17] One may easily see, however, that this passage provides important support for two main themes of the encyclical, namely (1) the criticism of autonomous morality and teleologism (VS #36-37, 74-75)[18] and (2) the doctrine of intrinsically evil acts (VS #79-83). Concerning the first, the person's being a "nature" created by God limits the scope of reason's autonomy because the "natural" moral law thereby has a religious foundation, that is, God as its author: reason "participates" in this law, but it is not for the human person "to establish" the eternal law (VS #36).[19] Concerning the second, many if not all intrinsically evil acts mentioned in *Veritatis Splendor* 80 harm the living body which, as bearer of human

15. Rhonheimer, *Natur als Grundlage der Moral,* p. 90: "Wenn die natürliche Neigung nicht von der Vernunft geregelt ist, kann sie . . . unmenschliche Folgen zeitigen."

16. Ibid., p. 90: "Die sittliche Tugend ist also . . . die Vervollkommnung der natürlichen Neigung aufgrund deren 'conformitas ad rationem.'"

17. E.g. the extensive popular commentaries published in *Osservatore Romano* autumn and winter 1993-1994 only briefly treat this topic (Janet E. Smith, 5 January 1994, and Bernhard Fraling, 19 January 1994, remain narrative). The book *Moraltheologie im Abseits? Antwort auf die Enzyklika "Veritatis Splendor,"* ed. D. Mieth (Freiburg: Herder, 1994), does not analyze these passages. Protestant voices include, for example, Martin Honecker, "Wahrheit und Freiheit im Spannungsfeld des Pluralismus: Zur Moralenzyklika 'Veritatis Splendor,'" in *Materialdienst des Konfessionskundlichen Instituts Bensheim* 1 (1994): 6-11, and Schöpsdau, "Rekonfessionalisierung der Moral?"

18. One must here keep in mind that the subtitle of Rhonheimer's study is *Eine Auseinandersetzung mit autonomer und teleologischer Ethik.*

19. In his commentary on this point in *Osservatore Romano* 22/29 December 1993, Martin Rhonheimer summarizes the issue: "John Paul II's teaching focuses on the idea of a true human autonomy founded precisely on an original 'ontological' dependence of man on God." One may add that it is precisely this "idea" that Rhonheimer himself (1987) puts forward.

personality, is to be affirmed for its own sake. Although I will not treat these complex topics here, it must be pointed out that the intimate connections between nature, body, and person worked out in paragraphs 46-50 serve as a philosophical and even "ontological" foundation for these two main themes of the encyclical.

Veritatis Splendor 51 mentions "certain philosophical theories which are highly influential in present-day culture." These theories are similar to the ones already outlined in paragraphs 46-50; they presuppose a separation between the individual freedom and the nature which we all have in common. Such a separation "obscures the perception of the universality of the moral law on the part of reason" since the natural moral law refers to the common nature. But John Paul II claims that individual freedom in moral issues cannot be separated from this common nature since it is constitutive of the individual moral subject, the human person.

In keeping with this fundamental claim the immutable structure of "nature" is further emphasized. The natural law "involves universality." It "is universal in its precepts and its authority extends to all mankind" (VS #51). Human persons live in different historical periods and in different cultures, but the human nature "transcends those cultures" and "is itself the measure of culture." The truth of the immutable natural moral law "unfolds down the centuries" and can be "specified and determined" by the church's magisterium (VS #53).

The theory outlined in *Veritatis Splendor* 46-50 is thus in paragraphs 51-53 employed as a proof of the universal obligation of moral precepts. Since all human beings share in the same nature, specific circumstances cannot alter moral judgments which refer to this nature. In *Evangelium Vitae* 22 the concept of nature is employed in a similar manner. If nature is conceived as a merely physical nature, it loses its "transcendent character" and becomes a subject of manipulation. This is a state of "freedom without law." Interestingly, the opposite view of "divinizing" the nature by considering it unlawful to interfere in any way with it, is here also condemned. This view is labeled as "law without freedom." Both of these opposites misunderstand nature's dependence on the plan of the Creator.

Evangelium Vitae 22 employs the word "mystery" four times in order to underline that "nature" is not natural in any secular sense. The existence of man is something "sacred" and "transcendent." In other words, since human nature reflects the plan of the Creator, it is essentially *supernatural*,[20] although it should not become "divinized."

The contexts in which the notion of nature is mentioned thus show that this notion is employed in order to consolidate the absolute and immutable content of those moral precepts that prohibit harming a living human body. "Nature" and "natural" in the two moral encyclicals are neither opposites of "supernatural" nor synonymous with "secular." Human nature is something sacred and transcendent, a mystery.

2. Rejecting False Dualism: A Lutheran Affirmation

Protestant reactions to the view of nature presented in *Veritatis Splendor* have been rather negative. Commentators have pointed out that this view represents a "philosophical metaphysics of natural law" or an "objectivist" view of natural law. They emphasize that according to Protestantism God does not stand at our disposal; thus we cannot recognize God's purposes in nature's finalities.[21]

Although such views may point in a right direction, they do not give any detailed description of what Lutherans and other Protestants think of the fundamental matters described in *Veritatis Splendor* 46-50. Lutheranism does not have a tradition of such detailed moral philosophy and fundamental theology as does Roman Catholicism. But there are nevertheless topics in Lutheran theology, too, that converge with the argumentation presented by the pope. Let me outline three such issues.

1. Lutherans have often accused Roman Catholics of a false dualism between body and soul. Especially in the discussions concerning man's personal existence after death Lutherans traditionally object to the view that the soul in death becomes separated from the body and bears the personal identity during an intermediate state. According to

20. Rhonheimer (*Natur als Grundlage der Moral*, p. 420) finishes his study by concluding that when the errors of moral autonomy are avoided, "ist der Weg freigelegt zu einer wahrhaft übernatürlichen, christlichen, weil christozentrischen, Moral der Bergpredigt, der Seligpreisungen."

21. Schöpsdau, "Rekonfessionalisierung der Moral?" p. 164; Honecker, "Wahrheit und Freiheit," p. 9.

many Protestants, the biblical idea of the human person's unity as body and soul makes it anthropologically difficult to affirm a separate existence of an immortal soul.[22] When Roman Catholic theology now emphasizes this unity and the importance of the body for personality,[23] it rejects the traditions of Platonic dualism and contempt of corporeality; traditions Lutherans have always rejected as well.

2. The complex relations between neo-Kantian moral philosophy and Christian ethical teaching raise important questions for both Catholics and Protestants. Lutherans have often considered Kantianism, especially under a specific neo-Kantian guise, as a "Philosophy of Protestantism."[24] Following this line of thought, prominent Protestant theologians have considered Christianity to be essentially a domination of spirit over world and nature. In keeping with this view, the notions of person, freedom, and culture have been understood as antagonists of nature.[25]

The neo-Kantian dualism between person and nature has often led Protestantism to a contempt of nature and, consequently, to ethical consequences that are problematic and sometimes clearly false. Let me give one brief example. Many neo-Protestant theologians of the late nineteenth century taught that the human society develops from the lower state of nature to the higher state of culture, freedom, and

---

22. W. Schoberth, Tod. *Evangelisches Kirchenlexikon* 4 (Göttingen: Vandenhoeck, 1996), pp. 897-901, offers a standard view and a bibliography.

23. One can of course ask how the anthropology of VS is compatible with the Roman Catholic theology of death. See for example the new *Catechism of the Catholic Church* (London: Chapman, 1994), pp. 997, 1005, which teaches the separation of soul from body in death.

24. See Risto Saarinen, *Gottes Wirken auf uns. Die transzendentale Deutung des Gegenwart-Christi-Motivs in der Lutherforschung* (Stuttgart: Franz Steiner, 1989), and Risto Saarinen, "Kants Kritik der praktischen Vernunft als 'Philosophie des Protestantismus' bei H. Cohen und W. Herrmann," in *Akten des 7. Internationalen Kant-Kongresses,* ed. G. Funke (Bonn: Bouvier, 1991), pp. 629-38.

25. In Protestant theology this view was programmatically put forward by A. Ritschl (see, e.g., Albrecht Ritschl, *Die christliche Lehre von der Rechtfertigung und Versöhnung,* vol. 3.3 [Bonn, 1888], pp. 25, 199-200). Ritschl further considered this to be Luther's own view: "Denn wo anders findet sich die Voraussetzung aller Naturforschung, nämlich daß der menschliche Geist über die Welt mächtig und mehr werth sei als sie, vorbereitet, als in Luthers Idee von der Freiheit eines Christenmenschen" (Albrecht Ritschl, *Drei akademische Reden* [Bonn, 1887], p. 17).

spirit. Whereas family is a social form of the lowest "natural" stage, the universal state represents the highest "cultural" stage of this evolution. A Christian aiming at moral perfection should rise from natural stages to cultural ones. Consequently, as the prominent liberal theologian Wilhelm Herrmann writes:

> a home can only retain its ethical character when it contributes to the cultural work through the civil occupation of a family member, especially of the husband. A person who only lives for his family is immoral in the same sense as a person who only lives for his own health.[26]

Herrmann continues by pointing out that women are bound to nature and family, whereas men have the capacity of rising to the spheres of culture and freedom.[27]

This example appears today odd enough to reveal the problems related to a contempt of nature and a dualistic separation of nature from culture. But there are subtler forms of neo-Kantian dualism that have exercised their influence upon Protestant views concerning the theology of nature and creation, the relation between theology and philosophy, and the foundations of ethics.[28] It can be argued that tendencies to separate theology and religion from philosophy, metaphysics, and the natural reality often presuppose a dualism that displays a contempt of nature in its ethical applications.[29]

Given the strong and problematic impact of neo-Kantian "transcendentalist" philosophy in Protestantism, one is ready to believe that a similar impact in modern Catholic dogmatics may cause problems in the understanding of nature and other "realistic" themes of theology.

26. Wilhelm Herrmann, *Ethik* (Tübingen, 1901), p. 163 (my translation).

27. Ibid., pp. 152-58, 173-74. For the context of these views, see Risto Saarinen, "Die Kulturbedeutung des Protestantismus im Urteil der Luther-Interpreten. Von Albrecht Ritschl bis Friedrich Gogarten," in *Christentum und Weltverantwortung*, ed. J. Heubach (Erlangen: Martin-Luther-Verlag, 1992), pp. 25-49.

28. These are discussed by Ole Jensen, *Theologie zwischen Illusion und Restriktion* (München: Kaiser, 1975), and Saarinen, *Gottes Wirken auf uns*.

29. Discussions on ecology and theology, beginning from Lynn White, "The Religious Roots of Our Ecological Crisis," *Science* 155 (1967): 1203-7, and recently summarized by Jürgen Moltmann, "Ökologie," in *Theologische Realenzyklopädie*, vol. 25 (Berlin: de Gruyter, 1995), pp. 36-46, have to some extent realized these problems.

3. The place of natural law continues to be debated within Protestantism. Whereas recent Continental European Protestantism tends to be critical of it, much of Scandinavian Lutheran and worldwide Anglican ethical thought applies the idea of natural law. A recent comparative survey of the Christian churches' ethical teachings comes to the conclusion that Protestants and Anglicans apply a variety of ethical theories among which natural law and especially creation-based arguments play an important role.[30] Thus one should not postulate false basic differences between the ethical approaches of the churches.

Even in German Protestantism the recent philosophical popularity of virtue ethics and of some Catholic-inspired philosophical efforts has to some extent revived reflections on natural law. The above-mentioned criticism of "philosophical metaphysics of natural law" in *Veritatis Splendor* by Martin Honecker, for example, considers a "phenomenological" natural law theory to be an adequate approach and presents a "criterion-based situation ethics" as a Protestant alternative.[31]

The crucial question that emerges as a corollary to this third point of possible convergence is, however, whether the foundational or "ontological" view put forward in *Veritatis Splendor* 46-50 necessarily implies the straightforward Roman Catholic moral applications, especially in the field of sexual ethics. Let me summarize the ontological claims of the pope's view:

1. The person is a moral subject in the unity of body and soul that both together constitute the human nature.
2. A moral act cannot be dissociated from the bodily dimensions of its exercise.
3. Natural law refers to the nature of the human person.
4. Natural law is a rational order; therefore it is through the use of reason that this order can be discovered.
5. But this "natural" is finally supernatural or revelatory, since it represents the Creator's plan.

---

30. Mark Ellingsen, *The Cutting Edge: How Churches Speak on Social Issues* (Geneva: WCC, 1993), pp. 139-45.

31. Honecker, "Wahrheit und Freiheit," pp. 9, 11.

Roman Catholic corollaries of point 5 include the following: Natural law is "participation of the eternal law in the rational creature" (VS #43). It is Christ who, "having taken on human nature, definitively illumines it" (VS #53); it is the church's magisterium that specifies and determines the moral norms. Reason can to some extent discover the already existing moral truth, but it cannot invent or create moral positions on its own.

Points 1 and 2 are, I think, compatible with the teaching of all Protestant churches. Concerning point 2, Protestant churches certainly do not affirm such an "Abelardian" view according to which external actions would be morally indifferent.

Here something ought to be said about the frequent quotations of the Council of Trent's condemnation of Lutheran teaching on justification. Canons 18-21 of *Decree on Justification,* which anathematize the opinions that (a) good works are totally indifferent and that (b) Christians do not need to keep the commandments of God, clearly do not apply to Lutheran teaching. Joint ecumenical statements have pointed this out.[32] It is unfortunate that ancient condemnations of falsely understood Lutheran positions are quoted in order to control modern Catholic moral theology which, by the way, does not affirm the "Abelardian" view either.

Concerning the pope's points 3 to 5, those Protestant churches that affirm the idea of a natural moral law understand it as a rational order, not as a biological law. They also emphasize that "natural" here means something "created," which becomes illuminated when we follow Christ.[33] Thus natural moral law is essentially a theological

---

32. See, e.g. *Lehrverurteilungen — kirchentrennend?* vol. 1, ed. K. Lehmann and W. Pannenberg (Göttingen: Vandenhoeck, 1986), pp. 58-59, and Otto Hermann Pesch, "Die Canones des Trienter Rechtfertigungsdekretes: Wen trafen sie? Wen treffen sie heute?" in *Lehrverurteilungen — kirchentrennend?* vol. 2, ed. K. Lehmann (Göttingen: Vandenhoeck, 1989), esp. pp. 265-66. As Pesch here points out, Luther is totally misunderstood in canons 18-21.

33. See, e.g., Ellingsen, *The Cutting Edge,* pp. 139-40. The new document of the Joint Working Group between WCC and RCC, "The Ecumenical Dialogue on Moral Issues," *The Ecumenical Review* 48 (1996): 148, unmistakably understands "nature" as referring to human nature and to human reason. For the place of natural law in Protestantism in general, see Falk Wagner, "Naturrecht II," in *Theologische Realenzyklopädie,* vol. 24 (Berlin: de Gruyter, 1994), pp. 153-85.

perspective, a perspective that offers a platform toward secular morality but cannot be reduced to a secular discourse. And those currents in Protestantism that do not want to employ the idea of natural law proceed in their theological ethics from the biblical ideas related to creation and to the example of Christ, thus affirming that the final foundation of Christian ethics is revelation. In this sense most of the content of points 3 to 5 is compatible with Protestant ethics.

What remains problematic is the authority ascribed to the church's magisterium and, in particular, the philosophical question of whether all human persons literally share in the *same* nature. To this question we will soon return.

Approving the fundamental claims expressed in points 1 through 5 does not imply, however, that their Roman Catholic ethical applications need to be affirmed. Scandinavian Lutheranism, for example, can and in fact does adhere to almost everything claimed in these points but nevertheless draws opposite ethical conclusions in the issues of contraception and divorce. This observation raises the important but very difficult issue of practical inference: often it seems to be genuinely possible to make different and even contradictory judgments on the basis of the "same" fundamental convictions. This difficult issue, however, is not my topic here.[34]

I have above wanted to show that the three points of convergence and the five fundamental claims made in *Veritatis Splendor* are themes in regard to which an interconfessional discussion can be fruitful. But the last part of my article will be critical rather than irenic.

3. Rejecting False Monism: A Christian Critique

Veritatis Splendor obviously aims at avoiding the post-Enlightenment apotheosis of individualism. The Catholic position presupposes a universal human nature with an eminent moral significance. Into this nature the law becomes "impressed" (VS #51) from the archetype

---

34. E.g., Oliver O'Donovan, "Life in Christ," *The Tablet* (2 July 1994): 826-28, has critically discussed the situation in which two churches claim to share the same fundamental values although they draw different ethical conclusions from these values.

and thus the law's precepts oblige everyone in the same manner. Everyone shares in the same human nature. Moreover, this nature contains the fundamental values or "goods" which constitute human dignity. The notion of human or personal dignity is massively present everywhere in *Veritatis Splendor* and *Evangelium Vitae*. It is frequently employed in order to restrict human freedom, as if the human capacity for free decisions were a vice rather than a virtue.[35]

This feature is at variance with the history of the notion of dignity. Already Pico della Mirandola and in modern times especially Kant, whose usage many prominent legal and philosophical texts follow, saw human dignity as established in a person's free ability to choose.[36] In the Vatican's understanding, however, dignity is not founded on freedom but rather exists in continuing potential conflict with it. Such dignity is something sacred or even taboo rather than dignity in its modern Kantian sense. Even though the use of "dignity" and human "goods" in *Veritatis Splendor* and *Evangelium Vitae* sometimes approaches the so-called basic goods theory, *Veritatis Splendor* in my view opposes the Kantian features of this theory.[37]

In *Veritatis Splendor* dignity is not found in freedom but vice versa: the basic personal dignity establishes freedom and remains its measure. Since human dignity ontologically precedes human freedom, one must ask whether this dignity is in any way based upon persons as *individuals* or whether it is rather a character of *common* human nature in which the individuals have a share.

---

35. At least since Anselm's *De libertate arbitrii*, Western theology has clearly recognized that a true Christian freedom has to be something different from *posse peccare*. For Anselm's position, see Saarinen, *Weakness of the Will in Medieval Thought*, pp. 43-51.

36. See, e.g., R. P. Horstmann, "Menschenwürde," *Historisches Wörterbuch der Philosophie*, vol. 5 (Basel/Stuttgart: Schwabe, 1980), pp. 1124-27.

37. The basic goods theory is often attributed to Catholic ethicists J. Finnis and G. Grisez. According to John Finnis, *Natural Law and Natural Rights* (Oxford: Clarendon, 1980), practical reason does not infer what is good by observing human nature; it directly experiences or grasps this. Cf. Knut Haakonssen, "Natural Law," in *Encyclopedia of Ethics*, ed. L. Becker (New York: Garland, 1992), pp. 884-90. Haakonssen here describes the Kantian characteristics of Finnis's theory. For basic goods theory in VS, see Selling, "Context and Arguments," pp. 67-68. Rhonheimer, *Natur als Grundlage der Moral*, pp. 130 and 245-46, criticizes Finnis and Grisez (whose theories he in some other respects embraces) for voluntarism and lack of adequate rational teleology.

Veritatis Splendor evidently supports the latter view. The negative precepts universally oblige everyone never to offend "the personal dignity common to all" (VS #52). The nature is described as something "which all have in common" (VS #51). The human nature is "the measure of culture and the condition ensuring that man . . . asserts his personal dignity" and does not "call into question the permanent structural elements of man" (VS #53). The universal natural law which is "impressed" into the heart of man in turn "expresses" the dignity of human person (VS #51).

The personal dignity present in human nature is a permanent structure common to all. Thus it is something that ontologically precedes individuality. Presupposing fundamentally individual natures that would differ from each other would call into question the universality of natural law as the law of human nature. Dignity is not, as in modern times, a character of individuals but a universal character of common nature. It is an expression of the impression of the archetype of natural law in the human person.

This view in some ways resembles that of Thomas Aquinas, who considered that the specific dignity of human nature in comparison to other created beings consists in its being the image of God.[38] From one perspective, however, the encyclical's view conflicts with Thomism.

The perspective from which this conflict becomes visible is that of *Averroism* or *monopsychism,* that is, the view according to which human souls are finally clones that instantiate the one and the same archetype when they inhabit different individual bodies. According to *Veritatis Splendor,* individual human beings receive their personal dignity not because of any individual or unique characteristics but because they share in a common nature. Does *Veritatis Splendor* through this teaching approach the monistic Averroistic views that deny the uniqueness of individual souls? An Averroistic psychology is obviously problematic. Since Thomas Aquinas's criticism of it in the treatise *De unitate intellectus contra Averroistas* (1270), Averroism has been refuted a number of times as incompatible with Christian anthropology.

As far as I know nobody has raised the issue of Averroism or the problem of "individuation" of human persons in the otherwise ex-

---

38. Horstmann, "Menschenwürde," p. 1124.

tensive and critical discussions around *Veritatis Splendor.* At two places the encyclical letter itself, however, seems to be aware of this problem. In the first occasion its solution is surprising:

> This universality [of natural law] does not ignore the individuality of human beings nor is it opposed to the absolute uniqueness of each person. On the contrary, it embraces at its root each of the person's free acts, which are meant to bear witness to the universality of the true good. (VS 51)

The somewhat enigmatic English text[39] seems to say that individuality is to be sought in a person's free acts. This is an extremely weak notion of individuality. If the problem of modern autonomy was that "man would be nothing more than his own freedom" (VS #46), the opposite problem of *Veritatis Splendor* is that an individual person is nothing more than a sacred nature common to all, individuated only by the circumstance that singular bodies united with this common nature can perform acts which are "free" in the sense that they can go wrong and indeed do go wrong if they do not "witness the universality of the true good." A logical consequence of this view would be that a man who exercises his *own* freedom ceases to be a *man* since through ceasing to witness the universal good the person separates himself from universal humanity.

Another attempt to preserve individuality is made in *Veritatis Splendor* 85 in the form of a rhetorical question:

39. The German text here says: "Diese Universalität sieht nicht von der Einzigartigkeit der Menschen ab, noch widerspricht sie der Einmaligkeit und Unwiederholbarkeit jeder einzelnen menschlichen Person: Sie umfaßt im Gegenteil grundlegend jede ihrer freien Handlungen, die die Universalität des wahren Guten bezeugen müssen."

It is difficult to think that the German text could be a translation from English; perhaps here German is indeed the original language of the author. Be that as it may, the terms "Einmaligkeit" (singularity or once-ness) and "Unwiederholbarkeit" (unrepeatable-ness) are here even weaker than the English "individuality" since they only claim that the individuation of human nature as "Einzelperson" consists in its occupying specific positions within a time-continuum. Moreover, the phrase "Einzigartigkeit" does not exactly refer to individuality but rather to the uniqueness of human being as species. One thus reads the German text so that individuality there is almost nonexistent and the danger of Averroism consequently even greater than in the English text.

How can obedience to universal and unchanging moral norms respect the uniqueness and individuality of the person and not represent a threat to his freedom and dignity?

The rhetorical question is not directly answered in *Veritatis Splendor* 85-87. Reflections on freedom in those paragraphs can perhaps be regarded as indirect answers. These reflections stress that the "origin" of human freedom "is not in itself, but in the life within which it is situated" (VS #86). Freedom is given as a gift, it is "to be received like a seed and to be cultivated responsibly" (VS #86). We see that these enigmatic descriptions tend to regard true freedom as something impersonal which is not a mark of our individuality but a mark of universal life, which is received from outside and after that occupies the human soul. But such tendencies of course beg the rhetorical question and make the worry expressed by it even greater, since this interpretation of freedom obviously does represent a threat to a human person's freedom and individuality insofar as it is *his* freedom and *his* individuality. Thus the danger of monopsychism or Averroism remains.

One could of course say that any accusation of "Averroism" can only be put forward as a result of a malevolent and far-fetched reading of the encyclical since the "dignity common to all" is only meant to underline the equality of every person as an equal image of God. Of course the point of controversy in Thomas Aquinas's *Tractatus de unitate intellectus contra Averroistas* is not ethics in the first place. But if we look at Aquinas's argumentation closer, the analogies are not irrelevant.[40]

The Averroist Siger of Brabant claimed that the so-called potential intellect by which we can receive abstract concepts is one for all men.

---

40. The description of Thomas's argument follows the interpretation given in *The Cambridge History of Later Medieval Philosophy*, ed. N. Kretzmann, A. Kenny, J. Pinborg (Cambridge: Cambridge University Press, 1982), pp. 595-622. For a more detailed description of the complex issues, see *Individuation in Scholasticism: The Later Middle Ages and the Counter-Reformation, 1150-1650*, ed. J. J. E. Gracia (New York: SUNY Press, 1994), and *Individuum und Individualität im Mittelalter*, ed. J. A. Aertsen and A. Speer (Berlin–New York: Walter de Gruyter, 1996), esp. pp. 178-96, 249-302. In the following I use the English translation: Thomas Aquinas, *On the Unity of the Intellect Against the Averroists* (Milwaukee: Marquette University Press, 1968).

Analogically, in *Veritatis Splendor* it is the common nature as the foundation of morals by which we receive the abstract moral truths (e.g., "human dignity") expressed by natural law. In *Veritatis Splendor* #46-53 the universal nature that both ontologically establishes and cognitively illuminates the moral law thus displays a role and function similar to that of potential intellect in Siger of Brabant.

Thomas's criticism of Siger concerns the relatedness of cognition and individuality. He finds that the Averroistic position cannot account for individual persons actually thinking; according to Averroism we would only participate in some universal cognition. But this is contrary to our psychological experience. This experience can only be met by saying that although the universal object of our knowledge certainly is one, we must see that this object allows itself to be individuated in different human persons. Each individual intellect already possesses the so-called intelligible species which this process of reception and individuation requires. Knowing truth is not simply a participation in some given universal object or in a collective cognitive light; abstract concepts are always conceived by means of intelligible species present in the individual intellect.

Thus Thomas can insist on the individual nature of our understanding:

> It is therefore one thing which is understood both by me and by you. But it is understood by me in one way and by you in another, that is, by another intelligible species. And my understanding is one thing, and yours, another; and my intellect is one thing, and yours, another. . . . Now from this it is clear in what way there is the same knowledge in the pupil and in the teacher. For it is the same in relation to the thing known, but not, however, in relation to the intelligible species by which each one knows. For in this respect knowledge is individuated in me and in him.[41]

Without pushing the analogy too far, one can say that the problem of *individual cognition of universal truths* is not adequately met either in Averroism or in the views of Rhonheimer and *Veritatis Splendor*. We recognize these truths as individuals, and our application of them is

41. Aquinas, *On the Unity,* #112.

dependent on our being individuals. We have individual potential intellects which we must employ as individuals.

In his study *Natur als Grundlage der Moral* Martin Rhonheimer extensively discusses the Thomistic psychology from which he claims to derive his concept of nature. He does not, however, pay any attention to the problem of individuation and the danger of Averroism. On the contrary Rhonheimer massively emphasizes the unity of intellect in Aquinas.[42] According to him, the human intellect essentially is "participation in the divine light of knowledge."[43] Rhonheimer's interpretation of Aquinas thus extends the already very uncertain idea of the unity of the so-called agent intellect (as *lumen naturale*)[44] to the intellect as a whole and, consequently, brings the Angelic Doctor to the camp of the Averroists. Through the use of Rhonheimer's view of nature by John Paul II this Averroistic tendency becomes transmitted to *Veritatis Splendor*.

The philosophical (and theological) problem of the papal view is

---

42. Rhonheimer, *Natur als Grundlage der Moral*, pp. 210-31.

43. Ibid., p. 211: "Der menschliche Intellekt ist tatsächlich eine Teilhabe am göttlichen Erkenntnislicht."

See also p. 218: "Weil auch beim Menschen jede Erkenntnis in der Einheit der intellektiven apprehensio endet, besteht zwischen dem Intellekt der reinen Intelligenzen (Engel) und demjenigen des Menschen nicht ein Unterschied bezüglich wesentlicher Eigenschaften und Fähigkeiten; der menschliche Intellekt gehört zum gleichen Genus, wie derjenige der reinen Intelligenzen. . . . Die menschliche *rationalitas* ist somit also tatsächlich ein Derivat der göttlichen Weisheit."

According to *Cambridge History* (p. 608) Thomas "rejects those accounts of intellectual cognition which involve representations that are innate to the soul or that are sent into the soul from a higher being, and he likewise denies that the human intellect knows material things in the exemplars of the divine mind." See also next footnotes.

44. Aquinas himself did not think the agent intellect to be one either but considered that it is, like the potential intellect, multiplied according to the number of individual human beings. There exists, however, a respectable Christian opinion according to which God would be the only agent intellect who illuminates the human souls as *lumen intellectuale/naturale*. But, contrary to Rhonheimer, "it is clear that for Thomas God in fact has no special role to play in man's achieving knowledge of the natural order" (so *Cambridge History*, p. 614; see also pp. 607-14).

Moreover, as Finnis (*Natural Law and Natural Rights*, p. 36) points out, "for Aquinas, the way to discover what is morally right (virtue) and wrong (vice) is to ask, not what is in accordance with human nature, but what is reasonable."

that our knowledge of the natural law or of human nature is supposed to be an immediate participation in the divine light. In such a model the human intellect in its moral orientation is basically one, and individuality either does not play any role at all or is harmful since it separates the person from this truthful unity.

The view of Aquinas, however, stresses that although truth as such is universal, our cognition and understanding of it necessarily remains radically individual since our souls are individual souls provided with individual intellects. This is an epistemological fact based on Christian anthropology. Aquinas can even claim that the human person as a rational animal in a very deep sense "is intellect." This means that a person's individual intellect constitutes his or her identity; it is not essentially a participation in something else. For Thomas, this fact is also relevant in ethics:

> Now it is clear that the intellect is that which is the principal agent in man, and that it uses all the powers of the soul and the members of the body as if they were organs. And on this account Aristotle said subtly that man is intellect "or is principally this." If, therefore, there is one intellect for all, it follows of necessity that there be one who understands and consequently one who wills and one who uses according to the choice of his will all those things by which men are diverse from one another. And from this it further follows that there would be no difference among men in respect to the free choice of the will, but it [the choice] would be the same for all, if the intellect in which alone would reside pre-eminence and dominion over the use of all other [powers] is one and undivided in all. This is clearly false and impossible. For it is opposed to what is evident and destroys the whole of moral science and everything which relates to the civil intercourse which is natural to man, as Aristotle says.[45]

From this quotation we see that for Aquinas the existence of moral science witnesses the individuality of human souls. A view which relies upon the oneness of intellect is not only empirically false but offers a destructive model since it does not employ the *conversatio civilis*

---

45. Aquinas, *On the Unity*, #89. The reference to Aristotle pertains to the place in *Politics* in which the philosopher says that the human person is by nature a political animal (*Pol.* 1253a2-3).

through which human persons as by nature political animals must formulate their own rules of conduct. Averroists replace this process with a claim that the one light from above rules everything.

One may finally remark that the encyclical's emphasis on the human body is also interesting from the perspective of Averroism. We affirmed above the pope's attempt to give the human body a moral significance in order to avoid false dualisms. In Averroism, however, the human body is considered to be the "principle of individuation" in a very strict sense, that is, that individuals are distinguished by their bodies but not by their souls since the one soul is the universal form of all bodies. This strict application of the Aristotelian matter-form relationship was rejected by Aquinas in the case of human persons:

> In many bodies, therefore, there are many souls, and in many souls there are many intellectual powers which are called intellects. Nor on this account does it follow that the intellect is a material power, as was shown above.[46]

Now, *Veritatis Splendor* 49 claims that

> body and soul are inseparable; in the person, in the willing agent and in the deliberate act they stand and fall together.

Protestants have on the one hand every reason to affirm this holism. But on the other hand, if this holism is affirmed together with an idea that the soul's activity consists only in its participation in the divine light, then the body becomes the genuine principle of individuation and, consequently, the sole bearer of human personality. We noted this above in the connection of *Veritatis Splendor* 51 in which it was held that the person's free acts are the root of his or her individuality. In paragraphs 48-49 the body is, in unity with the soul, often described as bearer of personality, although the pope does not explicitly claim that the body is constitutive for human personality. Martin Rhonheimer, however, does not hesitate to take this last step and to say that

---

46. Aquinas, *On the Unity,* #103. Although Aquinas's anti-Averroistic stance is clear, he wrestled with this issue a lot. For further discussion, see *Individuation in Scholasticism,* ed. Gracia, pp. 173-94, and many articles in *Individuum und Individualität,* ed. Aertsen and Speer.

the body is "constitutive" for personality;[47] thus the Averroist view of the body as the only principle of human individuation which is implicit in *Veritatis Splendor* 48-49 becomes explicit in Rhonheimer's study.

Conclusion

I have above outlined how Pope John Paul II in his encyclical letter *Veritatis Splendor* understands nature as foundation of morals. *I have been sympathetic* to his claim that certain types of neo-Kantian philosophy separate the notions of person, freedom, and culture from nature in an inadequate and dualistic manner that leads to a contempt of nature. Examples of such a problematic dualism can be found in Protestant theology as well. Stressing *the unity of body and soul in a person* helps to overcome this dualism.

I have further been critical of the encyclical's almost monistic view of *unity between the individual person and the dignified nature common to all human beings*. I have argued that this view approaches an "Averroistic" position in which our true individuality gets lost because our human dignity would only consist of our sharing in a sacred reality common to all. For reasons both historical and theological, the notion of human dignity cannot be played out against the idea of individual freedom.

47. Rhonheimer, *Natur als Grundlage der Moral*, pp. 48, 409 (quoted above).

Conscience and Magisterium in *Veritatis Splendor*

THEODOR DIETER

THE ENCYCLICAL *Veritatis Splendor* is strongly concerned about "an overall and systematic calling into question of traditional moral doctrine." The root of such currents of thought is seen in "detaching human freedom from its essential and constitutive relationship to truth" (VS #4). According to the encyclical the "relationship between man's freedom and God's law is most deeply lived out in the 'heart' of the person, in his moral conscience" (#54).[1] Therefore conscience is a central problem considered by the encyclical. In the first part of this chapter I will describe the main aspects of the encyclical's understanding of conscience and magisterium; in the second chapter I will analyze several aspects and comment on them.

I

Conscience is seen by the encyclical "in its primordial reality as an act of a person's intelligence, the function of which is to apply the universal knowledge of the good in a specific situation and thus to express a judgment about the right conduct to be chosen here and now" (#32). According to this understanding, the relation to natural law is

---

1. The encyclical deals twice with the topic of the conscience: at first in the introductory remarks to chapter 2 (#31-32) and then in greater detail in paragraphs 54 to 64.

constitutive for the concept of conscience;[2] therefore this concept must change once "the idea of a universal truth about the good, knowable by human reason, is lost" (#32, cf. #54). In such a case, there is a tendency to grant "to the individual conscience the prerogative of independently determining the criteria of good and evil and then acting accordingly" (#32). Henceforth it is not a correspondence between the conscience and the "universal truth about the good" that is decisive, but "'being at peace with oneself.'" The criteria become sincerity and authenticity (#32). "In their desire to emphasize the 'creative' character of conscience, certain authors no longer call its actions 'judgments' but 'decisions'" (#55). In fact, however, conscience "is a moral judgment about man and his actions" (#59), as the encyclical says by referring to Romans 2:15-16.

Further, the "dignity of this rational forum and the authority of its voice and judgments derive from the *truth* about moral good and evil, which it is called to listen to and to express" (#60). Therefore the "duty to follow one's conscience" (#32) must not be separated from the "moral obligation . . . to seek the truth and to adhere to it once it is known" (#34).

Divine law is thus "the universal and objective norm of morality" (#60), while conscience as "the application of the law to a particular case" (#59) "formulates the proximate norm of the morality of a voluntary act" (#59) or "the proximate norm of personal morality" (#60). Admittedly, the encyclical maintains: "Conscience, as the judgment of an act, is not exempt from the possibility of error." "Conscience is not an infallible judge; it can make mistakes" (#62).[3] Errors of conscience can come about either through a false assumption about the law which is to be applied to a certain act or through false assumptions about facts belonging to the act under discussion. The latter case is not discussed in the encyclical. It does address the first case, where conscience "directs us to act in a way not in conformity with the objective moral order" (#62). Conscience can err by reason of an

2. Cf. #52: The "universal and permanent laws . . . are applied to particular acts through the judgment of conscience."

3. The two sentences are not perfectly consistent with one another because in the first sentence "conscience" is understood as a judgment, while in the second it is seen as the faculty of making judgments.

invincible ignorance, "an ignorance of which the subject is not aware and which he is unable to overcome by himself" (#62). Such an ignorance can be culpable or nonculpable. It is culpable "when a man shows little concern for seeking what is true and good, and conscience gradually becomes almost blind from being accustomed to sin" (#62). But even if a nonculpable error of conscience cannot be imputed to the agent, the act "does not cease to be an evil, a disorder in relation to the truth about the good" (#63). In spite of this fact, conscience does not forfeit its dignity in the case of nonculpable invincible ignorance because "it continues to speak in the name of the truth about that good which the subject is called to seek sincerely" (#62).

In view of the constitutive relation of conscience to law, conscience is in constant need of being formed. This forming of conscience is viewed in the encyclical in connection with the renewal of our mind (Rom. 12:2; cf. #64). A "sort of 'connaturality' between man and the true good" (#64) is required for true judgments of conscience. This connaturality is achieved by virtuous attitudes. The church's magisterium is of great help in the formation of conscience because it teaches the truth to which, by its nature, conscience is related.

The main aspects of the conception of the magisterium which can be found in the encyclical can be described in eight theses:

1. According to the Second Vatican Council, sacred Scripture or the gospel is "the source of all saving truth and moral teaching" (cf. #28).

2. In faithfully preserving what the Word of God teaches on moral action, the church "has achieved a doctrinal development" (#28). This development occurs with the assistance of the Holy Spirit: "Within tradition, the authentic interpretation of the Lord's law develops with the help of the Holy Spirit. The same Spirit who is at the origin of the revelation of Jesus' commandments and teachings guarantees that they will be reverently preserved, faithfully expounded and correctly applied in different times and places" (#27).

3. The whole people of the faithful who have received the anointing of the Holy Spirit "cannot be mistaken in belief" (#109). Nevertheless, "authentically interpreting the word of God" is the task of "the church's living magisterium, whose authority is exercised in the name of Jesus Christ" (#27). Theological opinions are "neither the rule nor the norm" of the magisterium's teaching. "Its authority

is derived, by the assistance of the Holy Spirit and in communion *cum Petro et sub Petro,* from our fidelity [i.e., the pope's together with that of all the bishops] to the Catholic faith which comes from the apostles" (#116).

4. The church's magisterium exercises its teaching office by intervening "not only in the sphere of faith, but also, and inseparably so, in the sphere of morals" (#110).[4] It makes "judgments normative for the consciences of believers" by describing those acts which are in themselves in conformity with "the demands of faith and foster their expression in life" and those which are in contradiction to them. It "teaches the faithful specific particular precepts and requires that they consider them in conscience as morally binding." Further the magisterium is "warning the faithful of the presence of possible errors, even merely implicit ones, when their consciences fail to acknowledge the correctness and the truth of the moral norms which the magisterium teaches" (#110).

5. Moral theology is part of the church's moral reflection. It is a science related to revelation as well as "to the demands of human reason." Insofar as it discusses the good and evil of human acts and of persons, "it is accessible to all people"; it is theology insofar as it is concerned with "the origin and end of moral action," which "are found in the one who 'alone is good' and who, by giving himself to man in Christ, offers him the happiness of divine life" (#29).

Moral theology (and theology in general) is "an ecclesial science because it grows in the church and works on the church" (#109). Moral theologians "have the grave duty to instruct the faithful . . . about all those commandments and practical norms authoritatively declared by the church. While recognizing the possible limitations of the human arguments employed by the magisterium, moral theologians are called to develop a deeper understanding of the reasons underlying its teachings and to expound the validity and obligatory nature of the precepts it proposes" (#110).

6. Nevertheless, God's eternal law can be known either by natural reason or — "in an integral and perfect way" — by revelation. In the first case we speak of natural law, in the latter of divine law (cf. #72).

4. Cf. John Mahoney, *The Making of Moral Theology* (Oxford: Clarendon, 1987), pp. 116-74.

7. The moral commandments of the natural law are universal and immutable, "particularly those which prohibit always and without exception intrinsically evil acts" (#115). One must seek out "the most adequate formulation" for these universal norms. While remaining "valid in their substance," they "must be specified and determined *eodem sensu eademque sententia* in the light of historical circumstances by the church's magisterium" (#53).

8. The encyclical intends to state the incompatibility of certain theological and philosophical opinions or even trends with revealed truth (cf. #29). In order to do so, it must explain some principles "drawing attention to those elements of the church's moral teaching which today appear particularly exposed to error, ambiguity or neglect" (#30).

II

Let us now explore and analyze some aspects of these doctrines of conscience and magisterium. The analysis is partly an analysis of the internal consistency of the encyclical, partly an analysis within a Lutheran perspective.

1. That conscience has its dignity and authority by speaking in the name of the truth about the good is common to the Catholic and Lutheran traditions insofar as in both traditions conscience is not an unmediated relation of the self to itself but is constitutively related to and dependent on a reality beyond itself. In the case of the Lutheran tradition this is the Word of God. At the diet of Worms (1521), when Luther was summoned to revoke some of his doctrines, he said: "Unless I am convinced by the testimony of the Scriptures or by clear reason. . . . I am bound by the Scriptures I have quoted and my conscience is captive to the Word of God. I cannot and I will not retract anything."[5] Here Luther does not appeal to his conscience as is often supposed, but to the Word of God to which his conscience is captive.

5. *Luther's Works,* vol. 32, p. 112. (*Weimarer Ausgabe* 7:838,4-7: "Nisi convictus fuero testimoniis scripturarum aut ratione evidenti . . . victus sum scripturis a me adductis et capta conscientia in verbis dei, revocare neque possum neque volo quicquam.")

Therefore in order to understand correctly what conscience is, one must look at that in the name of which conscience is speaking. According to Luther, this is the Word of God as law and gospel; according to a great line of Catholic tradition, this is natural law.[6]

2. Law can only bind a person if it is understood.[7] According to the Catholic tradition, conscience is the place where law is understood and related to concrete situations; therefore conscience is the place where law is speaking in its obligatory character.[8] But we soon notice that in conscience different persons hear the law pronouncing different commandments or different practical judgments in similar situations. Among other explanations, this divergence can be understood by the concept of the erring conscience. This is a crucial concept in the doctrine of conscience.

The encyclical says: "The council [i.e., the Second Vatican Council] reminds us that in cases where such invincible ignorance is not culpable, conscience does not lose its dignity" (#62). This sentence quoted from *Gaudium et Spes*[9] evoked the following comment by Joseph Ratzinger (1968): "With regard to the obligatory

6. There are also other lines in Catholic doctrine, especially a personalistic one stemming from Augustine. Cf. Eberhard Schockenhoff, *Das umstrittene Gewissen* (Mainz: Grünewald, 1990), pp. 70-77, 127-33.

7. Cf. Thomas Aquinas, *De veritate* q.17, a.3 corp.: "So, no one is bound by the command of a king or lord unless the command reaches him who is commanded; and it reaches him through knowledge of it. Hence, no one is bound by a precept except through his knowledge of the precept. . . . Thus, as in physical things the physical agent acts only by means of contact, so in spiritual things a precept binds only by means of knowledge. Therefore, just as it is the same power by which touch acts and by which the power of the agent acts, since touch acts only by the power of the agent and the power of the agent acts only through the mediation of touch, so it is the same power by which the precept binds and by which knowledge binds, since the knowledge binds only through the power of the precept, and the precept only through the knowledge" (Thomas Aquinas, *The Disputed Questions on Truth*, trans. J. V. McGlynn, vol. 2 [Chicago: Henry Regnery, 1953], pp. 327-28).

8. Ibid., "Consequently, since conscience is nothing else but the application of knowledge to an act, it is obvious that conscience is said to bind by the power of a divine precept."

9. "Not infrequently, however, conscience can be mistaken as a result of insuperable ignorance, although it does not on that account forfeit its dignity" (*Gaudium et Spes*, chap. 16 [*Decrees of the Ecumenical Councils*, vol. 2, ed. N. P. Tanner (London: Sheed & Ward; Washington, D.C: Georgetown University Press, 1990), p. 1078]).

force of erring conscience our text uses a somehow evasive wording. It says only that conscience thereby does not lose its dignity."[10] In contrast to the quoted statement of the Second Vatican Council and the encyclical, the question of erring conscience was more precisely and elaborately discussed in scholastic theology. In this respect the questions were: "Whether erring conscience obligates,"[11] "Whether the will which does not correspond to erring reason is bad,"[12] and "Whether the will which corresponds to erring reason is good" or whether it obligates.[13]

The question under discussion concerns the characteristics that render an act a moral act. Aristotle distinguishes acts of art *(techne)* and moral acts by pointing out that for the latter it is not enough that the act itself meets some requirements (this is sufficient for the result of an act of production [*poiesis*]) but that the acting person must fulfill several conditions, mainly that he or she must act with knowledge and intention (willing an act for its own sake).[14] If we extend this line of understanding the morality of an act, we can argue according to Abelard: "There is no sin unless it is against conscience."[15] Abelard expresses the consequence of this principle very sharply and boldly: If the persecutors of Jesus thought they would please God in doing so they could not have omitted their persecutions without committing sin.[16] This conclusion is totally consistent with his concept of morality, but it contradicts our deep intuition and conviction of the rightness or wrongness of acts.[17] So there is the task of mediating what we could call the subjectivity of intentions with the substance of law. Otherwise

10. *Lexikon für Theologie und Kirche,* vol. 14, 2d ed. (Freiburg: Herder, 1968), p. 330.

11. Cf., e.g., Aquinas, *De veritate* q.17, a.4.

12. Cf., e.g., Aquinas, *Summa Theologiae* 1.2, q.19, a.5 (Westminster, Md.: Christian Classics, 1981).

13. Cf. ibid., a.6.

14. Cf. Aristotle, *Nicomachean Ethics* 2.3; 1105a28-33.

15. Peter Abelard, *Ethics,* ed. D. E. Luscombe (Oxford: Clarendon, 1971), pp. 54-55.

16. Cf. ibid., pp. 54-57.

17. Aquinas is quoting from John 16:2: "the time is coming when anyone who kills you will suppose that he is performing a religious duty" (cf. *Summa Theologiae* 1.2, q.19, a.6 sed contra).

either the morality of a person or a moral act is void or the right
substance of an act lacks morality.

Thomas Aquinas strongly emphasizes the subjectivity of morality:
The goodness of the will depends on the object of the act.[18] But the
object of the will is presented to the will by reason.[19] Therefore, even
if reason is erring and the will, by contradicting it, performs the
substance of a right action, that will is nevertheless bad because goodness of will does not depend on the object in itself but on the object
as it is perceived. So will becomes bad in departing from erring reason
as long as the mistake of reason is not corrected. Thomas maintains
that this is not only the case in indifferent matters but also in acts
which are in themselves bad or good.[20] If someone would come to
the judgment that abstaining from fornicating is bad and he then
nevertheless willed to abstain, his will would not then be bad because
it willed an act (or non-act) bad in itself, but it would be bad because
it had willed an act perceived to be bad.[21]

On the other hand, Thomas maintains that the will which follows
erring conscience or erring reason is bad; the will is not excused in
doing so, unless there is an ignorance in conscience that makes the
act involuntary *(involuntarium)*. Ignorance can be directly voluntary if
the will intends it, or it can be indirectly voluntary if someone care-

18. Ibid., a.2 corp: "Consequently the goodness and malice of the act of the will
depend on some one thing. . . . Now that one thing which is the principle in each
genus, is not something accidental to that genus, but something essential thereto. . . .
Therefore the goodness of the will's act depends on that one thing alone, which of
itself causes goodness in the act; and that one thing is the object, and not the
circumstances, which are accidents, as it were, of the act."

19. Ibid., a.3 corp: "Now the will's object is proposed to it by reason. . . .
Therefore the goodness of the will depends on reason, in the same way as it depends
on the object."

20. Ibid., a.5 corp: "The will that is at variance with erring reason or conscience,
is evil in some way on account of the object, on which the goodness or malice of the
will depends; not indeed on account of the object according as it is in its own nature;
but according as it is accidentally apprehended by reason as something evil to do or
to avoid. And since the object of the will is that which is proposed by the reason . . . ,
from the very fact that a thing is proposed by the reason as being evil, the will by
tending thereto becomes evil. And this is the case not only in indifferent matters, but
also in those that are good or evil in themselves."

21. Cf. ibid.

lessly does not know what he or she ought to know. In none of these cases does erring conscience excuse.[22] Thomas sets the example: an erring reason makes the judgment that "man is obliged to have sexual intercourse with the wife of another man." The will which conforms to this judgment is bad because this error of reason derives from an ignorance of the law of God, which one ought to know.[23] So one could have the impression that erring conscience leads a person into a situation of perplexity: the will conforming to this conscience would be bad, even sinful, and the will not conforming to it would also be bad or would sin.[24] But there is another possibility: to change the judgment of conscience by detecting its error and conforming to the right conscience.[25]

Therefore there are two requirements which must be met if will is to be good: it must be directed toward something which is both good in itself and also perceived as good. The will becomes bad if either one of these requirements is not fulfilled.[26]

---

22. Ibid., a.6 corp: "And I call that ignorance *directly* voluntary, to which the act of the will tends; and that, *indirectly* voluntary, which is due to negligence, by reason of a man not wishing to know what he ought to know. . . . If then reason or conscience err with an error that is voluntary, either directly, or through negligence, so that one errs about what one ought to know; then such an error of reason or conscience does not excuse the will, that abides by that erring reason or conscience, from being evil."

23. Ibid., "For instance, if erring reason tell a man that he should go to another man's wife, the will that abides by that erring reason is evil; since this error arises from ignorance of the Divine Law, which he is bound to know."

24. Aquinas, *De veritate* q.17, a.4 ad 3: "A false conscience which is mistaken in things which are intrinsically evil commands something which is contrary to the law of God. Nevertheless, it says that what it commands is the law of God. Accordingly, one who acts against such a conscience becomes a kind of transgressor of the law of God, although one who follows such a conscience and acts according to it acts against the law of God and sins mortally. For there was sin in the error itself, since it happened because of ignorance of that which one should have known."

25. Aquinas, *Summa Theologiae* 1.2, q.19, a.6 ad 3: "Suppose a man's reason or conscience to err through inexcusable ignorance, then evil must needs result in the will. Nor is this man in a dilemma: because he can lay aside his error, since his ignorance is vincible and voluntary."

26. Ibid., a.6 ad 1: "As Dionysius says . . . , *good results from the entire cause, evil from each particular defect.* Consequently in order that the thing to which the will tends be called evil, it suffices, either that it be evil in itself, or that it be apprehended as evil. But in order for it to be good, it must be good in both ways."

This solution to the problem of mediating the subjectivity of morality with the objectivity of law does not seem to be convincing. The concept of erring conscience in Aquinas presupposes a combination of the subjective-intentional perspective of the acting person and the objective perspective of "that which one is obligated to know." The content of the latter seems to be precisely defined and knowledge of it is open to everyone, since ignorance in these matters is voluntary and can be overcome. Ignorance concerning the facts of acting can perhaps not be overcome and is therefore not sin, but ignorance concerning law is sin.[27] Ignorance in the latter sense and sin are understood in an objective perspective: the practical knowledge of an individual is compared with the objective "what one is obligated to know" and then judged as sin. But who is the (infallible) subject of the knowledge of "what one is obligated to know"? How can the access to such a knowledge be described in terms of morality, and, in the case of a lack of knowledge, be described as deviating from a former judgment of conscience about what one should do?[28]

Aquinas has good reasons for both sides of this combination — subjective and objective — but this does not mean that the mediation of them is successful. Rather, the two sides are simply juxtaposed.[29]

27. Aquinas, *De veritate* q.17, a.4, difficulty 5: "God is more merciful than a temporal lord. But a temporal lord does not accuse a man of sin in something which he did by mistake. Therefore, in God's sight a man is much less obliged under pain of sin by a mistaken conscience." Ad 5: "When the error itself is not a sin, the conclusion is true, as when the error is due to ignorance of some fact. But, if it is ignorance of a law, the conclusion is wrong because the ignorance itself is a sin. For before a civil judge, also, one who thus appeals to ignorance of law which he should know is not excused."

28. Aquinas reports the following argument: one has to obey the commandment of the higher power (e.g. of the emperor) and not the commandment of the lower (e.g. the proconsul) if they are in contradiction, so one has to obey God and not the conscience if they contradict one another. He objects that in the case of erring conscience the situation is similar as if one would think that the commandment of the proconsul is the commandment of the emperor but in fact it is not (cf. *Summa Theologiae* 1.2, q.19, a.5, difficulty 2 and ad 2). But this argument does not play a role in Aquinas's discussion of the objective aspect in morality.

29. According to Aquinas, right conscience binds absolutely *(simpliciter)*, whereas wrong conscience binds with some qualification *(secundum quid)*, that is, as long as the erring judgment of conscience endures (cf. *De veritate* q.17, a.5 corp). But this distinction of two types of obligation does not solve the problem.

The short discussion of some aspects of Aquinas's theory of conscience shows that the problem of the relation between subjectivity and objectivity in conscience is not only a problem of modern times but rather is as old as thinking about conscience. Conscience is itself the problem of mediating the subjectivity of morality and the objectivity of moral law or moral truth. Of course, the problem has become aggravated in our time because of the changes in understanding (natural) law, but the problem of mediation comes from the very center of the Christian tradition.[30]

Therefore discussing contemporary problems of conscience is impossible without discussing old problems. But it is insufficient merely to take up previous solutions of the problems because, as we have seen, even the solution of Aquinas had deficiencies. One would thus expect that the problem of such a mediation would be discussed in the encyclical. It does complain about "detaching human freedom from its essential and constitutive relationship to truth" (#4) while maintaining the dimension of subjectivity in conscience: conscience is seen as "the proximate norm of personal morality" (#60). Even if we keep in mind the encyclical's intention to stress the objectivity of natural law, it falls short when it says only that "there is profoundly

30. In modern times G. W. F. Hegel formulated the problem in the following way: "Conscience is the expression of the absolute title of subjective self-consciousness to know in itself and from within itself what is right and obligatory, to give recognition only to what it thus knows as good, and at the same time to maintain that whatever in this way it knows and wills is in truth right and obligatory. Conscience as this unity of subjective knowing with what is absolute is a sanctuary which it would be sacrilege to violate. But whether the conscience of a specific individual corresponds with this Idea of conscience, or whether what it takes or declares to be good is actually so, is ascertainable only from the content of the good it seeks to realize. What is right and obligatory is the absolutely rational element in the will's volitions and therefore it is not in essence the *particular* property of an individual, and its form is not that of feeling or any other private (i.e. sensuous) type of knowing, but essentially that of universals determined by thought, i.e. the form of laws and principles. Conscience is therefore subject to the judgement of its truth or falsity, and when it appeals only to itself for a decision, it is directly at variance with what it wishes to be, namely the rule for a mode of conduct which is rational, absolutely valid, and universal. For this reason, the state cannot give recognition to conscience in its private form as subjective knowing, any more than science can grant validity to subjective opinion, dogmatism, and the appeal to a subjective opinion" (G. W. F. Hegel, *Philosophy of Right,* trans. T. M. Knox, 2d ed. [Oxford: Clarendon, 1945], p. 91).

imprinted upon it [conscience] a principle of obedience vis-à-vis the objective norm which establishes and conditions the correspondence of its decisions with the commands and prohibitions which are at the basis of human behavior" (#60). This is only the assertion of a correspondence; it does not show how such a correspondence is possible.[31] We also fail to find an explicit discussion of whether and in which sense erring conscience is morally binding. In order to strengthen the objective side of morality, an attempt to mediate between the two sides would have been necessary on a theoretical level. We also would need a practical suggestion how to deal with a situation of perplexity when, for example, an individual reads in the encyclical that using artificial methods of contraception is in itself bad but cannot see that this judgment is correct. Conscience remains "the proximate norm of morality."[32] I know, of course, that many theologians are very glad that the encyclical does not give answers to such questions, but the result is that persons will look for their own solutions without the help of the magisterium. Therefore — against its will — the encyclical contributes to an individualistic approach to ethics.

3. On the one hand, the encyclical maintains: "The moral law has its origin in God and always finds its source in him: At the same time, by virtue of natural reason, which derives from divine wisdom, it is a properly human law" (#40). On the other hand, the same reason can (mis)understand itself as creating values (cf. #40), and conscience can, if accustomed to sin, gradually become almost blind (cf. #62) or, we could add, conscience is born and raised in original sin. Speaking in this way of nature and reason, however, is highly abstract. Reason is always embedded in an individual life history, language, society, and culture (e.g., "culture of death"). Moreover, the document claims on the one hand: "But here [i.e., in moral life] birth does not come about by a foreign intervention as is the case with bodily beings . . . ; it is the result of a free choice. Thus we are in a certain way our own parents, creating ourselves

31. For an excellent discussion of several questions belonging to our problem see Eberhard Schockenhoff, *Naturrecht und Menschenwürde* (Mainz: Grünewald, 1996), pp. 143-232.

32. What is the precise meaning of the sentence "when a man shows little concern for seeking what is true and good" (#62) — in view of the claim of the magisterium that under the guidance of the Spirit "the church's reply contains the voice of Jesus Christ, the voice of the truth about good and evil" (#117)?

as we will, by our decisions" (#71[33]). But on the other hand we read: "Accepting . . . the 'disproportion' between the law and human ability (that is, the capacity of the moral forces of man left to himself) kindles the desire for grace and prepares one to receive it" (#105 with reference to Rom. 7:24-25). *"Only in the mystery of Christ's Redemption do we discover the 'concrete' possibilities of man. . . .* God's command is of course proportioned to man's capabilities; but to the capabilities of the man to whom the Holy Spirit has been given; of the man who, though he has fallen into sin, can always obtain pardon and enjoy the presence of the Holy Spirit" (#103). Here we find different perspectives side by side, a theological one that stresses sin and grace and a theological or philosophical one that centers on nature and reason in its integrity. I can find no mediation or integration of the two perspectives. This criticism is not directed against thinking in terms of nature and reason in theology. It is clear that baptized and nonbaptized, or believers and nonbelievers, have much in common in relation to moral obligations. But there are sharp tensions between stressing the capacities of reason and nature on the one hand and the constant complaint about the "culture of death" *(Evangelium Vitae)* and the often repeated admonition "Do not be conformed to this world" (Rom. 12:2) on the other.[34] These problems of human freedom and sin, natural possibilities and grace, ethical engagement and the life of Christian love, can be addressed only in a doctrine of sin and grace. In my opinion such a doctrine should be the framework for dealing with the problem of nature. After the fall we cannot say only that grace presupposes nature, but we also must say that a theologically relevant concept of nature presupposes grace, both ontologically and epistemologically. A truly theological concept of nature can only be developed in a dialectical process between "gratia supponit naturam" and "natura supponit gratiam." There are of course many theories in Catholic theology dealing with this problem in a comparable way.[35] There are elements of an

33. Quoted from Gregory of Nyssa *De vita Moysis* 2,2-3 (*Patrologia graeca* 44, ed. J. P. Migne, pp. 327-28).

34. #88: "It is urgent then that Christians should rediscover the newness of the faith and its power to judge a prevalent and all-intrusive culture."

35. For example, we think of the "nouvelle théologie," Karl Rahner, Hans Urs von Balthasar, and others. For a helpful description and analysis of the problems, see Ulrich Kühn, *Natur und Gnade. Untersuchungen zur deutschen katholischen Theologie der Gegenwart* (Berlin: Lutherisches Verlagshaus, 1961). Cf. also Mahoney, *Making of Moral Theology,* pp. 72-115.

answer to our question in the encyclical, but as far as I see, there is no explicit and consistent answer.[36]

4. This deficit is linked to a failure adequately to distinguish between different terms of law. Of course it is correct to say that "useful distinctions [between different forms of law] always refer to that law whose author is the one and the same God and which is always meant for man. The different ways in which God, acting in history, cares for the world and for mankind are not mutually exclusive; on the contrary, they support each other and intersect" (#45). There is a fundamental difference, however, in the meaning of "law" when Paul says that "law brings only consciousness of sin" (Rom.

36. We find the following indications to the encyclical's opinion on this question:

(1) "Only God, the supreme good, constitutes the unshakable foundation and essential condition of morality" (#99).

(2) "The moral sense . . . is . . . rooted and fulfilled in the religious sense" (#98).

(3) Freedom "is an essential part of that creaturely image which is the basis of the dignity of the person. Within that freedom there is an echo of the primordial vocation whereby the Creator calls man to the true good, and even more, through Christ's revelation, to become his friend and to share his own divine life" (#86). Here the encyclical seems to talk about a twofold vocation of the human person (by the Creator and through Christ's revelation), but both are only added by the phrase "even more," which is not very clear. Does "the true good of man" mean the same thing as "becoming a friend of God," or is it something different? If the first, is it the case that everybody is then called to be a friend of God by creation? What then about the freedom of grace? If the latter is the case, what then is the relationship between the true good and becoming a friend of God? What then is the precise relationship between the two vocations?

(4) "In an individual's words and above all in the sacrifice of his life for a moral value, the church sees a single testimony to that truth which, already present in creation, shines forth in its fullness on the face of Christ" (#94). This follows a quotation from Justin Martyr concerning the *logos spermatikos*.

(5) "The crucified Christ reveals the authentic meaning of freedom" (#85). Christ "opens up to the faithful the book of the Scriptures and, by fully revealing the Father's will, teaches the truth about moral action" (#8).

(6) There is "the source of a deep rebellion" in man, "which leads him to reject the truth and the good in order to set himself up as an absolute principle unto himself" (#86, with reference to Gen. 3:5).

(7) "Consequently, freedom itself needs to be set free. It is Christ who sets it free" (ibid.).

As far as I can see, the encyclical does present a theory of its own, integrating these elements.

3:20b) or "Christ bought us freedom from the curse of the law" (Gal. 3:13), and when Thomas Aquinas states that "the law of the Spirit of life in Jesus Christ" (Rom. 8:2) can be understood as the Holy Spirit dwelling in the soul or as faith working through love (cf. #45). These (necessarily) different meanings of "law" entail different concepts of conscience because it is constitutive for conscience to be related to law (or the word of God).

5. Martin Luther understood law in a genuinely theological way and not simply as morality. In this perspective, fulfilling the commandments of the law must be seen in the light of Deuteronomy 6:5 ("You must love the Lord your God with all your heart and soul and strength"; cf. Matt. 22:26-40).[37] Therefore it is not enough to fulfill a commandment by an act of will and corresponding exterior action which, in agreement with right reason, have the right object and goal and attend to the required circumstances. Rather the law and each of its commandments require that one loves God with the "heart," that is, not only the will but the totality of one's being. Reluctance, sluggishness, lack of joy, reservations in acting in accordance with the commandments, or boasting about moral actions all show that a person is not totally directed to God. It does not lie in the power of the will to convert a person totally to God, and therefore the commandments viewed in this way are not perceived in the mode of moral philosophy. Theologically understood law requires such a totality, and where such a totality of loving God (and the other) does not exist a person violates the law of God. If law in this sense is heard in conscience it not only makes the person conscious of single acts of sin but also makes persons discover themselves as sinners. So law has primarily an accusing function, directed at the person. But when law requires totality and this totality is not in the power of the person, it says: "You must have Christ and his Spirit!"[38] Only something coming from outside but then dwelling in the innermost part of human beings can create in them a totality of love to God (which will last the

---

37. Deuteronomy 6:4-7 is quoted in #10 of the encyclical, but without drawing consequences for understanding what it would mean to fulfill the law, as meaning that only a person who is totally engaged in love to God is fulfilling God's will.

38. *Weimarer Ausgabe* 56:338,38 (*Luther's Works,* vol. 25, p. 327).

whole of their lives). So law disturbs and startles conscience; only the gospel — not any action of a person — comforts and pacifies the disquieted conscience. Faith is trusting the gospel and so participating in Christ's justice; therefore Luther says: "Faith is nothing other than a good conscience."[39] Conscience is the place where human beings exist before God (coram Deo).

Luther also has an equivalent to the concept of moral conscience. It is called "conscience toward or before men" (Gewissen vor den Leuten).[40] This conscience — or aspect of the conscience — is concentrated on the acts of a person. It is the consciousness of what one has done and whether it was done well or not (according to the law). In this conscience one can be certain that one has performed something well. It is then possible to appeal to conscience against the attacks of enemies. Such conscience cannot, however, withstand the judgment of God.[41] Nevertheless there is a correspondence between the two aspects of conscience: what Christ has done and communicated to the faithful through the gospel, they now are called to do to others, guided by the Ten Commandments, the precept of love, and the love realized in Christ.

In this sense a Lutheran could agree with the encyclical when it says: "These actions [of a Christian] are called to show either consistency or inconsistency with that dignity and vocation which have been bestowed on him by grace. In Jesus Christ and in his Spirit, the Christian is a 'new creation,' a child of God; by his actions he shows his likeness or unlikeness to the image of the Son" (#73). So what a Christian does expresses that he or she is a child of God, but this is not teleologically related to the "ultimate end (telos) of man" (#73), the eternal beatitude, because according to Paul we are "if children, then heirs" (Rom. 8:17). The heritage is given to the children because they are children, not because they have behaved in some special way (though their standing as children can be cancelled by their actions).

6. There is an ambiguity in understanding the phrase "morally good" in the encyclical, corresponding to the failure to distinguish different meanings of "law" (see above [4]). On the one hand we

---

39. *Weimarer Ausgabe* 20:718,19f.
40. Ibid., 36:363,16 (*Luther's Works,* vol. 51, p. 273).
41. Cf. *Weimarer Ausgabe* 36:362,39-363,31 (*Luther's Works,* vol. 51, pp. 273-74).

read: "The rational ordering of the human act to the good in its truth and the voluntary pursuit of that good, known by reason, constitute morality" (#72). This corresponds to the statement that moral theology, insofar as it discusses good and evil, is accessible to all people (cf. #29). On the other hand, the encyclical maintains: "Activity is morally good when it attests and expresses the voluntary ordering of the person to his ultimate end and the conformity of a concrete action with the human good as it is acknowledged in its truth by reason" (#72). Ordering an act to humanity's ultimate end (God or eternal beatitude) requires grace, but grace cannot be understood as a requirement of morality. In line with a highly questionable opinion of the Second Vatican Council, the encyclical maintains: "Nor does divine providence deny the helps that are necessary for salvation to those who through no fault of their own have not yet attained to the express recognition of God, yet who strive, not without divine grace, to lead an upright life" (#3).[42] There are atheists, however, who can act morally while at the same time explicitly and consciously rejecting God. Their ultimate end is neither God nor eternal life. On closer inspection, we find in the encyclical genuinely different concepts of morality side by side without mediation. Certainly, acts of believers and nonbelievers have much in common, but the frameworks of their respective actions are very different from one another. Luther takes this seriously in distinguishing between a theological and a moral concept of acting and between the two dimensions of conscience (*coram Deo* — *coram hominibus*). The ambiguity in using the phrase "morally good" in the encyclical has its starting point in understanding the question of the rich young man ("Teacher, what good must I do to have eternal life?" Matt. 19:16) as a question about morality (cf. #7). Great parts of the moral tradition (e.g., Aristotle and Kant) would not express the fundamental moral question in this way. Further: Do we ask "Christ the redeemer" about morality? The pope is quite right in opposing the "destructive dichotomy . . . which separates faith from morality" (#88). But integrating morality into the life of faith does not imply integrating elements of faith and grace into the concept of morality.

The encyclical contains many important and valuable insights and

---

42. The quotation is from *Lumen Gentium,* chap. 16.

thoughts. My criticism is that it fails to draw certain clear distinctions and thus provide the mediations between the distinguished aspects needed for a satisfying solution. Only by distinguishing what is different and then mediating between what has been distinguished can one avoid separating aspects that belong together. I fully agree that these aspects (e.g., faith and deeds) belong together; my disagreement centers on how to reach this goal.

7. There is also an ambiguity concerning the authority of the magisterium. On the one hand we read, as already cited: "The moral law has its origin in God and always finds its source in him: At the same time, by virtue of natural reason, which derives from divine wisdom, it is a properly human law" (#40). By reason, law becomes the law of human beings and gains its obligatory character for them. Therefore one would expect the authority of the magisterium to extend only as far as its arguments. But the faithful and the moral theologians are expected to accept precepts proclaimed by the magisterium as binding in conscience even if they recognize "the possible limitations of the human arguments employed by the magisterium" (#40). Here law or particular precepts do not become a person's own law by reason. Rather, the argument now is, that "the magisterium does not bring to the Christian conscience truths which are extraneous to it; rather it brings to light the truths which it ought already to possess, developing them from the starting point of the primordial act of faith" (#64). This is a different access to precepts and their obligation than that provided by reason. So there is in the encyclical a high esteem for reason side by side with a high esteem for authority, but no mediation between these two approaches to concrete practical truth.

8. The high claim for the magisterium's authority creates several difficulties. The problem is not that it proclaims precepts with a binding character for conscience. If we look into the Bible we find several such precepts as manifestations of the will of God, and theologians have to spell them out for — and together with! — the faithful. But, first, it is a truly awesome task to proclaim precepts to be accepted in conscience as morally binding, because to err in such a case is to torture consciences, something much worse than corporal torture. The magisterium consists of human beings, none of whom is free from sin and error, but they refer in such a strong way to the

assistance of the Holy Spirit that the voice of the magisterium is identified with the voice of Jesus Christ (cf. #117). It would have been helpful for the consciences of the faithful if the encyclical had more clearly distinguished between the magisterium and the voice of Christ in the sense that the magisterium itself is on the way to finding the will of God, especially in questions in which there is great dissent among the faithful.[43] This is not said in the name of "freedom" from moral obligation but for the sake of grounding the conscience of persons in truth. Even for the magisterium it is difficult to exclude every possibility of error, and appealing to the guidance of the Spirit even against counterarguments comes near to a spiritualistic attitude which appeals to the immediate inspiration of the Spirit.

The encyclical maintains that the precepts of natural law are universal and immutable, especially those which prohibit acts inherently evil. An oft-cited example of such a precept is the prohibition of torture. Aquinas, however, accepted the torture of innocents as part of regular court procedure,[44] and the church itself often used torture in persecuting heretics and witches. Another example is the prohibition of lending money at interest in the patristic church and in the medieval ages. This prohibition was a fundamental principle of medieval economy, which created many problems. But now Catholic theologians state that the theological and philosophical arguments in favor of this prohibition proved untenable.[45]

Therefore one would expect that the magisterium would exercise a self-imposed moderation, at least in questions that are highly controversial throughout the church, as, for example, the question of artificial contraception (cf. #80). I do not find such moderation in the encyclical.

43. In its criticism against "certain moral theologians," the encyclical states: "No one can fail to see that such an interpretation of the autonomy of human reason involves positions incompatible with Catholic teaching" (#37). The mere fact of criticism shows that some theologians can fail to come to the same conclusion as the encyclical. Therefore appealing to an "obvious fact" which is obviously not the case is not a very helpful and convincing exercise of magisterium.

44. Cf. Eberhard Schockenhoff, *Naturrecht und Menschenwürde*, p. 209.

45. Cf. W. Kerber, art. "Zins," in *Lexikon der Wirtschaftsethik* (Freiburg: Herder, 1993), col. 1341.

Another problem appears when we note that the encyclical not only proclaims and explains moral precepts, but also intends "to reflect on the whole of the church's moral teaching" (#4). In some sense the latter is an implication of the former and therefore an object of the magisterium's decision; but on the other hand there is a qualitative difference between dealing with particular precepts and dealing with the whole of the church's moral teaching. In discussing a doctrine as a whole, there are many more possibilities of error, and the arguments are more distant from their point of origin in revelation.

The encyclical also discusses and makes judgments about theories and methods of moral argumentation (cf., e.g., #69-83). In doing so "the church's magisterium does not intend to impose upon the faithful any particular theological system, still less a philosophical one" (#29). It wants "to state that some trends of theological thinking and certain philosophical affirmations are incompatible with revealed truth" (#29). It seems obvious that stating such incompatibilities belongs to the tasks of the magisterium. But again there are many possibilities of error in understanding the criticized theories and also in claiming such incompatibilities, since the concepts and the levels of discourse in such theories are sometimes different from those of revealed truth. So arguments for such incompatibilities are not easily made.[46] At least the degree of authority of the church's proclamation here is not the same as it is in other parts of its moral teaching.

My main concern, insofar as the magisterium teaches a concept of conscience, however, is the following: Catholic and Lutheran tradition agree that conscience does not rest in itself but depends on a divine word which is heard in conscience. For the Catholic tradition this is the word of the law. But because the law accuses, the person who is a transgressor of the law must also within the conscience hear the gospel which liberates from the accusation of the law through the forgiveness of sin. So — at least in a theological perspective — conscience cannot be understood only as the act of moral judgment (cf.

---

46. E.g., Christians saw (and sometimes see) such incompatibilities between the Bible's view of the world and the heliocentric view of the world, or between the concept of creation and a theory of evolution. It is clear that the latter problem especially is a highly complex one.

#32). We find a moral concept of conscience in the encyclical but not a genuine theological concept related to and rooted in the word of God (law and gospel). Because different meanings of "law" are not distinguished, law and gospel are then not distinguished. As a result, the encyclical's concept of conscience is not convincing if it intends to be not only a moral but also a theological concept. As a moral concept, it is helpful, even if, because of its deficits in mediating subjectivity and objectivity, it is less than totally satisfactory. Nevertheless, because the encyclical maintains that "the moral life, caught up in the gratuitousness of God's love, is called to reflect his glory" (#10), its concept of conscience falls short.

At the end of *Veritatis Splendor* the pope states: "The church's reply [to the question of the faithful] contains the voice of Jesus Christ, the voice of the truth about good and evil" (#117). And he continues: "Again the apostle Paul invites us to have confidence" (#117). Whom does he mean by saying "us" and what is the object of confidence? I suppose that "us" means the pope together with his brother bishops. They could have fear before the task of speaking as the voice of Jesus Christ,[47] so the pope reminds them that "our competence is from God, who has made us competent to be ministers of a new covenant" (quoting from 2 Cor. 3:5-6, 17-18). In 2 Corinthians 3 Paul opposes sharply *kaine diatheke* and *palaia diatheke*. *Palaia diatheke* (3:14b) does not mean "old covenant," because Paul says that "of Moses" (3:15) is read out loud in the synagogue; so it means the Torah of Sinai.[48] Correspondingly *kaine diatheke* means the gospel, and Paul as *diakonos kaines diathekes* (3:6) says the same as "servant of the gospel" (cf. Rom. 1:1, 9; 15:6; Phil. 2:22; Col. 1:23; Eph. 3:6-7). Paul understood his task as opposed to the task of Moses, who was in charge of the law: "The law, then, engraved letter by letter upon stone, dispensed death, and yet it was inaugurated with divine splendour" (3:7). In spite of its splendor (!), law *(palaia diatheke)* brings death with it because this

---

47. Cf. Johannes Paul II, *Die Schwelle der Hoffnung überschreiten* (Hamburg: Hoffmann und Campe, 1994), pp. 31-42. Here the pope is meditating on Luke 5:10 (" 'Do not be afraid,' said Jesus to Simon").

48. Cf. Otfried Hofius, "Gesetz und Evangelium nach 2. Korinther 3," in *Paulusstudien* (Tübingen: J. C. B. Mohr [Paul Siebeck], 1989), pp. 75-120.

is the truth of law about the sinner.[49] It is a pity that in his citation
the pope omits the sentences about Moses and the law of Sinai in
2 Corinthians 3. If he had quoted them, the necessity of clear distinctions between different types of law would have been evident. "For
if that which was soon to fade had its moment of splendour, how
much greater is the splendour of that which endures!" (3:11). So the
church is in service of the splendor of the gospel, which indeed enables
human beings to fulfill God's will. *Veritatis splendor:* this is the splendor
of the gospel, the splendor of the Lord (3:18), this is God's creative
truth about men and women.

---

49. Ibid., pp. 82-83: "Die Tora als 'das Geschriebene' hat es stets mit dem
Menschen zu tun, der ihren Forderungen aufgrund seiner Verfallenheit an die Sünde
prinzipiell nicht zu genügen vermag, so daß im Lichte des in ihr bezeugten heiligen
Gotteswillens das gänzlich unheilige Sein des Menschen ans Licht kommt. Eben
deshalb aber gilt: *to gramma apoktennei* (2 Kor 3,6b). Gemeint ist: Die Tora vom Sinai
als das Geschriebene und Vorgeschriebene behaftet den Sünder bei seiner Sünde und
spricht ihm das Todesurteil."

Freedom and Truth in *Veritatis Splendor* and the Meaning of Theonomy

LOIS MALCOLM

VERITATIS SPLENDOR is written to address a specific problem: the lack of harmony between the magisterium's teaching and "certain theological positions, encountered in seminaries and faculties of theology." The pope perceives a trend within the Roman Catholic Church — "the spread of numerous doubts and objections of a human and psychological, social and cultural, religious and even properly theological nature, with regard to the Church's moral teachings" (VS #4-5). He hopes to correct this trend by reinforcing, among other things, the universality and permanent validity of natural law, the link between faith and morality, and the magisterium's authority beyond intervening "only to 'exhort consciences' and 'propose values'" in light of which individuals make their decisions and life choices independently (VS #4-5). But his concern with ecclesial authority is rooted in a deeper concern over the rising individualism in contemporary society. He questions whether the individual's conscience — and its criteria of "sincerity, authenticity, and 'being at peace with oneself'" — should be the supreme tribunal of moral judgment (VS #32). He questions the loss of an idea of universal and absolute truth, wondering whether a relativistic conception of morality can provide the very warrants needed to speak out against the violation of human rights and serious forms of social and economic justice. Can relativism ensure the values of "justice, solidarity, honesty, and openness" that are often identified with individual free-

159

dom (VS #98)? Thus the core issue in *Veritatis Splendor* is not simply the question of ecclesial authority but the more profound modern problem of "detaching human *freedom*" from its "essential and constitutive relationship to *truth*" (VS #45, my emphasis). In raising this question, the pope can be classed with a range of theologians, philosophers, social scientists, and moral theorists who question whether a moral discourse restricted to the decisions and choices of autonomous moral agents is rich enough to provide moral resources for the pressing problems of our time — human rights abuses, social and economic injustice, and so on — in the face not only of cultural pluralism but the rise of technological power.[1]

Veritatis Splendor contributes to this discussion by defining true freedom as a "theonomy" that links freedom with absolute truth. In developing his understanding of freedom, the pope criticizes what he understands to be the "autonomous" thrust of "recent Roman Catholic moralists." Much of his own proposal is developed as a specific critique of key themes in the Roman Catholic moral theology following the reforms of Vatican II — for example, its understandings of the "fundamental option," "intrinsically evil acts," the role of the magisterium in shaping conscience, and so on. The pope's critics, in turn, question whether his position does not simply substitute a "heteronomous" norm for an "autonomous" one.[2] This issue between the pope and his critics is important theologically because it drives at what lies at the heart of a Christian understanding of "theonomy."[3]

1. Compare the pope's argument with, among others: Christopher Lasch, *The Culture of Narcissism* (New York: W. W. Norton, 1978); Alasdair MacIntyre, *After Virtue* (Notre Dame, Ind.: University of Notre Dame Press, 1981/1984); Robert Bellah et al., *Habits of the Heart: Individualism and Commitment in American Life* (New York: Harper & Row, 1985); and more recently, William Schweiker, *Responsibility and Christian Ethics* (New York: Cambridge, 1995).

2. See, e.g., the following "revisionist" responses to the pope: Charles E. Curran, "*Veritatis Splendor*: A Revisionist Perspective," in *Veritatis Splendor: American Responses,* ed. Michael E. Allsopp and John J. O'Keefe (Kansas City: Sheed & Ward, 1995), pp. 224-43; Bernhard Häring, "A Distrust That Wounds," in *Considering "Veritatis Splendor,"* ed. John Wilkins (Cleveland: Pilgrim, 1994), pp. 9-13; in that volume, see also Richard McCormick, "Killing the Patient," pp. 14-20, and Josef Fuchs, "Good Acts and Good Persons," pp. 21-26.

3. See Paul Tillich's definitions of "theonomy," "autonomy," and "heteronomy" in *Systematic Theology* (Chicago: University of Chicago, 1951), 1:83-86, 147-50; for a

In my analysis of the encyclical, I propose that the pope is weaving together two major conceptual patterns for defining freedom: one rooted in traditional conceptions of natural law and magisterial authority, and the other rooted in the encounter of call and response, dialogue, and communion between Christ and Christian believers.[4] My thesis is that the latter conception of freedom — which is ultimately rooted in Christ's self-giving on the cross — is the more comprehensive understanding of freedom in the encyclical and that it offers an ongoing, reflexive witness against both a false autonomy and a false heteronomy.

The pope's definition of freedom cannot be isolated to a single section or genre in the encyclical. Although the most explicit and technical definition is found in the middle section, we cannot ignore either his exegesis of Matthew 19 (in the first section) or his discussion of martyrdom (in the final section). My analysis, therefore, begins with an interpretation of his exegesis of Matthew 19. This exegesis enables us to identify the central question of this paper: whether the pope collapses a theonomous into a heteronomous conception of freedom by identifying Jesus' absolute call to discipleship with the magisterial authority of the church. With that question in mind, I turn to an analysis of the central themes in the notion of freedom provided in the second part of the encyclical. I then compare that definition, which focuses on freedom's relationship to natural law, with the other more personalist pattern for understanding freedom — and its overarching context within the theme of Christian martyrdom — found in the third part of the encyclical. On the basis of this comparison, I conclude that the latter understanding of freedom is more comprehensive and that it serves as an ongoing source

---

different but related definition of these three terms, see Karl Barth, *Church Dogmatics, The Doctrine of the Word of God,* vol. 1 (Edinburgh: T & T Clark, 1956). See also Robert Scharlemann, "Autonomy," in *A New Handbook of Christian Theology,* eds. Donald W. Musser and Joseph L. Price (Nashville: Abingdon, 1922), pp. 49-54.

4. For an analysis of an analogous contrast, see Janet E. Smith, "Natural Law and Personalism in Veritatis Splendor," in *Veritatis Splendor: American Responses,* ed. Allsopp and O'Keefe, pp. 194-207. See also these primary sources on the pope's personalism: Karol Wojtyla, *The Acting Person,* trans. Andrej Potocki (Boston: D. Reidel, 1979); and *Person and Community: Selected Essays,* trans. Theresa Sandok (New York: Peter Lang, 1993).

and norm that empowers and corrects both autonomous and heteronomous forms of freedom.

I. An Exegetical Context

The pope's proposal for a definition of freedom cannot be divorced from the story of the rich young man in Matthew 19 since it is in his exegesis of this story that he introduces his central assumptions regarding the meaning of true freedom. By situating his discussion of freedom within the context of the dialogue between Jesus and the rich young man, the pope situates it within the context of an "encounter" with Christ and the "call from God who is the origin and goal of all human life" (VS #6-7). This call to follow Jesus is "the essential and primordial foundation of Christian morality" (VS #19). At the heart of Christian ethics is the call to partake in Jesus' life and destiny, to share his free and loving obedience to the Father's will, to "imitate" him along the path of love: in other words, to be "conformed" to Christ. Jesus' response to the young man's question — "What must I do?" — indicates that the Christian moral life is not simply about rules but about the "full meaning of life" — the "aspiration at the heart of every human decision, the quiet searching and interior prompting which sets freedom in motion" (VS #7). By starting with this story, the pope situates the moral life within its theological and religious context; following Jesus touches the "very depths" of one's being. Jesus' answers regarding what is good and evil have to do with a "profound process" of appropriating and assimilating the whole reality of the incarnation and redemption. In his answer to the rich young man, Jesus brings the moral question — "What must I do?" — back to its religious foundations, back to the acknowledgment of the reality of God, that is, in his words, the "fullness of life," the "final end of human activity," indeed, "perfect happiness." The moral life is understood to be a response to God's gift and love for human beings. Its fulfillment only comes as a gift from God, who offers a share in the divine goodness revealed and communicated in Jesus. God alone is Good; no human effort succeeds in "fulfilling" the law. The "secret," then, of the "educative power" in Christian morality, according to the pope, lies not in doctrinal assertions or appeals to moral vigilance but rather in "constantly looking to Jesus."

Nonetheless, the law is not only *fulfilled* in Jesus Christ. It also has a *pedagogic* function to help sinful humans become aware of their powerlessness in the face of sin, to strip them of their presumption of self-sufficiency, to lead them to ask for and receive the life in the Spirit that can help them conquer sin. Further, this pedagogic function is intrinsically linked not only with its fulfillment in Jesus Christ, as we have already noted, but with its *positive* function as law. This positive function is the explicit assertion of the two main commandments within Christian faith, the commandments to love God and the neighbor. Hence these commandments not only serve a pedagogic function in helping us become aware of sin and they are not only already fulfilled in Christ — who interiorizes their demands as the living "fulfillment" of the law, fulfilling their authentic meaning, giving grace to people to share in his life, and providing them with the strength of their witness to that love in personal choices and action — but they also simply serve the function of asserting what positively needs to be done in order to be good and right. We have noted the intrinsic connections the pope makes between the fulfillment of the law in Jesus, its pedagogic function, and its positive function as law. In turn, these positive commandments to love God and neighbor are linked with both *natural law* and the *divine law,* both *Old* (as found in the Decalogue) and *New* (as, for example, in the Sermon on the Mount or the summary found in Rom. 13:8-10). In doing this, the pope makes it clear that Christian discipleship entails obedience to the injunctions found in the Decalogue that safeguard persons and protect their goods, specifically, its negative precepts that protect human life, the communion of persons in marriage, private property, truthfulness, and a person's reputation. Finally, the pope adds yet another form of law to this list. The disciple's encounter with Christ is mediated over time through the *church,* the "living tradition" of apostles, and this living tradition has, like the early apostles, been "vigilant over the right conduct of Christians" throughout its history.[5]

A number of observations can be made at this point. First, this

5. This analysis presumes the Reformers' distinctions among the "uses of the law." See John Calvin, *The Institutes of the Christian Religion,* vol. 1 (Philadelphia: Westminster, 1960); and Martin Luther, "On Temporal Authority," in *Martin Luther: Selections from His Writings,* ed. John Dillenberger (Garden City, N.Y.: Doubleday, 1961).

move to situate Christian ethics within the context of the call of discipleship, the "encounter" between Jesus and his disciples, has strong parallels with the attempt by mid-century theologians to situate theological ethics and theology within the context of an I-thou encounter. We might observe that this exegetical context serves as a kind of "fundamental ontology" for the pope's ethics, situating his conception within a particular frame of reference with regard to the ultimate structure of the divine-human encounter.[6] Instead of, say, the Neoplatonic scheme of exit and return that served as the frame for Thomas Aquinas's ethics, a dialogical or "personalist" frame serves as the conceptual matrix for the pope's moral theology. Further, by starting with this encounter between Jesus and the rich young man, the pope begins his moral theology with a profound sense of the intrinsic connection between morality and religion. On the one hand, religion is deeply moral; the love of God must be translated into the love of neighbor, otherwise the attempt to speak on behalf of God can become a form of heteronomous power that falsely absolutizes its own authority without correctives and checks. On the other hand, morality is deeply religious. For the Christian, empowerment for the moral life is found in Jesus Christ. Over and against a strictly autonomous ethics, the Christian moral life is essentially a participation in the divine life, the compelling "imitation" of Christ, the entering into the life of God through Jesus.

With these observations, we arrive at what is distinctive about this passage. Its central theme is that Christian morality finds its center and criterion in the person of Jesus. The rich young man may keep all the commandments, but he lacks one thing: a total commitment to the person of Jesus Christ, a commitment that entails renunciation of everything that keeps him from discipleship. This passage collapses what can be identified as the difference between justification and sanctification. On the one hand, it is about gift — the call to encounter with Christ, who is the origin and goal of human life, the source and saving power of Christian morality. On the other hand, it is also a call

6. On this, compare Andrew Tallon's discussion of Emmanuel Levinas, Karl Rahner, and Bernard Lonergan as resources for analyzing the pope's fundamental ontology, "The Role of the Connaturalized Heart in Veritatis Splendor," in *Veritatis Splendor: American Responses,* ed. Allsopp and O'Keefe, pp. 137-56.

to obedience, a command to live life in a certain way. If it offers a vision of life that inspires and empowers — that responds in a profound way to the aspirations of the human heart — then it also presents a mandate and an imperative.

So far we have outlined a fairly standard reading of this passage. But the pope offers an additional twist. If the usual reading — and one could argue, the passage itself — collapses gift and command in the call to discipleship, then the pope collapses two further distinctions in his reading of the passage: the absolute and unconditioned call of discipleship with the moral teaching of the church. He equates Jesus' call, the primordial foundation of Christian morality, with the "living tradition" of the church and its interpretation of Jesus' commands and teachings. We arrive, then, at a central tension at the heart of the pope's interpretation of this passage: Is Jesus' ultimate and unconditioned call to discipleship to be equated with the church's judgments about how best to "put into practice" Jesus' commandments and teaching in specific historical and cultural contexts (VS #25)? If so, why? If not, then how is Jesus' call to be related to the church's teaching?

This question is a complex one. From a subjective standpoint, it grapples with the question of how the moral agent's response to Jesus' call is related to concrete moral judgments and acts. From an objective standpoint, it grapples with how the very absoluteness of moral norms is related to concrete judgments made in particular circumstances. We address these questions in the rest of the essay, but before we do so, we need to outline the more technical definition of freedom that the pope proposes in the second section of the encyclical.

II. A Natural Law Understanding of Freedom

After his exegesis of Matthew 19, the pope presents a comprehensive definition of freedom in the middle section of the encyclical. Not only does he propose a rich and subtle definition of freedom, but precisely because of its comprehensiveness, this definition can also serve as a kind of miniproposal for an ethics that has theonomous freedom as its first principle or root conceptual pattern. In examining this definition, my task will not be to analyze the accuracy of the pope's reading of existing "autonomous" positions — the positions he argues against in presenting his own constructive proposal. Rather, I focus specifically on the content of the pope's critique and his constructive position.

The pope's definition of freedom in this section has three dimensions.[7] The first dimension, which essentially deals with the nature and locus of the good, is entitled "freedom and law." The question the pope addresses in this dimension is the fundamental question of whether the ultimate "good" of freedom is to act as one wishes for one's own individual good (as one defines that good), or whether it is to will and act in conformity with the moral laws that inhere in human nature. The second dimension, entitled "conscience and truth," discusses how the agent — through the guidance of conscience — arrives at the norms that are to govern actions. The question here is whether conscience ultimately forms "decisions" of the individual's will or "judgments" that enact general laws in particular instances. The last dimension — which focuses on the practical question of who one should be and what one should do in specific circumstances — deals with the relationship between one's "fundamental option" and specific moral acts. The question here is whether an agent's moral identity is defined primarily by existential acts that shape the whole course of his or her life (what has been called in Roman Catholic moral theology "fundamental option"), or by judgments and actions regarding the object of particular acts, such as the fact that certain acts are "intrinsically evil."

I begin with the pope's discussion of "freedom and truth." In this discussion of freedom's ultimate good, the pope asserts the thesis of the encyclical: that freedom divorced from the fundamental truth of reality is not true freedom but arbitrary choice. He identifies a freedom divorced from truth with an "autonomous" conception of freedom that severs human freedom — the human capacity to choose and decide — from some understanding of "nature" — the inherent value of human and natural reality. He is especially critical of two forms of such an autonomous freedom, both of which locate morality solely

7. Note how these three dimensions mirror the distinctions in ethics among (1) the nature and locus of the good; (2) criteria for judgment and action; and (3) the character of the moral self. On this see James Gustafson's first chapter in *Christ and the Moral Life* (Chicago: University of Chicago Press, 1968).

in the rationality and will of the moral agent: (1) a consequentialist
ethics that presupposes a separation of "fact" from "value" and treats
all moral phenomena — except the will's actual capacity for choice —
as empirical phenomena to be studied by means of scientific methods;
and (2) a rights-based ethics that treats all other dimensions of human
and natural experience — for example, the material and biological —
outside of human creativity as raw material for human agency and
power. Both approaches to morality, the pope argues, lead to some
form of relativism because they allow no other substance to determine
the will's choices beyond its own preferences.

In lieu of such an autonomous ethics, the pope argues for a
"participated theonomy" in which human reason and will are oriented
not toward their own predilections but participation in divine wisdom
and providence.[8] Of course he does not negate the reality of human
reason and will; he even affirms that God has given human beings
"dominion" in the world. By means of their intelligence and will,
human beings do have some capacity to discover the values and laws
of created things and decide best how to use or appropriate them.
This capacity enables them not only to perform moral acts but to
shape a moral identity and therefore strive for moral perfection. What
the pope wants to stress, however, is that such autonomy does not
create its own values and norms. Rather, these values and norms are
contingent on divine wisdom and providence — what could also be
called divine law. In the pope's view, such an approach to morality is
not simply a heteronomy, in which the reason and will blindly follow
a strange law wholly external to them, but a theonomy — or more
specifically a "participated theonomy" — in which human beings, by

---

8. Compare the pope's distinction between (1) autonomous freedom and
(2) theonomous freedom with Mortimer Adler's distinction between, on the one
hand, (1) the acquired freedom of self-perfection and, on the other hand, (2) the
circumstantial freedom of self-realization and (3) the natural freedom of self-determination in *The Idea of Freedom: A Dialectical Examination of the Conceptions of Freedom*,
vols. 1 and 2 (New York: Doubleday, 1958 and 1961). For an analogous framework,
see Richard McKeon's essay on "Freedom and History" in *Freedom and History and
Other Essays*, ed. Zahava McKeon (Chicago: University of Chicago Press, 1985), pp.
160-241. See also the discussion of freedom, from a sociological perspective, in
Orlando Patterson's *Freedom in the Making of Western Culture*, vol. 1 (New York: Basic
Books, 1991).

the lights of natural reason and divine revelation, participate in their own finite way in the wisdom and providence of divine law, the divine pattern or exemplar that governs the ordering of existence.

Given this contrast between an "autonomous ethics" and a "participated theonomy," we turn to the second dimension in the pope's definition of freedom: his discussion of "conscience and truth," how he understands conscience to discern and enact the values and norms that inhere in created reality. In line with his rejection of an autonomous view of freedom's good, the pope rejects a view of conscience that emphasizes its creative character, that is, its capacity to make "decisions" as opposed to "judgments." Such an approach emphasizes concrete existential considerations rather than the application of general norms articulated at a doctrinal or abstract level. The pope rejects such a view because it stresses not the objectivity of moral norms but the "creative and responsible acceptance of personal tasks entrusted to one by God." Such a position tends to minimize the importance of objective norms for moral behavior, understanding these merely to be "general perspectives" that assist one in forming personal decisions.

What the pope offers instead is a view of conscience that highlights the way its "judgments" apply the natural law to specific circumstances, for example, the first principle of practical reason, that one must do good and avoid evil. In this, conscience is a "witness" to whether human beings are faithful or unfaithful to the law. Conscience, therefore, entails primarily a dialogue with God, the author of the law "whose voice and judgment penetrate the depth of the human soul" (VS #58). In serving as this witness, conscience manifests "conflicting thoughts" that either accuse or excuse a person. And since one's conscience can make faulty judgments, the pope calls Christians to have their consciences formed — to make them "the object of a continual conversion to what is true and to what is good" (VS #64). Such a task entails not merely having a general knowledge of God's law but having a kind of "connaturality" with the true good, a "connaturality" developed through the cultivation of the virtues, both cardinal (prudence, justice, temperance, and courage) and theological (faith, hope, and love). The function of the church's magisterium is precisely to assist Christians in the formation of such a conscience.

We have so far depicted the pope's conception of the good, which freedom is to enact, and how one's conscience discerns and applies that good — or that "law" — in specific circumstances. We turn now to the third dimension of his definition of freedom: how he defines the character of the moral self, the way an agent defines her identity over time by specific actions and judgments. The central issue the pope grapples with in this discussion is the relationship between a person's "fundamental option" and the specific choices she makes in concrete circumstances. At the outset, we should be clear that the pope does not wholly reject the concept of the fundamental option. He has a place in his ethics for a "fundamental option": those decisions which determine the course or direction of one's life, whether, say, one defines one's life as being for or against the Good and Truth. Indeed, he notes that the concept has deep biblical roots as the "obedience of faith," the act of "faith working through love," what forms the "core" of a person's "heart," the radical and unconditional decision demanded by the kingdom of God (Matt. 19:21).

What he criticizes in his treatment of the fundamental option is any disjunction of the way one's character or agency is shaped and the actual moral acts one performs. Freedom, he contends, becomes "slavery" when an act of faith — an act that shapes one's fundamental option — is separated from the specific moral acts one performs. Hence he criticizes the strict identification of one's fundamental option with what Karl Rahner would call the "transcendental" or "prethematic," an identification that would separate a "deeper" and "different" decision from the other more specific and "categorical" decisions one makes throughout the course of one's life.[9] He is also critical of any attempt to define these categorical acts merely as partial signs and symbols which never give one's fundamental option full definitive expression.

The pope's chief difficulty is with the development of two levels of morality, one centered on how the moral "good" and "evil" is dependent on the will and the other centered on ascriptions of "right"

---

9. On Karl Rahner's definition of the "fundamental option," see Karl Rahner, "Theology of Freedom," in *Theological Investigations* (London: Darton, Longman and Todd, 1969), 6:178-96; see also his *Foundations of Christian Faith: An Introduction to the Idea of Christianity,* trans. William Dych (New York: Seabury, 1978).

and "wrong" based on a "calculation" of the "premoral" and "physical" goods and evils that result from that action. The reason the pope is critical of any separation of these levels is that it diminishes the sense to which moral acts do have an "object," an object that has a "teleological" character essentially linked with humanity's final ends. The pope is critical of any disjunctions of two types of values: (1) those pertaining to the moral order, that is, properly "moral" values such as the love of God and neighbor and justice; and (2) those pertaining to the "premoral" order such as the mental, emotional, or physical advantages or disadvantages that can accrue to the self and others in specific actions (e.g., with regard to life, death, physical integrity, or the loss of material goods).

In sum, in this section, I have traced the pope's contrast between a "theonomous" and "autonomous" conception of freedom. The pope's theonomous position is a corrective to a autonomous ethics that solely identifies ethical judgments with decisions of the will. But is his position actually theonomous (in that it truly maintains a place for human freedom in relation to God) or is it finally heteronomous (based solely on obedience to a "strange" — *heteros* — "law" — *nomos*)? This leads us to ask what role the *individual* plays in the pope's work. The pope himself speaks of the importance of the fundamental option, but how is this option — this decision to creatively define one's life — related to the objectivity of laws that are to define one's actions? What role does a person's unique individuality play in the pope's definition of freedom? We return, then, to the questions raised at the end of our exegetical section: How is the gift and command of Jesus' call related to the shaping of the individual self? And, if the overarching shape of one's life is linked with specific norms and mandates, then wherein lies the absoluteness of those norms, which shape the self? I address these questions by examining yet another definition of freedom offered in the encyclical.

III. A Personalist Understanding of Freedom

In the previous section I examined one of the definitions of freedom in the encyclical — what we can call a traditional "natural law" view that locates freedom's end in a moral law or ideal befitting human nature.[10] I traced how the pope contrasts this definition with an "autonomous" view that locates its end within the agent herself, in her decisions about what she should be and do. The pope argues that the former definition is superior to the latter because it establishes criteria external to the self for determining how the self's freedom should be used. The autonomous view, by contrast, locates the norm for judging freedom within the agent's own capacity to exercise freedom of choice — for example, her own self-legislation (as in forms of Kantian ethics) and capacity to choose among possible good outcomes (as in forms of consequentialist ethics), or, on a popular level, in terms of such criteria as "sincerity, authenticity and 'being at peace with oneself'" (VS #32). Such individualistic forms of grounding moral norms do not, according to the pope, provide a strong enough basis for preserving the very freedom valued in democracies — for criticizing, for example, social and economic injustice, political corruption, and the violation of human rights, or for providing the kind of "radical personal and social renewal" needed to ensure "solidarity, honesty, and openness" (VS #98). The reason: they locate the norm for evaluating the human use of power (human freedom) in the actual use of that power — in the capacity to make choices and decisions. The danger in making the exercise of freedom the sole value to be preserved is this: value is not perceived to inhere in reality itself (e.g., in the intrinsic value of human beings) but in the capacity to exercise freedom (the use of power). But, if power is the only value, then what value or norm is to judge the use of power other than the very use of that power? Given this problematic, the pope attempts to ground the human good in an understanding of the "True" and the "Good" — beyond simply the exercise of power — because, in his view, only such a conception of truth and goodness external to the self can overcome "the various forms of totalitarianism" and "make way for the authentic *freedom* of the person" (VS #99, my emphasis).

And yet there is a difficulty with the pope's "natural law" view of freedom: it focuses on what human beings share — their knowledge of the law, the "True" and the "Good" — and not on what makes them *unique* and *individual*.[11] Such an approach meets the requirement

---

10. Compare Smith, "Natural Law and Personalism in *Veritatis Splendor*."
11. My argument here is influenced by William Schweiker, "Power and the

of providing a norm external to the self for evaluating the self's exercise of power. Nonetheless, the pope also stresses that it is precisely one's "obedience to universal and unchanging moral norms" that leads one to "respect the *uniqueness* and *individuality* of the person" (VS #85, my emphasis). But: Why ought an individual's uniqueness to be valued when any real, actual individual is always less than perfect? What is it that confers value on the individual, who is always contingent and imperfect?[12] Does the self, in all its individuality, need to be effaced in order for the individual to be morally good and true? Even in his depiction of the "natural law" view of freedom, the pope has a place for a strong sense of individuality and the human capacity to define and shape one's character and identity creatively. Even in that context, he makes reference to a person's "heart," which, in turn, is defined in terms of one's "fundamental choice which qualifies the moral life and engages freedom on a radical level before God." Such "fundamental choices" are the "decisions of faith" described in the Hebrew and Christian Scriptures — for example, in Israel's capacity to make covenants with God (cf. Josh. 24:14-25; Exod. 19:3-8; Mic. 6:8), the Christian's response to the call to discipleship and perfection (Matt. 19:21), and the radical and unconditional nature of the decision demanded by the reign of God (VS #66). But how is this conception of individuality — and one's capacity to change one's character creatively by deciding what one shall do or become — related to the focus on conformity to the "good" and "true," the moral law or ideal

---

Agency of God," *Theology Today* 52 (July 1995): 204-24. See also his comparison of Christian and Platonic approaches to ethics in "The Sovereignty of God's Goodness," in *Iris Murdoch and the Search for Human Goodness,* ed. Maria Antonaccio and William Schweiker (Chicago: University of Chicago Press, 1996), pp. 209-36. For a fuller development of his position, see his *Responsibility and Christian Ethics.*

12. Compare Risto Saarinen's observation that the pope's concept of nature tends toward an Averroist conception of the unity of the human intellect. See his essay in this volume. As Saarinen notes, commentators have pointed out that VS #46-50 follows Martin Rhonheimer's analysis of nature in *Natur als Grundlage der Moral: Eine Auseinandersetzung mit autonomer und teleologischer Ethik* (Innsbruck: Tyrolia, 1987). See, e.g., W. Schöpsdau, "Rekonfessionalisierung der Moral? Beobachtungen aus evangelischer Sicht zur nachkonziliaren Entwicklung und zur Enzyklika *Veritatis Splendor,*" in *Abschottung statt Dialog? Das Lehramt der Kirche und die Moral,* ed. S. Pfürtner et al. (Luzern: Exodus, 1994), pp. 149-70, see esp. pp. 163-64.

befitting human nature, so stressed in the pope's "natural law" view of freedom?

To address this question, I turn to a somewhat different pattern for understanding freedom in the third section of the encyclical, what we will call the pope's "personalist" conception of freedom. This other pattern is defined primarily in terms of the Christian's response to Christ's call to discipleship, even to the point of martyrdom. In my exegesis of this personalist pattern, I deal with how it depicts the relationship between (1) God as the source of the absolute moral claim on human life — as the "crucified Christ" — and (2) the moral agent who stands in relation to God — as the disciple who responds to God's call.

There is an eloquent passage at the beginning of the third part of the encyclical that depicts the pope's personalist conception of freedom. It begins with the observation that "rational reflection and daily experience" demonstrate both the *"weakness"* and the *"tragedy"* of human freedom. The weakness of human freedom lies in the fact that it is "real" but "limited." This weakness is demonstrated in three ways. First, it is demonstrated in the fact that human freedom has a truly "absolute and unconditional origin." Although human freedom is — like its origin — absolute and unconditional, this freedom itself originates from a reality other than itself; hence, it always finds itself situated within reality. For this reason, freedom always belongs to human beings as a gift. Humans are creatures who receive their freedom as a given, a gift. This is what it means to have a "creaturely image." And it is this creaturely image that constitutes "the basis of the dignity of the person." Second, this freedom is at once an "inalienable self-possession," on the one hand, and an "openness to all that exists," on the other. Further, this openness is defined more specifically in personal terms as the "passing beyond self to knowledge and love of the other." What this means is that true freedom is not merely oriented towards one's self in self-possession but is "ultimately directed toward communion." This freedom "is an echo of the primordial vocation" whereby "the Creator calls human beings to the true Good," and further, "through Christ's revelation, to become God's friend and to share his own divine life." Finally, although this freedom is a given, it is "received like a seed" that must be a "cultivated responsibility." And this leads us to the *tragic* dimension of freedom: that human beings face the constant temptation to sin. In a "mysterious way," the pope observes, we are "inclined to betray our openness to the True and the Good" and instead "choose finite, limited, and ephemeral goods." Such betrayal can take a variety of forms: for example, setting one's self or some other person or thing up as an absolute principle or, we might add, negating or denying the inviolable worth of created reality. Hence, there is a continual need for the ongoing conversion, imitation, and perfection of a life, the "contemplation of" and "communion with" Jesus so as to reorient one's inclinations so that they "conform" to Jesus' own pattern of self-giving (VS #86).

This depiction of freedom is expressed in more personalist language: it makes reference to freedom as part of the "inherent dignity" of the person, to its "openness to all that exists" and finding its culmination in "communion" and the "knowledge and love of the other" (VS #86). It is also deeply Augustinian in its focus on the tragedy of the freedom being its substitution of finite goods for the ultimate good (VS #86). We can identify two main themes in this definition of freedom. If it stresses the individual's "inalienable self-possession," then the goal of this self-possession is to pass "beyond self to knowledge and love of the other." Hence, stress is placed on both (1) the uniqueness of human persons and their irreducible moral worth, on the one hand, and (2) the source and goal of that uniqueness, on the other — communion with God and others. These two norms or values — the inherent dignity of individuals and their orientation toward communion — are depicted as absolute and unconditional, that is, linked with an "openness to all that exists." Indeed, the tragedy of sin is precisely the human failure to recognize the weakness of that freedom, which is always both "real but limited," the fact that its source and goal is rooted not in itself, or in finite, ephemeral goods, but in God, the True and the Good.

This personalist conception of freedom is situated within the broader context of a meditation on Christian martyrdom. Such martyrdom is rooted neither in human heroism nor the constancy of good intentions, but in the crucified Christ. We might say that the crucified Christ is the nature and locus of the good of this personalist conception of freedom.[13] The pope situates this conception of martyrdom in relation to the apostle Paul's understanding of his mission:

13. Compare James Gustafson, *Christ and the Moral Life*.

> Christ . . . sent me . . . to preach the Gospel, and not with eloquent
> wisdom, lest the cross of Christ be emptied of its *power*. . . . We
> preach Christ crucified, a stumbling block to Jews and folly to Gen-
> tiles, but to those who are called, both Jews and Greeks, Christ the
> *power* of God and the *wisdom* of God (1 Cor. 1:17, 23-24).[14]

The source and norm of freedom in this personalist view is the
crucified Christ who reveals the authentic meaning and truth of freedom by living it fully in the total gift of himself and calling his disciples
to share in this freedom as self-giving (VS #88). In the pope's words,
Jesus is the "living personal summation of perfect freedom in total
obedience to the will of God." His "crucified flesh reveals the unbreakable bond between freedom and truth"; in turn, "his resurrection from the dead is the supreme exaltation of the fruitfulness and
saving power of a freedom lived in truth" (VS #87).

What is the significance of having the crucified and risen Christ
as source of the absolute moral claim on human life? We might ask
the same question of the other ways of thinking and speaking of God
and God's relationship to human beings that we find in *Veritatis Splendor*, ways that stress the sense to which God is a personal God (for
example, as Creator and Redeemer, as the one who made covenants
with Israel, as one who calls believers to discipleship, or in relation to
the reign of God). What we find in these ways of speaking about God,
and especially in the testimony to the self-giving Christ, is not merely
a depiction of an impersonal Good unconcerned with the fate of
individuals — a Good that does not respond to or recognize what is
other than itself — but a God who has through Christ given God's
very self for human beings. Christians believe that God has not only
endowed creatures with value but has, through Christ, shared our
humanity in order to overcome sin, pain, death, and even demonic
powers. The significance, then, of Christian belief in a personal God
lies precisely in the affirmation that God, as ultimate power, has bound
God's very identity to the worth of created reality, not only by endowing it with inviolable worth but by giving of Christ's very self on
the cross. There is yet a further point about this Christian naming of

14. Note how the words "power" and "wisdom" are redefined by the "folly"
of the cross.

God: that this very act of divine power — of Christ's self-giving for humanity — actually defines what God's nature, God's character, is for us.[15] What classical christological and trinitarian belief affirms is that Christians know who God is — what God's character is like — based on how God has acted in creation and redemption, in the work of the Father, Son, and Spirit. What is affirmed in this Christian naming of God is that although God is the sole origin of power in the world, God is not simply an absolute power. Christians, for example, affirm that God is that reality who (as "Creator") endows created reality with value, and (as "love") gives of Christ's very self to finite existence. In these affirmations, both creation and love are instances of power in which power generates value or bestows value on another. But in such acts of bestowal, power *alone* does not define value. Rather, what defines value is the very act of *bestowing value*. Hence Christian moral theology is not based on a strictly empirical account of reality or one based solely on human creativity and freedom — or even a conception of an absolute and impersonal Good or Power. Rather, what undergirds Christian morality is this very divine *transformation* of power whereby ultimate power binds itself to the creation and redemption of finite existence.[16]

We turn to the anthropological corollary to this christological grounding of ethics. In the same way that Jesus' act of self-giving for his brothers and sisters on the cross constitutes his identity as the crucified and risen Christ, so the faith — the contemplation and communion — that responds to this gift "gives rise to and calls for a consistent life commitment." There is, then, an intrinsic relationship between faith and morality in this personalist conception of freedom: the "worship of God" and "contemplation of Jesus Crucified" is the "never-ending source" from which the church draws to live in freedom and love and service. Jesus' self-giving is the "source, model, and means" for the witness — the "confession" — of his disciples. If

---

15. This is the core insight for identifying a relationship between the economic Trinity and the immanent Trinity. See the classic statements on this in Karl Barth, *Church Dogmatics*, vol. 1, *The Doctrine of the Word of God* (Edinburgh: T & T Clark, 1956), and Karl Rahner, *The Trinity* (New York: Seabury, 1974).

16. On this discussion of the identity of God, compare Schweiker, "Power and the Agency of God," esp. pp. 207-8, and *Responsibility and Christian Ethics*.

Christ's identity is defined by the act of self-giving, then, his very gift of self is the "grace" and "responsibility" that enables human beings to do as he did. In their "trusting abandonment to Christ," Christian disciples are bound to the "profound love of God and our brothers and sisters" (VS #87-89).

But if charity is the believer's supreme "witness" or testimony, this charity contains justice in itself as its unconditional element.[17] In the pope's words: "Faith also possesses a moral content" (VS #89). If love is the ultimate truth that defines the Christian life, then its very quality as charity *(caritas, agape)* entails that justice — the recognition of the irreducible worth and dignity of each human person — is not violated. As I noted in my introduction to this personalist definition of freedom: the very act of (1) "passing beyond self to knowledge and love of the other" entails that one also (2) respect the uniqueness and irreducible worth of the other person — and, I might add, one's self — even in the attempt to share one's self with that other.[18] Charity requires that one give unconditioned respect to the personal dignity of each person as its condition. And such respect does not merely entail a "thin" abstract theory of the human good. Rather, it entails a concrete witness to the particular goods that constitute the inviolable dignity of humans — goods that entail the prohibition of certain acts as "intrinsically evil" (as found, for example, in the Ten Commandments). It is within this context of speaking about the Christian witness to the inviolability of human worth that the pope speaks of martyrdom — of giving of one's self in the act of witnessing to the moral order, that is, the inherent goodness and evil of particular acts (VS #90-94). In the same way that Christ has bound his existence to the inviolable worth of humanity, so we are to bind our existence,

17. Compare Paul Tillich, *Morality and Beyond* (Louisville: Westminster, 1995), pp. 38-39.

18. A theme that would need to be examined more closely is the relationship between self and other with regard to this conception of radical self-giving. This theme is especially salient in the feminist criticisms of *Veritatis Splendor.* See, e.g., Kathleen Talvacchia and Mary Elizabeth Walsh, "The Splendor of Truth: A Feminist Critique," in *Veritatis Splendor: American Responses,* ed. Allsopp and O'Keefe, pp. 296-310. For a discussion of the central theological issues at stake in this issue, see Kathryn Tanner, *The Politics of God: Christian Theologies and Social Justice* (Minneapolis: Fortress, 1992).

even to the point of death, to give witness to the inviolable worth of others.

What I have offered in this section is a reading of the pope's personalist understanding of freedom. This section has, in a nutshell, been an exegesis of his claim that "the Supreme Good and the moral good meet in truth — the truth of God, as creator and redeemer, is also the truth of humans who are created and redeemed by God" (VS #99). The foundation for the Christian morality in this personalist view is neither an abstract and impersonal good nor an absolute conception of power, but Jesus' self-giving for his fellow human beings. This self-giving, in turn, is the pattern human beings are empowered to follow — the "grace" and "responsibility" of Christian discipleship (VS #87). As Christ's identity — Christ's exercise of freedom and power — is constituted by self-giving, so the way of discipleship is constituted by obedience to the radical and unconditioned command of the gospel, in the pope's words, the constant "conformity" or "imitation" of the pattern of Christ's life (VS #89). Such truth is an ongoing corrective to both a false autonomy that would set individual freedom up as an absolute and, I might note, it also serves as a corrective to a false heteronomy that would establish a false social unity as an absolute — a "communion" that did not recognize the inviolable worth of individuals. Why? Because it asserts that the primordial ground of Christian morality is not power itself as an absolute but the divine power that has bound its very identity to the creation and redemption of finite life. Hence any act of human freedom that "echoes" this "primordial vocation" must itself be an act that reflexively witnesses to the irreducible worth and inviolable dignity of human beings (as creatures), even as it gives of itself to others in charity (in love) (cf. VS #86).

IV. A Concluding Comparison

In the section on the pope's exegesis of Matthew 19, I asked whether a tension could be discerned between the unconditional demand of the gospel, on the one hand, and the specific teachings of natural law and the church, on the other. I ask an analogous question in this section. Is there a tension between the two definitions of freedom we have outlined? The one stresses our communion between God and human beings, a communion which presupposes the inviolable dignity and worth of each individual. The other stresses the need for obedience to an immutable and universal natural law, a law that is also commensurate with the church's magisterial teaching; it emphasizes the way human rationality and will can discover and enact the norms and values that inhere in creation. Are these two conceptions of freedom distinct or are they the same? What is the relationship between them? My task in this final section will be to discuss the implications of the pope's personalist conception of freedom for these two issues: (1) how the moral agent is related to concrete moral judgments and acts and (2) how the very absoluteness of moral norms is related to conscience and the concrete judgments made in particular circumstances. I conclude with related reflections on the role of an "autonomous" ethics in moral theology.

I begin with the question of how the moral agent is related to concrete moral judgments and acts. I have noted that the pope is critical of a tendency he perceives in some modern Catholic moral theology to draw too sharp a distinction between a deeper "transcendental" or "prethematic" self that makes "moral" decisions regarding good and evil (which deal with more abstract ethical notions like justice and love) and the actions one actually performs with regard to "premoral" goods regarding, say, the mental, emotional, or physical advantages or disadvantages that can accrue to the self and others in specific actions (which deal with the concrete objects of specific moral acts). But he also presents a rich understanding of the concept of "heart" in the encyclical: that it has to do precisely with the "conversion" and "perfection" of one's life, one's loves and actions, by "conforming" oneself to the "pattern" of Christ. Indeed, at the heart of the pope's personalist view of freedom is the intrinsic link drawn between Christ's crucified and risen flesh and the way of Christian discipleship. It locates freedom's end not simply in (1) the will's decisions nor (2) a moral law or ideal befitting human nature but in (3) an act of faith, what he calls the "heart" of a human, the fundamental decisions and choices that define her identity and character over time. This act of faith presupposes a fundamental correlation between who Christ is and who we are — that we are to contemplate and imitate Christ so that we can enter into his act of self-giving for others. Hence, although the pope is critical of an approach to ethics that would sever one's fundamental option from specific behaviors, he does not reject the concept of fundamental option. Indeed, the very call of Christian discipleship requires a decision about the totality of one's life. But if this decision is not solely defined in terms of the "autonomous" will's decisions abstracted from concrete goods, then it is also not solely defined in terms of discrete or isolated acts of obedience to an external "heteronomous" law. Rather, it is the ongoing perfection and conversion of a life, a perfection that takes place in the actual judgments and actions that enact concrete goods or evils, goods or evils that either witness to or negate the inviolable worth of human dignity.

Now, it is precisely at this point that we are led to the role of conscience and the question of what constitutes the absoluteness of moral norms.[19] In the pope's personalist conception of freedom, his emphasis is not simply on how conscience perceives an immutable and universal law. Rather, what conscience perceives are the concrete goods — and evils — that either respect and enhance or violate a person's worth. These goods, and their implication that some acts are intrinsically evil, are precisely what is protected by the Ten Commandments or the church's moral teaching. But, if the authorization of these teachings does not simply lie in one's own individual "authentic" resonance with them, then it also does not simply lie in inherited moral convictions. Rather, their authorization lies in the irreducible worth of the particular goods themselves.[20] It is to this inviolable dignity that conscience gives

19. See the classic essay by Josef Fuchs, "The Absoluteness of Behavioral Moral Norms," in *Personal Responsibility and Christian Morality* (Washington, D.C.: Georgetown University Press, 1983), pp. 115-52.

20. Compare Jean Porter's observation: "The implication of affirming the independent significance of the object of an action, for Aquinas, is that moral judgment must be carried out in terms of the meanings of the basic moral concepts, such as murder and legitimate execution, for example, which form the framework for moral judgment and discourse for the whole society. Our understanding of these basic notions can be refined, and we can and do change our minds, individually and collectively, about the moral quality of some kinds of actions. Yet we cannot 'get behind' the basic moral concepts to some simpler and more fundamental units of moral analysis. The wisdom and commitments to the good that are embodied in these basic notions set the fundamental terms for moral judgment, whether that wisdom and those commitments are seen as coming from the human community and natural reason alone, or we trace them ultimately, as Aquinas himself would do, to the wisdom

witness; it is precisely this irreducibility that serves as an ongoing — and, one might add, reflexive — check on both individual and corporate uses of power. Thus, even though *Veritatis Splendor* stresses the magisterial authority of church teaching and in places absolutizes this teaching by stressing its immutability and universality, its own witness to the irreducibility of human worth articulates a reflexive norm that provides an ongoing test and correction of the very articulations of any such norm. What conscience perceives is a standard that tests not only one's own proclivities and preferences but the cultural forms which mediate a community's — including the Christian community's — norms and values. Although this standard is immutable and universal, its immutability and universality lie not in an impersonal principle nor a particular cultural articulation of that standard, but in the very inviolable worth of creaturely reality, a worth grounded in God's own personal creative and redemptive activity.

Of course, individuals and communities need each other in the formation of conscience. On the one hand, the "living tradition" has a role to play in the shaping of the individual's conscience. On the other hand, however, an individual may be led by conscience to question ecclesial and cultural authorities. Thus, before the emperor in Worms, Martin Luther insisted that it was not right to do something against the conscience; and even Thomas Aquinas stated that he would disobey the command of a superior to whom he had made a vow of obedience if this superior asked something against his conscience.[21]

---

and love of God" ("The Moral Act in *Veritatis Splendor* and in Aquinas's *Summa Theologiae*: A Comparative Analysis," in *Veritatis Splendor: American Responses,* ed. Allsopp and O'Keefe, p. 293; see also "Moral Reasoning, Authority, and Community in *Veritatis Splendor,*" *The Annual of the Society of Christian Ethics* [1995]: 201-19). See a fuller development of her position in Jean Porter, *Moral Action and Christian Ethics* (Cambridge: Cambridge University Press, 1995).

21. See how Paul Tillich distinguishes the Reformation's conception of theological freedom from the Enlightenment's notion of freedom of conscience: "The quest for 'freedom of conscience' does not refer to the concrete ethical decision, but to the religious authority of the inward light that expresses itself through the individual conscience. And since the inward light could hardly be distinguished from practical reason, freedom of conscience meant, actually, the freedom to follow one's autonomous reason, not only in ethics, but also in religion. The 'religion of conscience' and the consequent idea of tolerance are not a result of the Reformation, but of sectarian spiritualism and mysticism" (*Morality and Beyond,* p. 73).

The pope's very intent of providing a witness that can ward off in both "*civil society* and within the *ecclesial communities* themselves a head-long plunge into . . . the confusion between good and evil" entails that the unconditional and irreducible nature of these goods *in themselves* be maintained precisely so that they can serve as an ongoing and reflexive test and corrective to the existing values of those very civil societies and ecclesial communities (VS #93, my emphasis).

These reflections on conscience, in turn, lead us to the role of an autonomous ethics. The pope articulates an important critique of an autonomous ethic that would sever the link between freedom and nature, locating good and evil solely in the decision-making power of individuals, and thereby separating "valuing" decision-makers from the "facts" of reality. His very attempt to situate morality within the broader context of faith is an attempt to overcome the secularization of created reality, both human and nonhuman. This is an important point: the eyes of faith affirm the teleological character of such created reality, since they see all as finally participating in the divine life. Nonetheless, this point need not negate the recognition that all human beings, and not only Christians, have a capacity to learn morally. In fact, the pope himself refers to the fact that in their witness to the absoluteness of the moral good, Christians are not alone but "are supported by the moral sense present in peoples and by the great religious and sapiential traditions of East and West, from which the interior and mysterious workings of God's Spirit are not absent" (VS #94).

It also need not negate the importance of being attentive to the actual empirical and prudential goods — physical, psychological, social, and spiritual — that define human existence (cf. VS #112). Indeed, these premoral goods, in all their empirical richness, are precisely the values to be transformed by the conscience's insight into their unconditioned worth or "teleological character." The very condition of communion is the recognition of the inviolable worth of created reality. The Christian norm of agape presupposes these goods as its unconditioned element. The theological task is precisely to perfect and enhance these goods. It is possible, then, to have a place in an ethics for the empirical and prudential study of human goods, without negating their teleological character. Strong theological precedent can be found for this not only in Aquinas's differentiated concept of reason (in the distinctions between nature and grace, reason and revelation) but in the Augustinian transformation of the natural virtues or the spheres in the earthly cities in terms of the norm of love.

We return, then, to the question raised throughout the paper. Is the pope's proposal for freedom heteronomous or theonomous? We have addressed this question by focusing on the fundamental link he draws between faith and morality. Ostensively, this encyclical was written in order to bolster the magisterium's power. But there is a deeper theological goal that informs this encyclical: the goal of fulfilling the church's mission to speak out against injustice and affirm with other human beings and the other great religions the inviolability of human worth. The pope's argument is that the modern constriction of morality to the rights and freedoms of individuals undercuts the very bases for protecting those rights since it offers no other reference point for making moral choices than the choices — the acts of power — of individuals. In articulating his own constructive proposal, however, he presents what appear to be two understandings of freedom, one that defines it as obedience to the natural law — the true and good external to the self — and another that defines it in terms of one's communion with God and other human beings. In a comparison of the two conceptions of freedom, I have suggested that the latter offers the more encompassing framework. It locates the truth of freedom neither in the will's choices nor simply in an impersonal conception of the true and good, but in the Christian trinitarian and christological affirmation that, in Christ, ultimate power has constituted its identity not only by endowing human beings with inviolable worth (in creation) but by giving the divine self in Christ for the sake of witnessing to their irreducible worth.[22] It is only with reference to this source

22. I have attempted, in this argument, to work within the theological frame of reference of *Veritatis Splendor* itself and therefore have appropriated the pope's *material* conception of the Christian life as a form of "perfection" and "imitation." Nonetheless, the *form* of my theological argument is distinctly Lutheran in that its final norm for making theological judgments is the "crucified Christ" encountered in the Christian gospel. A classic depiction of this form of theological argument — in which the crucified and risen Christ is the theological criterion for moving beyond either legalism (a false heteronomy) or antinomianism (a false autonomy) is found in Martin Luther's "The Freedom of a Christian," in *Martin Luther: Selections from His Writings,* pp. 42-85.

and norm — which radically transforms their own exercise of freedom and power, whether as individuals or as church — that Christians can witness to moral truth in response to the pressing ethical, social, and political problems of our time.[23]

---

23. I am grateful to the following people for comments that have helped me to sharpen my argument in this paper: Theo Dieter, Reinhard Hütter, James F. Keenan, Gilbert Meilaender, Eberhard Schockenhoff, and William Schweiker.

"Intrinsically Evil Acts"; or, Why Abortion and Euthanasia Cannot Be Justified

BERND WANNENWETSCH

"THEREFORE, BY THE AUTHORITY which Christ conferred upon Peter and his successors, and in communion with the Bishops of the Catholic Church, *I confirm that the direct and voluntary killing of an innocent human being is always gravely immoral.* . . . The deliberate decision to deprive an innocent human being of his life is always morally evil and can never be licit either as an end in itself or as a means to a good end. . . . 'Nothing and no one can in any way permit the killing of an innocent human being, whether a fetus or an embryo, an infant or an adult, an old person, or one suffering from an incurable disease or a person who is dying. . . . Nor can any authority legitimately recommend or permit such an action'" (EV #57).

This passage is the heart of the papal encyclical *Evangelium Vitae,*[1] in which the pope attacks fundamental threats to human life in the present day. This encyclical letter is closely connected with *Veritatis Splendor,* published two years earlier, which dealt with questions of moral theological principle. In particular, *Veritatis Splendor*'s teaching about "intrinsically evil acts" provides the background to the statements of *Evangelium Vitae* on abortion and euthanasia. This is the connection I wish to explore, raising the question to what extent this

---

1. Cited as EV; VS stands for *Veritatis Splendor.* Subsequent citations of both encyclicals will refer to paragraph numbers and will be given parenthetically in the text.

teaching brings our current moral assumptions into clearer focus. My approach, then, differs somewhat from the (mostly intra-Catholic) responses to *Veritatis Splendor* and their characteristic preoccupations: how well the pope had understood the moral theologians he criticized there; whether his highlighting of "intrinsically evil acts" does justice to the complexity of moral judgment as their theories present it.[2] My argument will proceed along the following lines: having remarked on some distinctive features of the encyclicals, I shall first discuss three theoretical core-problems raised by the teaching on intrinsically evil acts: (1) in what sense commands can be given justification or reason; (2) what we mean by the "object" of an act; and (3) how community is related to moral language. The second part will then look for points of convergence and conflict with the ethics of the Reformation. Here, by way of comparison with Luther, we shall identify agreements on (1) the moral meaning of the body, (2) the emphasis on concrete responsibility for the neighbor, and (3) the understanding of suffering as intrinsic to the Christian ethos. Critical questions will arise, especially about the correspondence between faith and the "internality" of acts, and about the implications of this for the so-called works of supererogation.

1. The Character of the Two Encyclicals

There is no doubt that *Evangelium Vitae* is meant as a prophetic word. The visionary interpretation of the present situation as a large-scale "objective conspiracy against life" (EV #17) is prophetic in itself. Here the pope has in mind not only particular tendencies of thought and practice that undermine respect for life; he is aware of a "new quality" in the threat to life that comes about through systematic planning and through public, even legal, legitimation. The pope raises his voice

2. See Dietmar Mieth, ed., *Moraltheologie im Abseits? Antwort auf die Enzyklika "Veritatis Splendor"* (Freiburg: Herder, 1994), and John Wilkins, ed., *Considering "Veritatis Splendor"* (Cleveland: Pilgrim, 1994). Two notable exceptions, which suggest a reading of the encyclical as a response to the general cultural ethos rather than to professional moral theology, come (not by accident, perhaps) from a Catholic non-theologian and a non-Catholic theologian. See the contributions of Mary Tuck and Oliver O'Donovan in *Considering "Veritatis Splendor."*

against this false prophecy as well as against the tendencies it fosters. Prophetic, too, is his use of Scripture, on which we can only touch in passing. As in *Veritatis Splendor,* everything in *Evangelium Vitae* is concentrated upon a single passage: in the former the present situation was read through the story of the young man asking about eternal life (Matt. 19:16-22), in the latter through the story of Cain's murder of his brother (Gen. 4:1-16). The shadow that fell across Cain's face when "his countenance fell" falls now across the conscience of a society that refuses to be "my brother's keeper" and so becomes the murderer of countless innocent beings. This deliberate, and load bearing, "intratextual"[3] use of Scripture is especially striking to the Protestant reader, who is used to a bureaucratic rather than prophetic use of Scripture in church documents: a careful list of "relevant" biblical passages set out in a "balanced" manner so as to make sure they will finally cancel each other out. This prophetic call to repentance is also political. It is interested in far more than sustaining individual morality. Running counter to the trend to privatize morality (e.g., in the search for a "morning-after pill" that will make it possible to withdraw abortion from public control) *Evangelium Vitae* insists that this question should remain a matter of public responsibility (EV #13).[4] Hence its attack on the heretical imperative of private morality, that we should each bite into the fruit of the knowledge of good and evil for ourselves. So the limits imposed on "authority" in the passage quoted above must be understood to include the privatization of morality as well. Public authority may not legitimate action in defiance of the divine command; no more may it absolve itself from responsibility by de-publicizing acts that it should prevent from being committed. Therefore the pope calls for public action in a specifically political sense. For instance, instead of trying to resolve the problem of overpopulation in developing countries in the cultural-imperialist way, by exporting such blessings of technological civilization as contraceptives

3. George Lindbeck, *The Nature of Doctrine: Religion and Theology in a Postliberal Age* (Philadelphia: Westminster, 1984).

4. The manner in which VS especially does not only bring the authority of the magisterium into the moral discourse but tries to safeguard it against it as well, must however run counter to the intention indicated above and eventually serve the individualized morality that it attacks here. See Theodor Dieter's contribution in this volume.

or sterilization, the pope calls for an explicitly *political* approach to improving the conditions of life within those countries (EV #16).

In a situation that he diagnoses as a "war of the strong against the weak," he pronounces some words that claim an exceptionally high level of authority for encyclical letters. As Manfred Balkenohl remarks in his commentary on the German edition of *Evangelium Vitae*,[5] there are three points at which the encyclical uses "formulations of the highest magisterial degree" (#140), claiming, at least implicitly, "doctrinal authority." These passages, which are highlighted by their special introductory formula, are the ban on killing innocent life (quoted above) and two others that apply that judgment to abortion (EV #62) and euthanasia (EV #65). The highest magisterial authority, then, is claimed precisely at those points that spell out the content of "intrinsically evil acts." Admittedly there is something confusing about the status of such "not-quite-dogmatic" formulations; nevertheless it confirms the importance of the doctrine[6] for the moral theology of the Roman magisterium, as illustrated by the quotation with which we began, words that contain its material application. In a densely packed definition, *Veritatis Splendor* describes those acts as *intrinsece malum* which are evil "*always and per se,* in other words, on account of their very object, and quite apart from the ulterior intentions of the one acting and the circumstances" (VS #80). The interesting question is precisely what this definition rules out when it refuses to admit criteria on the basis of which we could so evaluate an act as to emancipate us from "simple obedience." We do not have to look far to find candidates: they range from "conscience" to "circumstances," from "good ends" to "good consequences" and "good reasons"; even "decision" — a favorite child of moral philosophy — has its wings clipped. For when we have to do with acts that are evil in and of themselves, there is nothing to decide, there are no options to

---

5. *Frohbotschaft des Lebens.* Commentary by M. Balkenohl, epilogue by Luitpold A. Dorn (Stein a. Rhein: Christiana Verlag, 1995), p. 140.

6. The doctrine is found as early as in Aristotle, who calls adultery, theft, and murder "intrinsically negative acts," to which his theory of "the mean" cannot be applied. "These and all other like things are blamed as being bad in themselves and not merely in their excess of deficiency. It is impossible therefore to go right in them; they are always wrong; rightness and wrongness in such things (e.g., in adultery) does not depend on whether it is the right person and occasion and manner, but the mere doing of any one of them is wrong" (*Nicomachean Ethics* 1107a, 12-17).

choose among, nothing to reason about, nothing to weigh up. They have simply to be avoided.

Since conscience is the site of these deliberations and decisions, the pope first makes clear (VS #54-64) that conscience, whatever its importance, cannot function as the final appeal in moral questions. It is the means of applying natural or moral law to concrete cases; it cannot be elevated to become the *source or criterion* of the good.[7] Conscience as the court of final appeal in deliberation and decision is the common factor in those moral theories which the pope rejects under the designation "teleological." By this he means that family of concepts which make the judgment on an act depend not only on its *content,* strictly defined, but on the quality of the subjective intention, the foreseeable consequences ("consequentialism") or the proper weighing-up of goods ("proportionalism," VS #65-78). The essential conviction which underlies talk of "intrinsically evil acts" is that the basic opposition of good and evil cannot be reduced to the relative oppositions of good and better or good and less good. Since we cannot decide for ourselves about good and evil, and are therefore dependent upon "the one who alone is good" (Matt. 19:17, VS #9), the moral quality of an act can be called "good" only insofar as it is capable *"of being ordered* to God" (VS #78). Here I understand the logic of the pope's argument to be as follows: If we ask what acts are exclusively God's prerogative to undertake, that will provide a key to what must be "intrinsically evil" in terms of human action and fall under the divine prohibition. "It is mine to put to death and to bring to life," says the Lord (Deut. 32:39). This must exclude any act that would take the divine privilege into human hands, disposing of life itself in its beginnings, its nurture, or at its end. This, I think, must be the reason why the pope views the "sacredness" and "inviolability" of human life to be at the very heart of the Ten Commandments, concentrated in the command "Thou shalt not kill." The commandments stand, he says with St. Augustine, "at the outset of ethics." Keeping them intact is the condition *sine qua non* that allows the positive aspects of the moral life to flower. Foundational, then, we may conclude so far, to any morality or ethical theory, the commands are not in need of justification, simply of obedience. But to this question of the relation

7. For a more detailed discussion of the role of conscience, see Theodor Dieter's contribution in this volume.

between command and justification we must attend in greater detail, since it is the framework within which we can read the doctrine of "intrinsically evil acts" in the strongest sense. In what follows I propose a reading of this doctrine that in some respects goes further than what the encyclicals say explicitly but is, I believe, consistent with their general line of argument. From time to time, however, I mark points of disagreement.

2. Basic Problems

(a) Command and Justification: Living Within Creaturely Bounds

To say that divine commands are not subject to rational justification means, to put it positively, that they describe the limits of creaturely life: life that neither has nor wills to have absolute self-disposal. This point may come to the fore when we place the two encyclicals side by side. For the acts that are denounced in *Evangelium Vitae* as assaults on human life are not mere occasional infringements of the commands; they go hand in hand with a diminishing sense of the commands as elementary statements that correspond in their very form to the creatureliness of human life. It is not simply that these commands approve of life and protect it. Their function is not independent of their form, that is, their apodictic phrasing as straightforward affirmations without explanation. This should not be taken as a defect demanding to be made good by a series of moral rationalizations or as a hangover from the age of "heteronomy." Their "nonfoundational" character *(Begründungslosigkeit)* means, rather, that we should neither admit nor submit to any pressure to justify them. The commands that function to promote and protect life do so *only while they are not understood functionally but apodictically,* that is, while they are not subjected to legitimation at the court of any other rationality than their own.

It follows, then, that obedience to the commands does not come from acknowledging some ground of justification for them but from the logic of the First Commandment itself. This again has no ground of justification; but it does have a preamble, "I am the LORD your

God." Obeying God's instructions, then, is no more and no less than living as God's creature; it means not presuming to "invent oneself," not even to invent one's own morality! Notice a distinction here: the "life" which the commands have in view, and which intrinsically evil acts destroy, is not "life in and of itself" but, quite precisely, life within creaturely bounds. That "life as the highest good" is not simply "life as such" does not, perhaps, emerge consistently and unambiguously from the encyclicals. In fact, talk of "life" in *Evangelium Vitae* is problematically smooth in that it relates the general human (biological) existence all too harmoniously to its eschatological coming into life in Christ.[8] Yet at least the pope's discussion of the moral significance of the martyrs leaves us no room to suspect a vitalism in Christian dress. Talk about the "value of life," whatever contingent features may be mentioned, is essentially about that creaturely life which, in the last analysis, would rather die than live in contradiction to God's commands (EV #47). It is, I think, along these lines that one can understand best the critical remarks of the pope about research in gene-technology, *in vitro* fertilization, and the artificial prolongation of life. Do practices like that not aim at preserving and producing life "as such," *while transgressing the limits of creaturely life?*

Perhaps the expression "foundationless commands," as I suggested it, may strike some as too sweeping. Not only is the history of

---

8. The problem of the wide analogical use of "life" in EV is traced back by Oliver O'Donovan to the surprisingly marginal role played by the cross and resurrection in John Paul's argument. While Saint Paul from this angle had kept his talk of "life" in an essential tension ("It is sown a perishable body, it is raised an imperishable"), the papal argument lacks this tension and is therefore in fact less capable of performing theological cultural-criticism than it intends. What it overlooks is that the modern "culture of death" has or even is at its root a certain "culture of life." It is exactly the unsaturated greed for life, the desperate attempt to give meaning to its limited time, which brings about the "culture of death." Therefore O'Donovan rightly brings a stark charge against the pope's analogical vision of "life": "with only categories of life-enhancement at his disposal, he ends up reinforcing certain vitalist perceptions which are fueling the cultural conflagration that he can dispute so forcefully." See O'Donovan's review of EV in *Studies in Christian Ethics* 9 (1996): 93-94. A similar smoothness characterizes John Paul's concept of "law" — a concept that in its linearity (from teacher in moral life to its fulfilling with the help of Christ) has no room for the biblical notion of the law that puts to death. See the contributions by Reinhard Hütter and Gilbert Meilaender in this volume.

moral thought full of such justifications for divine commands, but
one can find them in the Bible too. Yet they are more "reasons of"
than "reasons for," they are rather *explications* than *justifications* in the
strong foundational sense, that is, supporting the validity of the command itself. By displaying the beneficial circumstances that attend
obedience *for God's sake,* they describe the working-out of the command — its "blessing," one might say — rather than its "ends." In
traditional teleological terms we can express this by saying that *telos*
has two senses. It can mean the consequent explanation of a command
which clarifies its sense; alternatively it can mean an *ulterior* end. An
ulterior end is pursued by "means"; the "sense" of something, on the
other hand, is the illumination of what that thing really is. There is
no formal intellectual technique by which the light can be turned on;
it simply has to *dawn.* Talk of the "sense" safeguards us against the
idea that the reasoning is somehow manipulable — provided that we
are not misled into a literal understanding of what it means to "make"
sense! So we may speak of the commands as unfounded in a primary
sense, while allowing that they are open to explanation. Explanation
is not a way of justifying the command, yet it is not superfluous or
marginal. Why should we not be allowed or authorized to explain the
commands of a God who loves humankind in terms of his love? That
the commands are unfounded, in a primary sense, does not imply any
form of absolutism; on the contrary, it requires that explanation should
be forthcoming.[9] From here we can see another point: Unless we
grasp this decisive aspect of the commands, their foundationless status,
we will not see how the acts which they exclude can have a quality in
themselves which is independent of their ends. For a rational foundation has to be given in terms of ulterior ends that make the command and its observance intelligible. But ends are always sovereign
over means; they can always be pursued in more than one way and
through different types of acts. So the apodictic form of the command,
excluding absolutely certain definite ways of acting, will be analytically

9. VS, too, talks of the "need to find ever more consistent rational arguments in
order to justify the requirements and to provide a foundation for the norms of the
moral life" (VS #74). From the logic of the irreducible validity of commands, it
should be clear that this can only be a weak notion of "justification" that does not
claim a foundational status.

meaningless. For if the end of a command can be described in itself — as the logic of justification assumes — one cannot evade the possibility that some action may be eligible as a means which the wording of the command actually excludes. Though this may be seen as exceptional, it reveals a connection that is true in principle: the logic of rational foundation and ulterior ends is at the same time the demonstration of, and the instrument for, the "value-creating" sovereignty of the acting subject. Put theologically: the justification of the command lays claim upon the very position which belongs to the First Commandment and its preamble.

Objecting to the "tyranny of foundations," Robert Spaemann[10] has introduced some fresh considerations into the discussion that cohere with the position I have outlined so far. He describes ethics as the *"Regellehre des Handelns"* — the doctrine of rules of action.[11] This may serve as a reminder of Wittgenstein's argument, that rules cannot be justified; for that would presuppose there was a knowledge of the "end" (purpose) of the game which could exist apart from the rules. In fact, all we can say is, "then the game is not played properly"; and when we describe the game itself, all we can do is refer back to the rules that constitute it. One rule may be explained by reference to another, the second by reference to a third. The whole sequence of explanations cannot, however, itself be explained. There is no "original" rule to which all these explanations can be taken back. But Spaemann offers a further thought, helpful in our context: a rationally justified ethic would be an "eschatological idea" that presupposed that the endless discourse of reasons and counterreasons could be brought to a conclusion within time. Action, however, is always by its very nature limited in time; *ars longa, vita brevis* (p. 77). Every foundation for moral reasoning, then, we may conclude, is forced to occupy an eschatological standpoint that goes beyond the state of creaturely life: as though all the consequences of an action really could be foreseen;

10. "Wovon handelt die Moraltheologie?" in *Einsprüche: Christliche Reden* (Einsiedeln: Johannes, 1977). Numbers in parentheses refer to the pages of this volume.

11. Spaemann, too, points out that justifications for the essential moral norms are secondary and assume their validity. The freedom from foundational justifications explains why, as Spaemann sees it, secondary justifications of one and the same norm can have historical variation, partly as a result of the development of differing philosophical categories that do not have to be as homogenous as the norm itself.

as though the ends really could be completely explored; as though all goods really could be weighed upon a single pair of scales. Spaemann does not deny that the Christian ethos can be described in teleological terms. But the form the *telos* assumes is quite strange. Since it is the praise of God, it cannot be *put to work* in any way. The *telos* of the Christian ethos is as distant from any worldly *telos* as faith is from any "motive" of action. God is glorified when his commands are obeyed, and this obedience is not regarded as the object of any "decision." Otherwise one would apply the hermeneutics of suspicion, the distinction between "saying and meaning," to the divine commands; as if their verbal sense were different from what they were really after. Here, again, we meet the "transcendent" point of view which does not honor God *as* God, but thinks it has to *do* him some honor: of rehabilitating him before the court of reason as a "good" God, or of showing that the commands are, despite their unpleasant taste, really quite well meant. But when the law of God is celebrated — as in the *cantus firmus* of *Evangelium Vitae* — as the "law of life" (Sirach 17:11), what is meant is that the commands serve the will of God for human life. That will, however, is and will always be the will of the *living* God. So we cannot "see into" it, strip off the commands which "provisionally express" it, and take it over as a perspective of moral theology which may then be given effect in ways which even, from time to time, may make us so free as to dispense with the commands.[12] With the commands, as Spaemann puts it, there is always a "hard core" beyond the scope of deliberation. That unarguable character attaches to the fundamental goods: of life (do not kill!), of language (do not bear false witness! for as language is ordered to communication, it may not be made a means of deception), and of sexuality (for like life and language sexuality is not an instrument that serves other ends, but is an end in itself, an element of life; pp. 86-88).

These considerations afford a better view of the status and role which belong to such conceptions as "life," "nature," and "person" in moral discussion. They are not terms of justification; they do not

---

12. That we cannot see into God's will does not, as Josef Fuchs thinks, argue against the idea of an absolutely valid command, but, on the contrary, dissuades us from trying to get "behind" it to the author's "deeper motivation." See "Die sittliche Handlung: das intrinsece malum" in *Moraltheologie im Abseits?* p. 183.

refer to things which might provide a rational argument for the validity of a moral norm. Rather, they indicate the scope of the foundational moral rule and its unarguable claim. They mark out the sphere in which it is not something *for* or *about* human beings that is at stake, but living human beings themselves, a sphere in which you cannot think distinctly about ends, since the human being is, so to speak, an end. A term like "person" is really a *critical notion.* If we thought such a term referred to a particular kind of entity, the logic of the commands would have been abandoned. This may address a certain tension in the argument of the encyclicals. Natural law reasoning and personalism may create the impression that "personality" is a sort of substance that revelation can disclose and liturgy reinforce. Here we should recall Nietzsche's insight when he attacked supposed "absolute" moral values such as "preservation and advancement of humankind" with the words: "But this definition is an expression of the desire for a formula, and nothing more. Preservation *of what?* is the question one immediately has to ask. Advancement *to what?*"[13] Indeed, Peter Singer's argument about abortion and euthanasia shows how the concept of "person," invoked to determine the "value of life," can lead to the opposite side of the street from the pope.[14] But instead of treating the concept of "person" as a "purely moral notion," distinct from the concept of human life and qualifying it, Christians ought to be clear that notions of that kind serve an *ostensive* function. They represent something that attaches to human life as a God-given quality, not, in a faculty-psychology sense, something that belongs to it. On the horizon of the pope's argument, on the one hand, we can at least discern this emphasis: "The Gospel of God's love for man, the Gospel of the dignity of the person and the Gospel of life are a single and indivisible Gospel" (EV #2). Yet the fact that this needs to be said points to the danger we have mentioned, the danger to which a natural law argument is exposed by its leaning towards foundational concepts. Here we face a tension within the pope's argument of which he does

13. Friedrich Nietzsche, *Daybreak: Thoughts on the Prejudices of Morality,* trans. R. J. Hollingdale (Cambridge: Cambridge University Press, 1982), p. 61.

14. See Berthold Wald, "Über den Mißbrauch des Personenbegriffs zur Rechtfertigung von Abtreibung und Euthanasie," *Zeitschrift für Medizinische Ethik* 42 (1996): 79-89.

not seem to be fully aware. At least when we understand the doctrine
of intrinsically evil acts along the lines of "foundationlessness," as I
have tried to show it is understood best, the encyclical's leaning toward
foundational concepts such as "person" may seem to unwillingly
weaken the theological thrust of the doctrine, since the doctrine itself,
by its very logic, resists the tyranny of foundations in that it supposes
a kind of quality that acts have in themselves, their "object." To the
meaning of this term we now turn.

(b) What Have I Done? The Objective Teleology of Acts

From the perspective of the encyclical neither the subjective intention
nor the circumstances nor the consequences of an act are at the center
of moral judgment. Instead: "The primary and decisive element for
moral judgment is the object of the human act, which establishes
whether it is *capable of being ordered to the good and to the ultimate end,
which is God*" (VS #79). But how are we to conceive of the "object"
of an act? It is, as I wish to suggest, best understood from the angle
of "objective teleology."[15] According to Aristotle, acts can be seen as
part of a more encompassing activity *(praxis),* to which they are
directed as a *telos.* And what he describes at the beginning of the
Nicomachean Ethics in terms of the teleological relation of different
"arts" to each other, we can conceive of the relation of "practice" and
"praxis" as well. When someone plays the flute, for example, she is
making music; she participates in the good called "music" and at the
same time contributes to its continuation. This would be the case even
if the flute-player only intended to do breathing-exercises with a
resonant piece of wood. Proximate ends like this are compatible with,
and connected to, the real *telos* of the activity. (The connection can be
grasped, by listener as well as player, with very different emotional
responses; this, though, does not affect the connection as such.) So it

---

15. VS does not use this term in order to describe its own position but reserves
the term "teleological" for theories it rejects as "consequentionalist" or "proportionalist." Here the pope conforms to a tendency, prevalent since the fifties, to
reduce the scope of teleology and misses, in my opinion, an opportunity to clarify
the issue.

would be unreasonable to deny the connection of an action and its *telos;* yet the reasonableness in question here is quite different from the reasonableness of a particular act when we judge it in conformity with natural reason or some other kind of rationality. This difference is implied by the logic of intrinsically evil acts in the encyclical. The correspondence of act and *telos* applies negatively, too; and the fact that those who perform such acts delude themselves precisely about that correspondence makes them even more disastrous. A "deed" can only be an "action" if the subjective intention *(finis operantis)* is coherent with the objective *telos* of the activity *(finis operis)* in which the action participates. Without music there would be no playing on the flute or harp, and so on. For then we would never recognize these performances as action-complexes that are part of some *"praxis."* They would be breathing-exercises with wood, finger-exercises with strings; they would have nothing to do with each other. To perform an action, however, always means to participate in a teleological nexus of connections that is laid out before us in advance. The agent does not have the *telos* of her action at her disposal; the *telos* cannot be "posited" in terms of sheer intentionality. In this respect, the problem with the subjective-teleological theories that are under fire from the pope's argument is not that they would deny objective teleology altogether. They do, however, seem to assume that when it comes to making moral judgments, subjective *teloi* can be weighed on the same pair of scales as objective ones.

Thomas Aquinas put the connection of the "object of an action" in quaestio 18 of the prima secundae like this: The moral evaluation of an action presupposes a teleological framework. Just as each movement receives its species from the *telos* it is directed to, the species of an action is given from the object it is directed to. It is from this object that an action receives its very form, it is its *"materia circa quam"* (a.2). Though the object determines "in a primary and fundamental way" the moral quality of an action, beside this main source there are other sources of morality that Aquinas points to: the "circumstances" and "ends" of an action. The decisive fact, however, is that only all these sources together determine the morality of an action. Here Aquinas quotes Dionysius: "Quilibet singularis causa defectus malum, bonum autem causatur ex integra causa." An action, to be good, must be good in every respect. However: If it is bad in respect to its object, it can be healed neither by good ends nor by the circumstances (a.4, ad 3). To take the latter into account — if someone has, for example, stolen many things or only a few — will affect the judgment only in terms of moderation, never in its substance.

Consider how the problem of abortion throws this connection into sharp relief. Can a physician who has performed an abortion claim that he *simply* helped a woman in need? This end, honorable as it is in itself, cannot be presented as the "meaning" of his act. For the object of the practice is the killing of a human being. This teleological clarification helps us see why it is logically right to keep speaking of "the life of the unborn child." For if the *personal object* of the act is the child,[16] it cannot be left out of the description, reduced to a mere state of the mother's health, which can be altered by an intervention ("interruption of pregnancy"!). If the objective teleology of such an act is clearly in view, the justification needed for it appears in a different light as well. For then the justification, to be really justification, has to give account of *what the life is* which will be erased, *what the death means* to which we sentence a human being, and *to what extent* another mortal may claim such authority over it. So the justification of abortion and acts like it must go into all those "nice metaphysical points" that we are usually glad to confine to the nooks and crannies of theology and keep off the grass of everyday life. Nothing less, however, is logically required to justify such acts — leaving aside the question of whether the justification in any given case is self-consistent and conforms to the basic principles of any given morality, humanist or Christian. The accusation, then, of "not keeping to the point that really counts in practice" is not to be made against those who try to keep these questions alive in the debate. On the contrary, it is they who keep completely to the point, that is, to the object and *telos* of the act in question, by insisting that there are no short cuts when it comes to justifying it.

16. The identification of the personal object is part of the identification of the object of an act in terms of its content or substance. For only if that is made clear, can it be said to affect this person (and not that), or to affect this person in a primary way though affecting others as well. To be sure, an abortion affects always both, woman and child. But the difference as to what "to be affected" for each means — to be killed or to face hardships — may not be leveled in moral respect. Here talk of the "personal object" of an act, as I suggest it, may serve as a reminder for this much-overlooked necessity.

What is at stake here can be nicely illustrated by the example of the modification of the German abortion-law recently carried through by the federal state of Bavaria. The German law stipulates that an abortion may be performed with impunity in the first trimester if the woman has first undergone a compulsory but "open-ended" process of counseling. The Bavarian "extra" extends the mother's duty to accept counseling to a duty to give reasons. The reasons for the abortion must be given in the course of the counseling, though no evaluation of the reasons is made before the certificate of counseling is issued. This "extra" has been heavily under fire in public debate: it is said to impose yet another "humiliation" upon the woman. At first hearing this may sound strange, assuming that it is the mark of a responsible person to give an account of what she is doing. Should not this duty to give reasons be taken as a sign not of women's humiliation but that they are taken seriously as independent agents?

Yet the emotional intensity of the debate is explicable when we look at it from a different angle. What is at issue in the duty to give reasons is more than the imposition as a duty of an explanation that would otherwise, in the normal course of things, be offered quite spontaneously. It brings into view the fact *that the proposed act cannot be justified at all.* "Reasons" in this case — so it seems to be felt — must be something more than an account of the motives, something more than a description of the situation and the pressures it imposes. These could at most explain why a woman, or a couple, would have serious difficulties having a baby in the circumstances (or, analogously, looking on at the suffering of a dying person). But this is no sort of reason for killing. If justification *for this action* is needed, most of the explanations, statements, and arguments seem completely inappropriate. They would never be enough — even to the minds of most of those who give them — to justify the killing of a dependent human being. Is it, perhaps, an inkling of this fact that makes the duty to give reasons seem gratuitously officious? If one really wanted to take up the challenge, one would either *knowingly* act without sufficient reason, or one would avoid the action altogether, or, a third possibility, one would adopt the type of argument that someone like Peter Singer advances. This, however, is extremely unpopular, since it lets the morality we practice see itself in the mirror of the theory that corresponds to it, expressed in language of such clarity that most people would be

ashamed. The same point could be made analogously for euthanasia.
To say "to end her suffering" would not really answer the question
posed by the act, "What are you doing, if you . . . ?" A real reason
would have to be something like: "Because all suffering is meaningless
unless it leads to new possibilities of life, because 'life' is simply the
living-out of the personal powers to consume, to enjoy, to achieve
etc., and because the right to life is tied to the exploitation of such
powers."

If the object, or primary *telos,* of an action is decisive for moral
judgment, that does not mean, as we have seen in Aquinas's argument,
that collateral ends which may ensue from it, or subjective intentions,
are ruled out of account.[17] Yet how we weigh them will be governed
by the object of the act itself. If killing innocent life is evil in itself,
collateral ends may qualify, but clearly cannot alter substantially, the
way we judge such an act. But the crucial role of the object requires
us to go further into that connection. It also means that even the
motives *as such* cannot be evaluated in isolation from the *telos* of the
action. Killing for compassion, for example, cannot be analyzed simply
as an intrinsically evil act performed with a good intention. It is more
appropriate to say that the intrinsically evil act affects the evaluation
of the supposedly good intention. The object of the act exposes the
motive as "false mercy," which differs from true mercy in that one
does not stand by the sufferer in his or her suffering but finds both
the other's pain and one's own compassion unendurable.[18] The essential problem with the overvaluing of motives, intentions, and ends,
however, is its tendency to treat the whole burden of justification as
a sideshow, thus concealing the fact that for the act in question — in
the moral judgment of most people, not to mention Christians — no
justification at all can be given. This tendency, of which moral theologians, Protestant as well as Catholic, are not wholly innocent, has a

17. The distinction between *finis proximus* and *fines remoti* is found in Aquinas
just at the beginning of the moral-theological treatise in *Summa Theologiae* 1.2 q 1,3
ad 3: "One and the same act, in so far as it proceeds from the agent, is ordained to
but one proximate end, from which it has its species; but it can be ordained to several
remote ends, of which one is the end of the other."

18. The distinction between true and false mercy, made in EV #66f. with respect
to euthanasia, should be read in connection to the general observation in VS #70:
"Consequently, *the fundamental orientation can be radically changed by particular acts.*"

serious effect on the morality of everyday life and the level at which it is discussed.

This shift away from the object may contribute to the well-reported fact that many women who have had abortions suffer grave psychological strain and are haunted by the question "What have I done?" This question haunts them, not because moral agencies impose it from outside, but because it cannot be answered while the object of the action is suppressed. Whatever is suppressed will raise its head again. The psychological preoccupation with the question "What have I done?" may suggest that the answers we have given so far, and others have urged on us, have not hit the mark. Did we really "decide according to the circumstances"? Did we really "protect a future baby's right to be a wanted child"? Did we really "acknowledge our own limitations"? and so on. All hope of a real answer to our question, and a deliverance from its insistent presence, has to begin from viewing the act frankly in terms of its objective teleology, facing up to the fact that we have killed our child. Good therapy and pastoral care will encourage us to confront this reality and not let us be lured back into the swamp of rationalizations that can afford no absolution.

So far we have tried to show how the doctrine of intrinsically evil acts can be seen as a serviceable way of focusing moral judgment on the heart of the matter, the object of the act. But now we have to turn our attention to how the *subject* of the act relates to its object. This relation is dealt with in the encyclicals in terms of *intention*. "The morality of the human act depends primarily and fundamentally on the 'object' rationally chosen by the deliberate will" (VS #78). To distinguish this concept of intention from that of subjective teleology, one must emphasize the terms "rationally" and "deliberate will": "rationally" is to be understood in terms of the *internal* rationality of acting, by which the acting person knows and wills what she is doing. That is to say, she has "deliberately . . . chosen" the intrinsic object of the action. As distinct from mere reaction or behavior, an action is distinguished by a rationality of its own, in which the subjective *telos* coincides with the objective, by deliberate choice of the will, and at the same time chooses the proper means. This feature is, or should be, as the encyclical makes clear, the normal case; and principles of moral judgment should be based on this rather than on the exceptional case where subjective and objective *telos* fall apart.

The normal case also underlies the assertion that to grasp the object of an action one must "place oneself *in the perspective of the acting person*" (VS #78). If, then, the intention cannot be separated from the object, and the object is the content of the intentional action, the judgment about the act cannot be split up into a morally significant intention on the one hand and a morally neutral state-of-affairs that it brings about on the other. As Martin Rhonheimer[19] has shown, that way of seeing it could arise only from an *observer's point of view* that would neglect the *act of intending* (p. 11). It would lose sight of both the act of intending and the *specific relation* that the agent has to the personal object of the act. In the observer's perspective there is no difference between causing someone's death and killing that person. The morally significant feature of an abortion, for example, would not be the *intentional destruction* of the unborn child but merely the *intention that led to* interruption of the pregnancy. Here Rhonheimer points to the important distinction between the desirability of a state of affairs (say, that someone will die soon) and the goodness of an action. One can properly say, "It is good that he has finally died," but not, "It would be good to make him die." The goodness of a state of affairs cannot serve unaided as the criterion for determining the goodness of an act. The class of absolute prohibitions always relates to some *intentional action,* that is to say *the* action taken as a whole, never to mere intentions, effects or states of affairs, or to some "wider" context composed of these elements.

Yet there are recognized cases in which it appears as if the object of the action is being redefined in terms of ulterior intentions. So the killing of a human being in capital punishment, for example, is described as an act of punishment the *telos* of which does not really lie in the killing of the criminal but in the reestablishment of justice. Similarly in the case of killing in self-defense, it is said that the death of the aggressor is a collateral consequence taken into calculation but not chosen as the end of the action. This classical form of argument, which is also advanced by the encyclical (EV #55), could simply mean: The attribution in this case of a morally different object (self-defense)

---

19. "'Intrinsically Evil Acts' and the Moral Viewpoint: Clarifying a Central Teaching of Veritatis Splendor," *The Thomist* 58 (1994): 1-39. Numbers in the text refer to pages in this volume.

to an act phenotypically identical with another (killing), is not a subjective or arbitrary redetermination, but is authorized by the logic of social institutions. Within the institutional framework of the law, this action has *objectively* a distinct object, so that it is not included in the prohibition of killing. Now the illuminating feature of the encyclical's argument is this: it is *precisely because* the magisterium reckons with institutionally authorized redeterminations of the object of an act that it reacts as sharply as it does against recent tendencies toward public legitimation of abortion and euthanasia. Those offenses cannot be interpreted along the lines of legitimate killing such as capital punishment, as though the child were an aggressor to one's own life (i.e., one's life plan or pattern) that had to be repelled or punished. No authority in the world may redefine the object of *those* actions, which is always the killing of dependent and innocent life.

(c) Community and Moral Language: The Moral Notions of the Church

As these examples reveal, the task of moral judgment is always connected to the task of description. Moral notions must be given clarity, as must the subsuming of given performances and relations under them. Even the brief apodictic phrases of the Ten Commandments are not unambiguous by themselves, but only when they are heard within a particular community that has learned to understand such moral notions as "murder" in the right way, that is to say, has grasped their scope. So the Fifth Commandment, for example, rests upon a linguistic convention by which the children of Israel know when a killing is murder and when it is allowed or even required. The short version "You shall not kill" presupposes an extended casuistry in the minds of the hearers that is heard together with the command itself.[20] In other words, the exceptions (legitimate killing, capital punishment, holy war, etc.) are already expressed in the linguistic convention, so that the prohibition of killing as "murder" claims unconditional and exceptionless validity. This example, again, illustrates the meaning of

20. See Bruno Schüller, *Die Begründung sittlicher Urteile. Typen ethischer Argumentation in der Moraltheologie,* 2d ed. (Düsseldorf: Patmos, 1980), pp. 17-26.

the intention of an action and the inherent task of description. It can only be called murder if the act has been performed with the deliberate will to kill; therefore the passage of *Evangelium Vitae* quoted at the beginning of this article necessarily stresses the notions "innocent" and "voluntarily" in order to exclude the matters of capital punishment and legitimate killing from that "killing" which is absolutely prohibited. Thus the encyclical makes a sharp distinction: it will always be necessary to attend to the intention in order to clarify the meaning of the action, that is, to recognize *which* action is in question. So the killing of a fatally ill person as an unintended consequence of giving a high dose of painkiller is described and evaluated in a fundamentally different way from intentional killing in the sense of "assisted death." Only the latter can be called "euthanasia" and regarded as a grave sin. In that instance, however, the secondary intention to put an end to suffering cannot serve as justification for the "intrinsically evil act" (EV #64f). Along these lines of thought, the description of abortion as murder (EV #58) is consistent, while it would be a grave *moral* misjudgment to describe as abortion, say, the loss of a baby due to carelessness.

These descriptive considerations remind us that the struggle for morality is always a struggle for language. For language is permeated with moral judgments. Its use within a linguistic community represents, as Wittgenstein has impressively demonstrated, not merely an agreement in definitions but an "agreement in judgments."[21] In the linguistic memory, this is particularly the case with value-terms which, as "moral notions,"[22] carry within their descriptions a moral judgment. We can appreciate the force of the prophetic denunciation of those who corrupt the judging function of language: "Woe to those who call evil good and good evil, who put darkness for light and light for darkness, who put bitter for sweet and sweet for bitter" (Isa. 5:20).

The care of language, which must be recalled as a primary task of theological ethics, implies a critical turn against an increasingly dominant fashion for "objective" or "neutral" patterns of description, which veil the real *actions* by refusing to articulate the judgment. Talk of "assisted death," for example, cannot be allowed to presume in

21. *Philosophical Investigations* #242.
22. Julius Kovesi, *Moral Notions* (London & New York, 1967).

favor of an action the object of which is to kill a person. To help a dying person die should mean to accompany the process helpfully instead of breaking it off prematurely. Following the logic of moral notions a statement like this from the encyclical may seem superfluous: "Procured abortion is the deliberate and direct killing, by whatever means it is carried out, of a human being" (EV #58). Since "abortion" as a term of moral judgment (and perhaps the name of a legal offense) already contains this definition, it may seem tautological. Yet it is necessary to repeat definitions as a reminder when moral notions begin to be dissolved by the superimposition of alien teleologies. This, of course, is the pope's diagnosis of our times and the reason for his recalling the linguistic tradition of the church, that has (in contrast to its pagan neighbors) always called both infanticide and abortion murder, for it saw human life at every moment from conception as the "personal object(s) of God's loving and fatherly providence" (EV #61 with supporting references). This reminder is not only a criticism of neutral language ("fetus," "cell-cluster," etc.); it implies, as the pope sees it, that the church itself is not authorized to redefine the object of these acts. The church, too, is included among those "authorities" that may not overstep their power in this respect.

Within such limits, however, we have always to struggle for clarity about which acts should fall under a certain moral description and which not. If, for example, Jesus radicalized the Jewish notion of adultery to encompass a betrayal of conjugal fidelity from *either* side, the church cannot go behind that description. Yet there will still have to be deliberation when new situations and possibilities, in terms of technology or politics, bring about new kinds of acts that must be subsumed under moral notions. In order to meet this challenge the encyclical goes into the relationship between contraception and abortion, pointing to the fact that some contraceptives are really means of abortion (EV #13).

Yet the way these judgments are reached and the points they make in detail are controversial. And here a critical question arises: Given the social-linguistic character of moral language, how can the pope insist on specific attributions and judgments that are (as in the case of artificial contraception) not accepted either by the majority of moral theologians or by the members of the church? Will his persuasive reminder of the fact that there are intrinsically evil acts — a point

hardly ever denied by such people — not be weakened by such isolated judgments on specific matters? Such questions,[23] as I see it, are
no less justified than the central teaching itself. The social validity of
the doctrine of intrinsically evil acts will always be as strong as the
praxis of judgment within a church called to the *common* effort of
proving which acts fall under which descriptions.

In Thomas Aquinas the possibility of identifying the object of an
action (and, in some cases, distinguishing it from its phenotype) has
to do with the "order of reason." His example is taking another's
property. It is usually irrelevant for moral judgment where it is taken
from — a house or a garden or wherever — since stealing is stealing.
But when it comes to robbing temples, it is another matter. The object
of this act, phenotypically identical to other thefts, is different. It has
changed because of the special nature of the place. It is no longer
simply a theft but an act of sacrilege. The explanation Thomas gives
is that the "order of reason" makes theft from a holy place unthink-
able. Place, then, becomes a decisive factor for the definition of the
object of this act (*Summa Theologiae* 1.2.18, a10). The similarity between Thomas's conception and what we have spoken of in terms of
"social validity" is obvious. Thomas, however, thinks more in terms
of a natural reason, while we situate the rationality of a moral language
and its concepts within a "communicative reason" — which must
prove "the good and perfect will of God" (Rom. 12:2).[24]

---

23. One voice among many: Richard McCormick, "Killing the Patient," in
Considering "Veritatis Splendor."

24. Along these lines, Jean Porter ("The Moral Act in *Veritatis Splendor* and in
Aquinas's *Summa Theologiae:* A Comparative Analysis," in *Veritatis Splendor: American
Responses,* ed. Michael E. Allsopp and John J. O'Keefe [Kansas City: Sheed and Ward,
1995], pp. 278-95) is right to point out that the idea of an object of an action is not
meant to provide a formula to help us make up our minds about all possible acts in
advance. On the contrary, only when the object of an act is clear can the other elements
be identified as "mere circumstances" that will not substantially affect the judgment.
However, as we have seen, the object of an act is not identified sufficiently by a
phenotypical description; it is itself discerned by an act of judgment. That is why
Porter can conclude that "the determination of the object of an act is the *outcome* of
a process of moral evaluation, not its presupposition" ("The Moral Act," p. 284).
This conclusion is perfectly correct, but it leaves out a great deal. When a community
practices moral evaluation, the "outcome" is a series of moral notions, which *at the
same time* the ongoing practice *presupposes.* These notions are already in form, not only

After all, moral notions are not just "declared"; they are shaped by linguistic convention. Hence the importance of the places and relationships within which the language of a community is formed. In most cultures this is within a specific narrative tradition. Only within such a framework can the meaning of morally permeated terms and phrases be grasped. For here they are not isolated from concrete patterns of speech and action; their meaning is determined by their use within the narrative. What love means, for example, cannot be presumed as a piece of knowledge that will provide the key to a love story. Rather, the story tells us what love is about. From that we can understand why the encyclical rejects one way in which the fundamental option and concrete choice may be related, which would allow us to evaluate the option (to "love") apart from its use within the concrete story of love's decisions and actions (VS #68). In this way "love" would be merely a value or principle, the content of which one could no longer anticipate. To return, then, to the question of in what sense an action can be said to have an object: We cannot speak in this way of *isolated* acts, only of "actions," which derive their intelligibility from being part of recognizable types of conduct, represented and passed on through narratives that give shape to community-identity. Talk about the object of an action makes sense only in the context of a "praxis." This determines where, specifically, particular acts belong, that is, of what praxis they are the practices. To isolated individual acts, however, we can attribute no object — not, at any rate, without falling into a kind of "value-positivism." However, the fact that the object or meaning of an action cannot be decided apart from a praxis, is no argument for subjective types of teleology. A type of conduct, or praxis, cannot be referred to simply as a "situation" or "circumstance." It confers an objective generic description upon the act which characterizes it beyond the limits of its sheer particularity.

---

in process. Moreover they include a variety of specific types of act that have been taken to belong to them. So abortion is traditionally included under the prohibition of murder, and killing in self-defense is not; and this distinction now belongs to the concept of murder as we know it. A "new" moral question — such as the disposal of unwanted fertilized ova in vitro — must be decided not only on the basis of the logic of the concept as such, but in relation to the way this concept has been worked out in a variety of applications that the tradition has performed.

The dependence of moral notions on a community context points to another issue, too. We do not obey the commands for the sake of the good it will achieve, not even for the sake of the community's good, but for God's sake. Yet we are able to do so because and inasmuch as we have experienced the good that God has granted us in our community and which the commands have protected. So we do not *first* have the principle of sacredness-of-life and *then* refrain from abortion. Rather, our capacity and will to refrain has to do with whether we have experienced ourselves as children accepted and loved; whether we are taken seriously as persons in our formative social relations; whether we have been introduced to the world of the biblical narratives that shape our patterns of perception both emotionally and intellectually. Little, perhaps, has been so important over the centuries for the attitude of Christians towards abortion as the liturgical tradition of Advent and Christmas:[25] the story of the young woman who in dangerous circumstances is having a baby that she did not plan, the story of the child "jumping for joy in his mother's womb" as he encounters the unborn Messiah. And anyone who has learned to pray with the Psalmist, "You created my inmost being; you knit me together in my mother's womb. I praise you because I am fearfully and wonderfully made" (Ps. 139:13-14), will not leave it to the exclusive competence of scientific research to determine when one may begin to speak of human life. It is therefore much more than an afterthought when the encyclical finally points to the catechetical-liturgical dimension of the gospel of life that will be "celebrated" (EV #82-85).

The patterns of biblical language confer on us the skill that determines our capacity to describe situations and actions in a truthful way.[26] This descriptive capacity is the other side of the subjective clarity as to what kind of people we are. That, again, sheds a critical light upon talk about the "dignity" that is expressed in the woman's competence to make her own decisions. In speaking in this general way of "a decision" to be made there is a measure of descriptive

25. See Paul Ramsey, "Liturgy and Ethics," *Journal of Religious Ethics* 7 (1979): 162-63.

26. Stanley Hauerwas, *The Peaceable Kingdom: A Primer in Christian Ethics* (Notre Dame, Ind.: University of Notre Dame Press, 1983), pp. 124-25.

inadequacy. *What* action has to be decided upon; *how does that action impinge* upon the agent's being? Breezy talk about a "right — in the last instance — to make the decision" may not actually respect the woman's dignity at all. It may even deny her the dignity of being a self-directing person who can do very well without a decision of *that* sort. What if the "right to decide" only conceals the fact that the decision is being *forced upon her* by pressing her into a position where a decision must be made? Here the encyclical is right to indicate the problems of prenatal diagnosis, which too often simply *constructs* a dilemma to which eugenic abortion then presents itself as solution (EV #14).

If "decision" comes to mean simply the resolution of a dilemma in which one has to choose between inescapable alternatives, rather than as the forming of an action which flows authentically from the agent's own self-understanding and convictions, then we are not far from a moral syndrome to which we may give the name "sin-proportionalism." This syndrome adopts the language of forgiveness and instrumentalizes it. It has produced a tendency to treat the acknowledgment *wrung from* Dietrich Bonhoeffer that in taking definite responsibility we cannot remain free of sin as though it were a general commonplace. So we reach a kind of proportionalism that no longer distinguishes sin from obedience but only weighs different sins against each other. Since everything is, in a more or less rarefied way, sinful — having a baby in an overpopulated world, claiming the right to a disabled child who will cost the public as much as a terminally ill patient — the difference in the sins of abortion and euthanasia is merely relative. Where everything is sin, nothing is really sin. Faced with this sin-proportionalism even the Protestant interpreter cannot restrain a cheer at the pope's insistence on "especially grave sins." The leveling of sin corresponds to an equally sweeping kind of "forgiveness-talk": sin, of whatever color, can be forgiven. This "can" all too easily suggests a supposed moral duty on God's part, a kind of "divine fate" that derives from the inevitability of sin. When everything is sin, everything *must* be forgiven. By this means sin-proportionalism provides absolution in advance for the decision; and it is not a "truly free decision" unless it has absolution in advance. After all, the agent is then able to choose between options belonging to the *same* category: sin-that-can-be-forgiven. Over against this the encyclicals remind us that God graciously bestows on us the capacity to keep his commands and that "concrete possibilities" can only be discerned "in the mystery of Christ's redemption" (VS #103). With respect to sins already committed, however, the pope quotes the words of Cain: "My sin is greater than I can bear" (Gen. 4:13, EV #21) and addresses a special pastoral word to women who have had an abortion. Without prevarication he calls their action "terribly wrong" and stresses the importance of facing up to it honestly. A word of forgiveness is not missing. But it is not delivered as a piece of information (". . . can be forgiven") but as a summons, "Give yourselves over . . . to repentance. The Father of mercies is ready to give you his forgiveness and his peace in the sacrament of reconciliation." God's forgiveness makes it possible also to ask forgiveness of the slain child, "who is now living in the Lord," and to become a witness for the right to life (EV #99).

3. How the Papal Teaching Relates to Reformation Ethics

(a) Convergence: The "Moral Meaning of the Body," the Neighbor, and Suffering

In considering the papal moral teaching in relation to Reformation ethics, my concluding observations will mark three points of convergence before turning to the most serious area of disagreement. First there is the emphasis on the *moral meaning of the human body.* To reckon with acts evil in themselves is to see whole human beings, in the inseparable unity of body and soul, as responsible subjects of their actions. So the doctrine resists the "personalist spiritualism"[27] that lurks in subjective-teleological concepts in that they tend to interpret bodily acts as material and instrumental to the purposes of the mental subject, which alone has moral significance (EV #18; VS #49). If the distinction between "fundamental option" and "concrete (bodily) acts" is understood in this way, it must rest on the unbiblical mind-over-matter

27. Martin Rhonheimer, *Natur als Grundlage der Moral. Die personale Struktur des Naturgesetzes bei Thomas von Aquin: Eine Auseinandersetzung mit autonomer und teleologischer Ethik* (Innsbruck/Vienna: Styra Verlag, 1987), p. 14.

metaphysics, in which moral significance is *attributed,* not present in the bodily act already.[28] The pope's high regard for the significance of the bodily dimension of acts could well have appealed to Luther, for whom bodily existence is at once the ground and the testing ground for good works. As Luther put it in his treatise *On the Freedom of a Christian,*[29] with the "outer man," who as a bodily being relates to himself and others, "works begin," while for the "inner man," man *coram Deo,* they have no meaning. In free submissive love our bodily outward-directed existence is conformed to the "new creation" that we have by God's grace become. So for Luther, too, the unity of the person is central, and any judgment on works flows out from it. "Consequently it is always necessary that the substance or person himself be good before there can be any good works." One is, however, according to Luther, a "person" not by virtue of a "spiritual core," to which the bodily existence should conform. Here one must remember Luther's turn against the Spiritualists, in that he sees the constitution of the "inner man" (i.e., "person") mediated exactly through the sensual means of word and sacraments: through the "ulterior word" that is spoken by human lips and cuts through to ears and hearts, through the waters of baptism that wet the skin, and through the gifts of the Eucharist that are smelled and tasted.

The second convergence concerns concrete neighborhood. While rule-utilitarian concepts have anybody and everybody potentially concerned in view, talk of intrinsically evil acts is, positively speaking, oriented to the *concrete* neighbor. It judges what A is doing to B in itself, and not by weighing up what consequences follow for C and D — the existing children of a couple contemplating abortion, the distressed relations of a candidate for "assisted death," the hopeful

---

28. For a philosophical deconstruction of the theory of a pre-bodily "meaning in the head," see Wittgenstein's analysis of pain and utterances of pain in *Philosophical Investigations.* See also Fergus Kerr, *Theology After Wittgenstein* (Oxford: Blackwell, 1986). Whether the idea of fundamental option should be understood in this sense is debatable. Josef Fuchs, for example, rejects the criticism of VS. Yet he seems to offer some evidence for this charge when he says, following Karl Rahner, that the "transcendental fundamental option" is present in the "core of the person" and therefore "at another level" from the concrete (bodily) acts ("Die sittliche Handlung," p. 24).

29. *The Freedom of a Christian,* trans. W. A. Lambert, Harold J. Grimm (from *Weimarer Ausgabe* 7, 20-38), *Luther's Works,* vol. 31 (Philadelphia: Fortress, 1957), p. 361.

beneficiary of organ-donation, or whomever. As we can speak of the object of an action as the *primary* end and *primary* consequence, so we can speak of a *primary* good: the life of the neighbor. There is moral sense, too, in the observation that not all relations are the same. There are primary relations which should be respected as such. We do not have responsibility for everybody but for those who are entrusted to us.[30] These are they, first of all, with whom we share certain morally characterized relationships in family, business, education, and so on. They do not constitute a statically defined group, the extent of which is limited in advance, for we can in principle be called upon to be a neighbor to *any* person. Yet that does not detract from the *concreteness* of the neighborly demand. Just as the encyclical points out that everybody is "his brother's keeper" (EV #19) and associates this with the priority of "those who are poorest, most alone and most in need" (EV #87), for Luther, too, the neighbor in his or her concrete need and predicament must be the measure and criterion for Christian action. "As our neighbor suffers hardship and is in need of our abundance . . . we should by our body and deeds help our neighbor without reward and everyone become a Christ for one another" (#27, Latin version).

The third convergence has to do with suffering as integral to the avoidance of intrinsically evil acts, and to obedience in general. While arguments for abortion and euthanasia tend to treat suffering as an absurd disaster, a denial, as it were, of God, which makes sense only in being eliminated, the encyclical states that suffering, when endured in faith, can turn out to be a "source of good" (EV #67). As for the practical difficulties that can motivate an abortion, it is said that they "can never exonerate from striving to observe God's law fully" (EV #13). Here, too, one has to remember that having children simply *does* involve suffering in the form of anxiety and disruption of our plans and of the patterns we have formed for our lives. Though there are, of course, differences in this respect that may be compensated for to an extent by fair policies, these can only be among relative degrees of suffering. Suffering does not function as a line *beyond which* decisions for abortion or euthanasia can be justified, thus weighing quality

---

30. See Robert Spaemann, "Wer hat wofür Verantwortung? Zum Streit um deontologische oder teleologische Ethik," *Herder Korrespondenz* 36 (1982): 348-50.

of life against life itself. What Luther has to say in his *Treatise on Good Works*[31] about suffering in faithfulness to God's commands can be read as a straightforward theological commentary on this point. While those without faith take suffering as "always an offense to them and harmful" and as caused by men and demons instead of God, for those who in their need have trust and confidence in God, sufferings may become "pure and precious merits, the costliest of treasures" (p. 28).

(b) Intrinsically Good Acts? Luther on Works of Faith

As can be inferred from the convergences described above, Luther would have had no problems with the idea of intrinsically evil acts as such, though his main interest is more in *good* deeds, as the positive side of Christian morality. Yet the connection is close. At the beginning of the same treatise Luther states: "there is no sin except that which God has forbidden. . . . Accordingly we have to learn to recognize good works from the commandments of God, and not from appearance, size or number of the works themselves, nor from the opinion of men or of human law or custom, as we see has happened and still happens because of our blindness and disregard of the divine commandments" (p. 23). The commands preserve us from falling prey to the "appearance" of works, that is to say, not knowing what we are really doing. So far, for Luther too, we can conclude, our actions have a kind of objective quality given them by their relation to the commands. This is so, since they derive their value not from "the opinion of men," not from our subjective opinions, intentions, or purposes, but from whether they are in accordance with the commands. Yet Luther goes deeper still, interpreting the "fulfilling of the commands" from the First Commandment, obedience to which is nothing more or less than faith, the "work of the First Commandment." So the idea of intrinsically evil acts is radicalized in the sense of Romans 14:13: "Whatever is not of faith, is sin." This, for Luther, can be said in reverse as well. Through faith, every deed is good without difference

---

31. *Treatise on Good Works,* trans. W. A. Lambert, James Atkinson (from *Weimarer Ausgabe* 6, 204-50), *Luther's Works,* vol. 44 (Philadelphia: Fortress, 1966). Numbers in the text refer to pages in this volume.

(p. 26). This has nothing to do with any intrinsic quality: "For the works are acceptable not for their own sake but because of faith" (p. 26). Good works, then, are characterized *from an ulterior point of reference*. They have an enhypostatic existence, so to speak: in faith, which is *God's* work in his people. Faith is, to be sure, neither a "motive" accompanying good deeds nor a *habitus*. It is itself a "work" that permeates every other work. It creates and implants a new *telos,* which is one and the same for every work of faith, the praise and glory of God. From this there follows an important corollary: "In this faith all works become equal, and one work is like the other; all distinctions between works fall away, whether they be great or small, short, long, many or few" (p. 26).

This, of course, sheds a critical light on Catholic teaching about "works of supererogation," a teaching found in the encyclicals, too, where the pope speaks of "heroic actions" that are "the most solemn celebration of the Gospel of life" (EV #86).[32] Luther, in contrast, affirms that "the higher and better the works are, the less show they make" (p. 41). They cannot be measured by their appearance, since their "perfection" is not intrinsic to them but conferred from beyond them, in their origin, which is faith, and their ultimate purpose, which is praise. The ulterior source of the goodness of good works poses the most serious question put to the papal teaching from the side of Reformation ethics: to what extent does it presuppose a systematic "knowledge" of the moral order or the moral law "from within," which can move confidently between a sphere of prohibitions (intrinsically evil acts), a sphere of duty (positive commands and the *nova lex* of the gospel of life), and a third realm of heroic and supererogatory

32. As an example of deeds that go beyond the commands, the pope mentions forgoing treatment with painkillers in order "to share consciously in the Lord's passion" (EV #65). It is remarkable, however, that apart from this outstanding heroism there is also praise for an "everyday heroism," for which the service and sacrifice of motherhood serves as an example (EV #86). This can be read at least as an approximation to Luther's revaluation of ordinary life — and perhaps as a cautious self-correction of the typical Catholic understanding of levels of moral achievement. As a further indication one may note the fact that the pope, in discussing the *locus classicus* of *"consilia evangelii"* does *not* claim Matthew 19:21 for that doctrine but takes Jesus' call to the young man as "meant for everyone" (VS #18). At the very least, the encyclicals display a certain ambivalence on this question, which is (consciously?) not resolved.

deeds? To the extent that moral theology proposes to retail such knowledge instead of giving "instruction in the art of correct asking about God's will and open hearing of God's command,"[33] an objection from the side of evangelical ethics cannot be suppressed. For God's will is not a scientific body of knowledge but something to be "proved" (Rom. 12:2), since it is always concrete. As we learn at any rate from Jesus' argument about the sabbath law, the claim to know the moral order can be used precisely to prevent such hearing and proving. Yet the doctrine of intrinsically evil acts, as should now be obvious, need not be put to that use. It is not, therefore, necessarily vulnerable to the critique of works-of-supererogation and of the systematized moral theology that goes with them. Used on its own proper terms the idea of intrinsically evil acts may teach us a way of asking about God's will *with the expectation that a concrete answer can be had.*[34]

33. Karl Barth, *The Christian Life: Church Dogmatics 4/4, lecture fragments,* trans. Geoffrey W. Bromiley (Grand Rapids: Eerdmans, 1981), p. 34.

34. I am extremely grateful to Oliver O'Donovan for having turned my poor English into real English and to Nancy Heitzenrater Hütter for having polished an earlier draft in that respect.

The Death Penalty in *Evangelium Vitae*

OLIVER O'DONOVAN

IN TAKING UP the question of the death penalty in *Evangelium Vitae,* we turn our attention to a matter that John Paul II hardly intended to be central. Abortion, euthanasia, and (to a lesser extent) suicide were the issues that moved him and shaped the thought of this encyclical; the death penalty is accorded one paragraph's discussion and a few brief allusions, and there is a note of uncertainty in what is said of it. The pope's publicists, however, in promoting the document in the weeks before it appeared, made rather a lot of the matter.[1] They evidently felt that the treatment of the death penalty offered a useful side-window on John Paul's doctrine of life that could go some way to offset the vulgar perception of him as a die-hard conservative. In the event those who looked for dramatic new departures must have been disappointed. Yet the publicists were not wrong, in my view, in thinking that the direction of John Paul's teaching can be gauged from this vantage point, and that it is not much out of tune with modern Western sensibilities.[2]

---

1. See *The Tablet,* 1 April 1995.
2. I must add a word to clarify the spirit in which I approach this discussion. Some aspects of this essay are critical; and anyone who criticizes John Paul II finds himself in the midst of a large company, with most of which I feel I have little in common. The chorus of dispraise which depicts him as a romantic conservative with his eyes closed on the world, tenacious of received tradition and resistant to new thoughts, inhibiting the voice of free dissent within the church he leads, could hardly, in my view, be wider of the mark. (As an assessment of his thinking, that is. On the question of how the pope's thought is reflected in the regime he heads, the internal difficulties that it wrestles with, and its failure to maintain the momentum of ecu-

For myself, I take up the question of the death penalty hoping that it may also shed some light on a puzzling *theological* feature in *Evangelium Vitae:* the almost total silence on the resurrection. How, one might wonder, can a Christian teacher proclaim the gospel of life without proclaiming the resurrection? Yet the seven references that I have identified (#26, 29, 50, 67, 82, 84, 105) all appear formulaic and nonload-bearing. Even more striking are the silences where one would expect an Easter reference as a matter of course: in paragraph 51 especially, but note also how the words of the ancient Easter liturgy, "trampling down death by death," are echoed shorn of a reference to their resurrection context in paragraph 102. In paragraph 36 the same fate, even more remarkably, befalls 1 Corinthians 15:45, "the last Adam became a living spirit." When Saint Paul wished to found a strong assertion of the personal significance of the life of the body, he did so by way of a series of analogies between "earthly" and "spiritual" bodies, in which the difference between the two was stressed quite as much as the correspondence: "It is sown a perishable body, it is raised an imperishable." John Paul, on the other hand, stresses throughout the *continuity* of life from the biological to the spiritual and eternal. Human life is in its very origins "almost divine" (#25), "a manifestation of God in the world" (#34). It is given to us with its own implicit moral and spiritual dimensions (#32), a "truth" of life disclosed in the commandments of God and fully grasped only in the light of the truth of God, man, and history (#48). It is the seed of an existence that transcends time (#34). There is a "single and indivisible Gospel" of life (#2), which "includes everything that human experience and reason tell us about the value of human life, accepting it,

---

menical engagement which it inherited, an Anglican theologian had best recognize that others are in a stronger position to comment than he is.) With the pope's turn from neoscholastic to patristic categories new occasions for ecumenical convergence have arisen, some of which are capitalized on in the later encyclical *Ut Unum Sint.* As for interest in the modern world, the sections of EV that analyze late modern culture (#19-23) show how a Christian teacher can attend to, and make use of, the reflections of his contemporaries on the crises of their times. I find much in EV to make me think John Paul something of a prophet, and in offering criticisms I would wish them to be seen as the service which the prophet can properly demand of the theologian.

purifying it, exalting it, bringing it to fulfilment" (#30). But not, apparently, astounding it with the news of the empty tomb.

One decisive innovation, however, articulates this continuum of life into a salvation-history: the "new principle of life" revealed in Christ, which is "self-giving" (#49). It must be acknowledged that, to offset any suspicions of a drift towards nature-mysticism, the pope insists very forcefully on the Christocentricity of the gospel (#29, 80); and to offset any hints of exemplarism or didacticism in the term "principle," he lays unimpeachable stress on the cross, the "very life of God . . . shared," the "source of life," the "meaning and goal of all history and of every human life" (#50, 51). Yet the place assigned to the cross in the history of life is, in effect, the place that should be occupied by the resurrection — or, more precisely, by the cross-*and*-resurrection, the Paschal mystery as a whole. And this draws our attention to the fact that the cross has little or no place in the pope's account of *death*. Much is said about the cross as the *conquest* of death, but nothing to suggest that the cross *is* a death, let alone a violent, unjust, or legally imposed death. To put it at its sharpest, one might say that *Evangelium Vitae* lacks any view of the cross of Christ as capital punishment.

We should not underestimate the significance of the death penalty as an issue of political ethics on which much else converges. Most Westernized societies abolished it for practical purposes a generation ago (the U.S.A. is the striking exception) and placed the burden of punishing serious offenders on their prison services. Most non-Westernized societies continue to make use of it, some simply out of custom, the Islamic ones out of strong religious conviction. Many of these societies could not begin to afford the kind of secure and humane prison system that Western societies (whether in good or bad faith) assume they can take for granted. It is, then, an issue that shows up the stark contrasts between "developed" and "developing" nations on which John Paul wrote so eloquently in *Sollicitudo Rei Socialis*. Furthermore, the ideological gulf between the different practices is hardening. When abolition was the trend in Western countries, it was largely justified on the grounds of practical humanity and penological relevance. Now, however, the abolitionist posture is increasingly re-interpreted as an issue of fundamental liberal principle — most notoriously by the decision of Amnesty International to treat the death penalty as a matter to be investigated along with torture. And these ideological developments in Western liberalism have had their theological equivalents. The death penalty has become a weapon within intra-Catholic polemics, where certain thinkers insist that it compromises the church's pro-life stance not to condemn it outright. It is also a weapon within intra-Protestant polemics, where penal questions have been drawn into the old controversy between Socinian (exemplarist) and Grotian (penal) accounts of the death of Christ.[3]

To this we add a further complicating factor for the Christian debate: no common front among the churches could be ecumenical if it ignored the theological moral tradition of the church; but that tradition is almost unanimously permissive of the death penalty, though within definite limits. Its more permissive side is represented by the judgment of Innocent III, who, against the Waldensians, allows that it may be "employed without mortal sin, provided (it is done) judiciously and without hatred, carefully and without haste." Its less permissive side is represented by Saint Ambrose, who, like most Christians of his period, saw it as a supreme virtue of Christian magistrates to avoid bloodshed: "Authority, you see, has its rights; but compassion has its policy. You will be excused if you use it; but you will be admired if you refrain when you might have used it."[4] The reluctance of Christians of that era, who genuinely loathed the death penalty, to rule it out, has, among other motivations, a theological concern to avoid Marcionism or Manichaeism. Ancient Israel's social arrangements, however inapplicable to the gospel era, must be understood as given by God and legitimate on their own terms.

Here, then, is a question on which Christians need a perspective that is ecumenical in the fullest sense of the word: uniting rich and poor churches, modern and premodern Christian insights, and different families of theological understanding. On what kind of argu-

---

3. See, e.g., Germain Grisez, *The Way of the Lord Jesus 2: Living a Christian Life* (Quincy, Ill.: Franciscan, 1993), pp. 891-94; Timothy Gorringe, *God's Just Vengeance: Crime, Violence and the Rhetoric of Salvation* (Cambridge: Cambridge University Press, 1996).

4. Innocent: "De potestate saeculari asserimus, quod sine peccato mortali potest *iudicium sanguinis exercere,* dummodo ad inferendam vindictam non odio sed iudicio, non incaute, sed consulte procedat" (*Enchiridion Symbolorum Definitionum et Declarationum de Rebus Fidei et Morum,* ed. H. Denzinger and A. Schönmetzer, 36th ed. [Barcelona: Herder, 1976], #795). Ambrose, *Epistolarum libri* 50.

ment might a Christian base opposition to the death penalty with theological integrity? And what kind of ideological temptations ought such a posture to beware of?

*　　*　　*

I propose to offer two readings of what John Paul has to say about the death penalty. The first will concentrate exclusively upon paragraph 56, the single formal discussion of the topic, and it will read it constructively, drawing out its potential for an ecumenically common standpoint. The second will take note of a few passing references to the topic elsewhere, and will then reassess paragraph 56 in the light of these, finding a more idealist and ecumenically less satisfying position. From this reading, finally, we return to the theological problematic posed in the introduction. The reason for this roundabout approach is to give full weight to the *ambiguities* surrounding the pope's view of the death penalty and to the dialogue he is conducting with the new Catholic Catechism *(C.C.).*

Paragraph 56 occurs near the beginning of the third chapter of the encyclical, which contains the bulk of its special ethics. From the command "You shall not kill" we are led to the only formal qualification which, in his view, this command is susceptible of: "legitimate defense," which includes not only personal self-defense but actions taken in responsibility for "the common good of the family or of the State" (#55 = C.C. 2265). This brings us to the section on the death penalty, which unfolds as follows:

(56a) He observes "a growing tendency," in and beyond the church, to favor limitation or abolition.

(56b) A methodological statement: The context must be "a system *(regula)* of penal justice ever more in line with human dignity."

(56c) There follows a concise statement (based on *C.C.* 2266) of the classical purposes of punishment: first, retribution, or "redress"; in a secondary place, the defense of public order and the rehabilitation of the offender.

(56d) The "nature and extent of the punishment" *(modum et genus)* — what kind of punishment and how much — has to be ordered "carefully" to the achievement of these purposes.

(56e) Capital punishment — "the extreme of executing the offender" — ought not to be invoked except in "cases of absolute necessity." This phrase is then explained to mean "when it would not be possible otherwise to defend society."

(56f) There follows disconcertingly upbeat generalization, clearly intended to emphasize the marginal nature of the concession just made to capital punishment: "Today . . . as a result of steady improvements in the organisation of the penal system, such cases are very rare, if not practically non-existent."

(56g) The section then concludes with a quotation from *C.C.* (2266) reinforcing the point that the principle of proportion requires "bloodless means" to protect public safety wherever they are sufficient.

Whether or not one is sympathetic to the pope's leaning away from the death penalty, and whether or not one is disappointed by his failure to go further, one is likely to feel that this statement leaves some important threads hanging loose. Three points are particularly in need of clarification. In the first place, what general state of affairs does the "upbeat generalization" (56f) suppose? In the second, what kind of situation does his talk of "absolute necessity" envisage? In the third, a more theoretical question: why, since the aims of punishment are stated, in a highly classical form, as primarily retributive and only secondarily defensive and remedial ("In this way authority also fulfils the purpose . . ." 56c), should the principle of proportionate defense (56e, 56g) exercise an overall constraint on the "nature and extent" of the punishment we inflict?

In the first place, we must suppose that in 56f John Paul is thinking only of modern, well-governed law-states. This most traveled of popes has seen the high level of social disorganization that poverty imposes on a considerable number of the world's nations. Furthermore, he himself lives in a land where the justice system has, for some decades, been unable to resist systematic corruption by the Mafia. Why, then, should he speak in terms that may possibly be appropriate in the majority of developed Western nations but can hardly be appropriate universally? One possibility is that he regards advanced economic development as the normal and normative condition of human civilization, an interpretation of which we might properly be cautious in the case of this pope, not only in view of the modernity-criticism adopted by the present encyclical, but in view of his warnings about the idea of development in *Sollicitudo Rei Socialis*.[5] It may be enough for the moment to say that this idealist characterization of the current situation is simply raised as a thought experiment on which no weight in the argument is reposed.[6]

The second question can be answered on the basis of indications in 56f. Cases of "absolute necessity" may be very rare (at least in well-governed law-states) *by virtue of the better organization of the penal system*. This separates the pope from any version of the thesis that certain types of crime, simply by virtue of their extreme gravity, constitute the necessity that justifies the extreme penalty. This is most striking since the Catechism (2266) gives every impression of supporting this thesis; when it authorizes "penalties commensurate with the gravity of the crime, not excluding, in cases of extreme gravity, the death-penalty." We must suppose that the pope understood the phrase "not excluding" to imply "but not requiring either." "Absolute necessity" is not a matter of the gravity of the crime alone — be it police-murder, child-murder, torture, indiscriminate terrorism, or whatever — but implies an element of *crisis*. Only so could the pope say that it arises very rarely in well-governed law-states; for, unhappily, no type of heinous crime is "rare if not practically non-existent" in well-governed law-states, which, indeed, have even tended to see the emergence of new types of specially heinous crime, pedophile child-murder for example. On the other hand, it does not seem that a *political* crisis fulfils the conditions either. If it is rare in well-governed law-

5. *S.R.S,.* especially #27-34.
6. The Latin version, which is supposed to be decisive for interpretation, reads: "Atqui hodie, propter convenientiorem institutionis poenalis temperationem, admodum raro huius modi intercidunt casus, si qui omnino iam reapse accidunt." It then continues, "Quidquid id est. . . ." This could plausibly be read in a way supportive of the minimizing interpretation of 56f. The connective "atqui" is commonly used to introduce a new thought — perhaps confirmatory, perhaps adversative, perhaps a new stage in an argument, but in any case somewhat oblique to the assertion that immediately preceded it. Followed by "quidquid id est," "however that may be," the whole of 56f looks like a parenthesis — a suggestion that may or may not be accepted, but which is not needed for the argument. The reasons that incline me away from this reading will emerge later in the discussion.

states that a state is threatened with disaster from subversion or civil war, that is credit not to the organization of its penal system but to the stabilizing effects of its democratic polity. On this interpretation, then, embattled regimes should take no encouragement from the pope's words to defend themselves by extraordinary measures involving the execution of opponents. (On an alternative reading of the passage, as we shall see, this point may not be quite so clear.)

The only scenario that seems to fit the description is a *breakdown of law and order*, in which government loses its control of crime and fails to protect society against its depredations. An organized penal system (i.e. a "system of justice," broadly understood to include detection, arrest, and conviction as well as punishment) has had much to do with obviating this type of emergency in developed societies; yet it is also plausible to think that in less elaborately organized societies the death penalty has played a significant role in containing forces of lawlessness and upholding public order. So on this reading John Paul sees the burden of maintaining order shifted, in well-governed states, from capital punishment to a sophisticated apparatus of detection and imprisonment. Given that the principle of proportionate defense demands a "bloodless" means where possible (56g), he thinks that this shift should be welcomed and consolidated; yet the liminal possibility of breakdown means that the death penalty is not disallowed categorically.

The third, more theoretical, question was why, if there are three purposes of punishment and retribution is the primary one, an overall constraint upon means of punishment should be that of proportionate defense. A consensus from the late eighteenth and nineteenth centuries would have said that *retributive appropriateness* was the final criterion for means of punishment. Our great-grandfathers and grandmothers thought the death penalty absolutely required, since only life could witness to the sanctity of life. The needs of social defense were almost irrelevant when set beside this great, all-mastering principle of justice. Alternatively, in the voice of a minority from the late eighteenth and early nineteenth century, which has found much sympathy in the twentieth, we could ask why *rehabilitation* should not count in determining the means of punishment quite as much as public safety. If there is some prospect of reformation, must the undoubted element of risk to the public speak decisively against it? Now, within paragraph

56 there is no answer to this question. So, for the purposes of this
first interpretation, I beg leave to improvise one that will give the pope
what I think he wants, which is an element of *social relativity* in determining the upper limits of what punishment may do.

If we know what we are about when we speak of a "retributive"
function of punishment, we mean that punishment is an "expressive"
act, an acted declaration of the truth about the offense in relation to
the moral order of society.[7] A punishment must pronounce judgment
on the offense, describing it, disowning it, and refounding the moral
basis for the common life which the offense has challenged. In this
sense punishment "gives back" the offense, not as an act of mere
retaliation, returning evil for evil, but in the sense of a true statement,
representing rightly that which has been done. If we then call retribution the "primary" end, we mean simply that such a pronouncement
is what punishing *is;* just as telling the truth is the primary end of
making a statement, because that is what "stating" is. Private vengeance or retaliation would be extrinsic, arbitrary ends; the distinction
between retaliation and the proper sense of "retribution" is essential
to any serious discussion of punishment.[8]

The secondary goods, of society and the offender, are also extrinsic
to the performance, though they are not arbitrary. These are the goods
that we may expect to follow, in the ordinary course of events, from
responsible punishment. Society is benefited because without such an
acted declaration in the face of disruption, its continued coherence is
put in question. The offender is benefited because, faced with the
truth of his act, he has an opportunity of self-knowledge which, under
the grace of God, may prove fruitful for his moral regeneration. Plato
sometimes speaks as if he thinks punishment *must* prove beneficial to
the offender; and, if we are optimistic, we are free to follow him in
this, provided that we take him seriously when he says it is the *justice*

---

7. On the concept of "expressive" punishment see J. Feinberg, *Doing and De-
serving* (Princeton: Princeton University Press, 1970), pp. 95-118; J. R. Lucas, *Responsibility* (Oxford: Clarendon, 1993), pp. 86-123.

8. This distinction is, as I read it, perfectly clear in the pope's (and *C.C.*'s)
formulation at 56c: "poena eo imprimis spectat, ut inordinato culpa illato occurratur,"
"to redress the disorder caused by the offense." This does not exploit the analogy I
advance between retribution and speech; but its objective social focus is clearly remote
from subjective ideas of vengeance.

of the punishment, and nothing else, that does the offender good.[9] It is not a question of some technique that will make a bad person good. The good is simply justice itself, the truth about the offense offered truthfully to the offender. (There may, of course, be incidental circumstances in the administration of punishment that derogate from its justice — the cruelty of warders or of other prisoners, for example — and it may be a proper matter for administrative technique to eliminate these.)

We have no reason, then, to say that the form of punishment should be determined by anything other than its expressive or "retributive" function. By fitting that function well, a punishment is more likely to achieve the secondary goods; if it fails to fit it, it fails the secondary goods as well. But, as in every expressive act, there is a *conventional* element in the correspondence of punishment to offense. Punishment is a kind of enacted language, and like all linguistic utterances, any one act of punishment can have a different meaning in different social contexts. There is no absolute vocabulary. Rather, as history has shown, there is a variety of possible systems of penal practice all of which satisfy the formal demand that offenses should be discriminatingly judged and pronounced on. The rule called by the Romans *lex talionis,* the infliction of equal and opposite harm, *appears* to promise an exact and universal tariff, but this is a chimera. Distinguished philosophers, Kant at their head, have sometimes confused it with the retributive form of punishment itself and so inferred that certain crimes (such as murder) must, as a moral principle, be answered with equal and opposite harm (the death penalty). Aristotle much more judiciously rejected the view that retaliation constituted just punishment, and so should we.[10] The chief usefulness of *lex talionis* is in assessing damages, not punishments. The equivalence of punishment to crime has to be a symbolic construct. Punishment is a language that evolves as the symbolic meaning of certain acts within the context of social expectation changes.

Montesquieu observed famously that in countries with mild laws inhabitants are as much affected by slight penalties as inhabitants of

9. E.g., Plato, *Gorgias,* in *Opera* iii, ed. J. Burnet (Oxford, 1903), pp. 476-78.
10. Kant, *Metaphysics of Morals* A.A.6.322-5. Aristotle, *Nicomachean Ethics* 1132b21-31.

other countries by severer ones.[11] Some languages of punishment are milder, some more savage than others; but they cannot tend to mildness or savagery independently of the conditions society offers. Consider what it means for British society, in common with many Western European societies, that it has been wealthy enough, peopled enough, and has enjoyed sufficiently effective communications, to organize and maintain a system of secure prisons, a police force with sophisticated detective techniques, and a control of firearms that makes it (even now) unusual for someone to be shot dead on the street. All this helps to determine the character of the death penalty in our society as disproportionate. Were these factors not to obtain, and were the sight of violent death to become common, then the whole symbolic meaning of capital punishment would change. A mild language of punishment supposes a mild experience of social life and, of course, the mild virtues that sustain it. A social trend towards immoderate and violent anger or to private revenge would certainly inflate the currency of punishment and produce harsher penal attitudes.

This seems to me to be the truth behind John Paul's suggestion that the outer limits of punishment are determined *relatively* to the needs of a society at a given time. The question remains why he confines this to the needs of *defense*. Those needs are a factor, certainly, since any heightened sense of danger must affect the symbolic meaning of acts taken to protect society. But the essential proportion is to society's *moral sensibilities*. There is good sense in the view that capital punishment is too severe if it is felt to be too severe. But John Paul, following *C.C.,* treats "legitimate defense" as a framework within which *all* the legitimate demands of social coherence against the life of a human being can be accommodated, and so proposes to read this criterion generously — to include, that is, the need to satisfy society's sense of justice. With this minor expansion of the principle of proportion, we can entertain the pope's general view of a penal system that is evolving to make capital punishment a more and more marginal possibility as the need for it disappears. "A penal system . . . ever more in line with human dignity" was the context in which capital punishment had to be addressed (56b). On the one hand, one cannot reach a moral view of capital punishment in isolation, apart from the whole

11. Montesquieu, *The Spirit of the Laws,* 6.12.

penal "language" of a society to which it must belong. On the other hand, one should look for a favorable evolution of that language, as society's sense of "human dignity" develops, making it possible, and necessary, to discard the ordinary use of the death penalty as it does so. What is the source of this evolutionary pressure? From the encyclical as a whole it is reasonable to suppose that it is the gospel itself. "Steady improvements in the organisation of the penal system" may be a result of this moral evolution, and they are certainly a precondition for its taking effect in this particular way; but mere efficiency, on its own, could not have achieved a moral revolution. The spread of the Christian message, not only outward but inward, changing the way we think about our social practices, is the force that has moved us so far, and can move us farther.

So far, then, we have extracted from paragraph 56 of *Evangelium Vitae* an account of John Paul's views on capital punishment that broadly supports Western trends towards abolition yet sufficiently acknowledges their contingency to keep faith with the tradition. On this reading paragraph 56 of EV seems to me to provide a hopeful foundation for a possible ecumenical consensus. It has not broken faith with the permissive end of the tradition, as represented by Innocent III's insistence that a magistrate might employ the death penalty without mortal sin if he did so responsibly; the only doctrine ruled out is that of Kant, Hegel, and their theological followers, that murder *requires* the death penalty as a matter of moral fitness. Yet its center of gravity lies closer to the patristic consensus summed up in Ambrose's "You will be excused if you use it, admired if you refrain." Absolute inviolability belongs only to *innocent* human life (cf. #57), so a society that has a necessity for capital punishment is not wrong to practice it. Yet there is a presumption that this situation will tend to disappear. A society that succeeds in responsible abolition is, to that extent, morally more advanced; while one that fails to abolish it once it has become disproportionate to its needs is at fault. Nothing in this approach decries a certain circumspection on the part of societies considering whether to do without capital punishment. The expectation that the *whole penal system* (i.e., system of justice) must evolve to greater recognition of human dignity introduces a precaution against any false consciousness that pursues this goal in isolation and ignores such things as the level of violence on the streets or the use of firearms

by the police. Ambrose knew of governors who, to avoid offending
the church with executions, left accused persons to die in prison
without trial. It might hardly be less cynical to strain at the gnat of
capital punishment and swallow the camel of execution-on-arrest by
a gun-happy police.

* * *

In our first reading of #56 we have proposed two small complements
to the pope's line of thought, one giving a more generous recognition
to the specially favorable conditions for abolition in the economically
developed world, the other filling out the ideas of proportion and
disproportion to give scope for the expressive character of penal justice. But is this interpretation true to the pope's intentions? There are
three other references to the death penalty in *Evangelium Vitae* which,
on the face of it at least, strike a different note. At best they require
integrating into our account; at worst they force us to revise it.

In paragraph 27, where the pope has gathered a number of "signs
of hope" to offset his depressing account of late modern culture, he
mentions "a new sensitivity ever more opposed to war" and "a growing public opposition to the death-penalty," and adds "even when such
a penalty is seen as a kind of 'legitimate defence' on the part of society."
This raises the puzzling question of how the pope can draw comfort
from a point of view that rejects his own (and the catechism's) insistence that the death penalty may be a "legitimate defence."[12]

12. This puzzle is easier to resolve from the Latin version: "latius usque publica
diffunditur opinio capitis poenae aversa, etiam veluti legitimae defensionis socialis
instrumentum, quandoquidem hodierna societas facultates habet crimina efficaciter
coercendi his usa rationibus quae hunc sontem reddant innoxium, hanc viam resipi-
scendi omnino non intercludant." The effect of the single sentence where the English
translation has two is to make it clear *why* the public is not impressed by the argument
of "legitimate defense": *since* "modern society has the means of effectively rendering
criminals harmless without definitely denying them the chance to reform." In other
words, public opinion takes the same upbeat view of the current penological situation
that we found the pope ready to entertain in 56f (together with its perplexing tendency
to normalize the Western law-state). Public opinion is turning away from the death
penalty because it thinks it no longer necessary. And from this public perception, even
if he is not sure whether he should wholly endorse it, the pope can derive encouragement.

In paragraph 40 the pope refers to the prohibition of murder in the Decalogue, adding: "Of course we must recognise that in the O.T. this sense of the value of life, though already quite marked, does not yet reach the refinement found in the Sermon on the Mount. This is apparent in some aspects of the current (i.e. *then* current) penal legislation, which provided for severe forms of corporal punishment and even the death-penalty."[13] The natural conclusion from this is that the Sermon on the Mount by implication *abolished* the death penalty when it "refined" the sense of the value of life.

Most striking of all, perhaps, is the passage in paragraph 9, where, in the midst of his exposition of the story of Cain and Abel, John Paul treats the "mark of Cain" as an illustration of the principle that "not even a murderer loses his personal dignity, and God himself pledges to guarantee this." Since we have been told that "God cannot leave the crime unpunished," we must assume that God's treatment of Cain represents the normative pattern of punishment, combining penal justice on the one hand with respect for the offender's dignity on the other.[14]

The drift of these three texts is to make John Paul appear far more of an abolitionist *in principle*. For they refuse to do what at first we took his methodological statement (56b) to be urging: to integrate the question of capital punishment into the general question of a humane justice system. For now, it seems, capital punishment is essentially a separable entity, an intrusive element in a penal order that has as its inner logic the recognition of human dignity. The methodological statement must therefore be read with fresh eyes. Viewing capital punishment "in the context of a system of penal justice ever more in line with human dignity" may not, after all, mean treating the death penalty as a part of that system. It may mean helping to free the system of an encumbrance by eliminating factors that occlude its true respect for human dignity. Nor is it as clear as it seemed on first reading that

13. "Nondum suavitatem Sermonis in Monte attingere, uti liquet ex aspectibus quibusdam iuris tum vigentis."

14. The subsequent quotation from Ambrose, *De Cain et Abel* 2.10.38, does not actually support the pope's point. It merely says that God intervened in mercy to preempt the precipitate exercise of human judgment. There is a great difference between mercy that *suspends* judgment and a respect for human dignity *displayed in* judgment.

the source of this evolutionary pressure on the penal system is the gospel. It seems, rather, to be a natural law principle of the inviolability of human life. Concessions to the death penalty, where required, are extrinsic to the inherent logic of this principle and have only to do with emergencies that beset institutions. Step by step these can be obviated through experience and organizational sophistication.

In support of this alternative reading we must observe how the pope has altered the treatment of "legitimate defense" that he found in the catechism. The decision to base *all* qualifications to the sixth command on that principle was already made there (2263-67). But in the central statement of the relevant section of the *C.C.* (2266) there was permission for the *ordinary* use of capital punishment, argued by the following compressed but clear steps: the need of public safety; the need to render aggression impotent; the need for a system of public justice based on discriminating retribution, such a system "not excluding" the death penalty "in cases of extreme gravity." The catechism then justifies defensive wars "for analogous reasons," before returning to the question of punishment to elaborate the three goods. Finally (2267) it makes the general statement, quoted in full at 56g, about proportionate defense, meaning this to apply analogously to all forms of "legitimate defense," that is, private self-defense, public justice, and defensive war. Although the order of the exposition is not without problems — the "analogous" remark about defensive war is uncomfortably sandwiched between two statements about penal justice — there is not much doubt that the catechism distinguishes three different forms of "legitimate defense," applies arguments to each that are analogous but not identical, and gives a special explanation of how penal justice derives from the general principle of defense.

But the pope elides the sequence of thought that links capital punishment to public safety by way of the system of retributive justice. The differentiating feature of penal order disappears, and capital punishment becomes an emergency provision just like war itself. This is the implication of his association of public opposition to war with public opposition to the death penalty (#27). Here is the significance, too, of his repeated use of what we have called the "upbeat generalization" (56f). For although he never quite affirms it — it is on the lips of others in paragraph 27 (in the Latin at least) and in paragraph 56 is followed by a distancing clause — the culturally triumphalist logic of the move is crucial to what has become, in effect, an *argument* with the catechism. The catechism seems to teach that capital punishment may be justified simply by the extreme gravity of the crime: "penalties commensurate with the gravity of the crime, not excluding, in cases of extreme gravity, the death-penalty." To which the pope replies: if you are serious about treating penal justice as legitimate defense, then the decisive factor is that the death penalty *can* be abolished without danger! Approaching 56f from this angle, we can no longer distance the pope from the appearance of a claim to universality. The condition of the modern, economically developed and well-governed law-state must be normative, since it has enabled punishment to be emancipated from the alien violence of self-defense. From this angle, similarly, we can see that the appeal to defensive proportion (which on our first reading we tried to widen) is meant to be kept narrow. When he quotes 2267 at 56g, he is asserting the primacy of defensive proportion in order to refute the catechism out of its own mouth. That principle renders the internal permissions of retributive justice quite irrelevant.

Here, then is our second account of John Paul's views. We find him less respectful of tradition and more convinced of the universal moral unfitness of the penalty of death. The differences in detail concern the way the methodological statement (56b) is read and how the "upbeat" statement (56f) and the quotation from the catechism (56g) are taken. Our second reading of paragraph 56 takes these last two strictly at their face value, where the first introduced exegetical qualifications. It also takes note of the passing mentions of the death penalty elsewhere in the document. It seems to be the reading that the pope's publicists gave it. On the other hand, because it sharpens the note of disagreement between the pope and the catechism, and sets him at an uncomfortable distance from the church's tradition, one should not say with too much haste that such an interpretation of a pope's words must be correct.

And, I am bound to say, the second reading is inherently less preferable, since the views that it highlights have some grave inconveniences. John Paul has exploited, on this reading, the catechism's attempt to derive the coercive powers of the state in criminal justice from "legitimate defense," thinking through the implications of this move even more resolutely. The truth is, one should never attempt such a thing. The right of the state to impose coercive measures against wrongdoers arises not from its need to defend itself but from its office of *judgment*. So the Western Catholic tradition, Augustinian and Thomist, Tridentine and Protestant, taught with undivided voice until the early modern period, basing their understanding upon Romans 13:1-7. Now, although the tradition of reflection nourished by the Social Encyclicals emphasized the constructive, organizational role of the state rather than the judicial, the role of judgment — often spoken of in terms of "safeguarding rights" — was not forgotten in it. And although there has been little discussion of the coercive implications of this task, nothing in the tradition (so far as I can judge) suggests that the state needs *any other source* for its coercive action, when required, than the authority which its judicial role confers on it. In other words, "legitimate defense" is an intrusion, even from the point of view of recent Roman Catholic tradition, suggesting a radically weakened view of political authority. And, indeed, *C.C.* 1897-1904 is weaker by far than *Gaudium et Spes* 74 (itself not strong), on which it is based. A small straw in the wind is the citation of Romans 13, which in the council's document extends to verse 5, in the *C.C.* only to verse 2. What Saint Paul thought central to the work of the state, the bearing of the sword, the encyclical tradition thought supplementary, the catechism thought must be supplied from another source, and John Paul, finally (on this second account), thinks is an extraordinary measure for emergency use only.

This is excessively restrictive to the state in its ordinary functions; but it is also excessively permissive to it in a crisis. Our first interpretation suggested a distinction between a political and a penal crisis, and assumed that the pope intended only the latter kind to benefit from extraordinary permissions. But with our second interpretation the distinction hardly amounts to anything substantial. For if the death penalty is never at home in ordinary penal practice, then it is never invoked for purposes germane to penology but only to shore up the institution upon which all penal practice depends, that is, the state. The idea of an "emergency provision," whether we meet it in John Paul or in some well-known Protestant exemplars, implies an inevitable drift towards statism; for once the power of the sword is notionally set free from the constraints of justice *in extremis,* there can be no function for the sword but to enforce the state's grip. We should hardly be surprised if the state that is refused the just use of force in ordinary operations but is promised a *carte blanche* in an emergency, sets about creating one.[15]

Correspondingly, the ordinary operations of penal justice are presented in an idealized light. So wide and unbridgeable a gulf is made between death and all other kinds of penalty, that it quite escapes notice that the other punishments are coercive too. But all forms of coercion exercise their hold upon us through our mortality. Punishments are effected against the person, property, or liberty of the offender; an attack on any of these is an attack on the limited and irrecoverable powers which any individual human being can dispose of in order to live his or her life. Two years in prison are "two good years of my life," two out of a finite number less than a hundred. A heavy fine is a drain on resources that I need to feed, clothe, and house myself if I am to live my full term of days. And so on. A flexible penal system has a wide range of intermediate penalties that stop short of taking an offender's life. But that *ultima ratio* is indeed the *ratio* of all the penultimate measures. If we were not mortal, none of them would have any meaning. Death is the gold standard from which the currency of punishment draws its credit. Failure to see the intrinsic relation between death and punishment means failure to see what we *always* do when we punish; failure, therefore, to see that the state, in exacting the death penalty, is doing just what it always does, one way or another, in response to crime. The fruits of this bad faith in relation to the penal system are seen in the recurrent crises that Western societies experience in relation to their prisons. In this field, perhaps, only a pope can command enough length of vision to discern "steady improvements"!

* * *

I return in closing to the theological issue raised at the start: the failure of the encyclical to achieve a clear focus on the resurrection and its

15. Cf. Karl Barth, *Church Dogmatics* 3/4, ed. G. Bromiley, T. F. Torrance (Edinburgh: T & T Clark, 1961), pp. 446-48. The same demoralizing effects of the concept of emergency can be seen in some attempts to marry nuclear deterrence with just war doctrine. See my *Peace and Certainty: A Theological Essay on Deterrence* (Oxford: Clarendon; Grand Rapids: Eerdmans, 1989), esp. pp. 93-98.

tendency to put the cross in its place, central to the salvation history of life but unrelated to the phenomenology of death. Now I can suggest a reason for this. John Paul's failure, on the side of civil justice, to identify the link between judgment and mortality is reflected in a failure, on the side of death, to link mortality and judgment. Politically we have justice without death, anthropologically death without judgment.

Consider, for example, the use he makes of Moses' speech in Deuteronomy, "See I have set before you this day life and good, death and evil" (30:15, #28). John Paul sees this as "very appropriate for us who are called . . . to the duty of choosing between 'the culture of life' and 'the culture of death.'" But death is only discussed as a false object of choice, not as a weapon of judgment in the hand of God, which is how Deuteronomy sees it. Elsewhere, stating that "human life and death are in the hands of God" (#39), he develops this in such a way as to ignore the second member of the pair. And throughout the encyclical a major role is played by a text from Wisdom (1:13ff., 2:23f.) which declares that "God did not make death" but created man for immortality. The godless, on the other hand, taking the part of death or the devil, came to experience it by their own wickedness and folly. Clearly, there is some sense in which all Christians have to assert that death is not part of God's "original" created order. Saint Paul, too, said that "by man came death" (1 Cor. 15:21) How this is to be developed in relation to a biological order which requires death for its perpetuation we need not discuss here. But whatever development we give it, we must not sink into the theosophical comfort that simply dissociates the occurrence of death from God's purposes. As a statement about created order, "God did not make death" has its own proper use and validity: but for a statement about history we need something about the dialectic of sin, judgment, and redemption: "Shall there be evil in the city and I, the Lord, have not done it?" (Amos 3:6).

Judgment is the link that binds God's omnipotence to the occurrence of death. Without the idea of judgment, God's role in the death of Christ becomes especially problematic. Either that role is simply played down, and we are content to see Christ as a victim of human injustice, "betrayed into the hands of wicked men and slain"; or (the direction taken in EV) Christ's death is lifted out of the sphere of death as a whole and treated as an event apart, wholly a voluntary self-offering, not a true suffering with all the horror of judgment in its train. It is not wrong, of course, to see Christ either as a victim of injustice or as a voluntary self-offering; both characterizations have their place in an account of the Paschal mystery. But to prevent them falling apart we need a central link to bind them together.

A generation ago, when the abolition of the death penalty was being discussed in Britain, my own sympathies being engaged for the cause of abolition, I remember being choked with rage at a clergyman who argued on the opposite side with these astounding words: "People should remember that our Lord suffered capital punishment!" It was the dizzying non-sequitur of the argument that upset me. If, after all, the Son of God was put to death judicially, did that not argue for the grave inadvisability of such measures? But since it is the fate of all thinkers to weave reasons to clothe utterances that appear in public naked, I now think that behind the baffling non-sequitur there was a theological point. Christ's death was more than the fate of one good man at the hands of several bad ones. It was a clash of authorities, human and divine, in which our representatives passed judgment on God and God passed judgment on our representatives, each in the person of the Mediator, representing God to man and man to God. The universal meaning of the cross hangs on the authority with which the agents acted. If the whole thing was *ultra vires,* a miscarriage of justice based on corruption or misunderstanding, then it was a mere accident of history; we are not implicated in it. The symbolic links of judgment and execution stand at the heart of what we understand about Christ's reconciling death. We may be rid of ordinary uses of the death penalty in most Western states; I am glad to live in one where we are. We may one day be rid of it elsewhere, in Third World countries, Muslim societies, and so on. If we can achieve that responsibly, it will be a fine achievement — though we must be on our guard against irresponsible, crusading attitudes which fail to take the context (legal, economic, social, and moral) seriously. But we cannot be rid of the symbolic role that the death penalty plays in relating death to judgment. There will always be a death penalty in the mind — if, that is, we are all to learn to "die with Christ," understanding our own deaths as a kind of capital punishment.

To the extent that John Paul turns away from this, he is (to use without prejudice a term that often carries prejudice) a true "modernist." Whatever conservative social and moral norms he defends, he accepts the deconstruction of the nexus of ideas and symbols that once made them intelligible. Perhaps the most important question we should ask about his thought is how John Paul, the modernist, relates to John Paul, the critic of modernity, and whether his life-affirming moral policies are compromised in any way by such an ambiguity. For at the root of our late-modern "culture of death" there lies a certain culture of life. Precisely because our brief span must (it seems to us) carry the whole meaning of existence, offering all the reconciliation we can ever hope to find; precisely because death (whether Christ's or ours) is allowed no role in this reconciliation; we become greedy of life, demanding to live each moment to the full, snatching from others opportunities to live that could compete with our own, making calculated sacrifices of the "worthless" lives to enrich the "worthwhile," and so on. Euthanasia is the loudest confession that death — real, passive death, where one is carried where one would not go — has no meaning for us. We can encounter death only in the disguise of action. Something very similar, it seems to me, has happened in John Paul's account of the death of Christ. I do not find there that affirmation of the Paschal mystery which invests our passive deaths with meaning: "He was given up for our sins, and raised for our justification" (Rom. 4:25).

A Consistent Ethic of Life (with a Few Blemishes): Moral-Theological Remarks on *Evangelium Vitae* and on Some Protestant Questions About It

EBERHARD SCHOCKENHOFF

THE TWO WORDS that stand as the programmatic title at the beginning of the most recent encyclical of Pope John Paul II form an unusual combination. Taken individually, "gospel" and "life" have always been key concepts within Christian religious speech. Grouped together as a leitmotif, they point to the basic theological concern that runs like a red thread through the moral preaching of John Paul II since his initial encyclical *Redemptor Hominis:* to recognize human beings in the personal worth of their existence and to give an unconditioned respect to this worth in all its forms. The encyclical uses the concept *"evangelium vitae"* for this basic anthropological conviction of Christian faith, which can be translated into modern languages as gospel *of* life or as gospel *for* life.

1. The Gospel of Life and the Worth of the Human Person

The sense of this combination is evident: The good news of redemption and salvation, of liberation from guilt and sin, which the church is commissioned to proclaim contains also a truth about human life without which the gospel cannot be understood. As a necessary implication of theological speech about the person, this anthropological basis is accessible to natural reason, but its depths can only be explored in the light of revelation. Assertions about the gospel of the kingdom of God and about the truth of the human person condition one another: when the worth of the person is disregarded and violated, then the gospel as the Word of God to this person is also disregarded and violated. Conversely, where the good news is ignored, persons run the danger of becoming alienated from themselves. This conviction, that where the sense for God is lost, the sense for the human person also disappears, the encyclical expresses in saying: "The Gospel of God's love for man, the Gospel of the dignity of the person and the Gospel of life are a single and indivisible Gospel" (#2; cf. #21).

This fundamental anthropological assertion takes up the classical two-level pattern according to which Catholic moral theology and church social teaching see the worth of persons and their natural rights grounded. On the one hand, this gospel of life "can also be known in its essential traits by human reason" (#29), because the worth and radical equality of all persons represents an original practical insight and is not dependent on the recognition of the historical revelation of the love of God. On the other hand, the fundamental coordinates of the philosophical understanding of the person receive a theological fullness of meaning in the light of revelation, so that the essential determination of persons for their most extreme possibilities of existence is brought to completion. The return to the anthropological assertions possible to natural reason — especially about the person's self-givenness, capacity for relation, and spiritual-physical unity — is a methodological abstraction from the determination by the historical fact of revelation of the sphere in which the concrete person already stands. Nevertheless, this abstraction is necessary in order to make visible the universal identity of the human being and to make clear that the logical basis of this practical truth about the person is not dependent on the biblical revelation.

When the classical scholastic natural-law ethic and most streams of contemporary Catholic moral theology speak of a two-level grounding of the worth of the person and of the norms that are anchored in this worth, they are also advancing a serious, philosophically testable claim to validity on this first level. The basis of moral norms must be demonstrable to human moral reason, especially when they seek to protect human worth in the strict sense, as is the case with the moral prohibitions or with inherently immoral actions. This does not imply that these norms lose their validity if approval is withheld on arbitrary grounds, from lack of insight, or from culpable incapacity. One need not deny, as Bernd Wannenwetsch rightly cites from Robert Spaemann, that there is a process of moral reasoning which in practice cannot be cut off, every argument finding a more or less adequate counterargument. Practical reason is discredited, however, if one understands the back-and-forth of moral argument as an in-principle limitation of the reach of practical reason and thus as a basis for its essential incapacity, in order then to legitimate an avoidance of binding moral insight or a suspension of moral commitment.

The rational legitimation of moral norms is not limited to the goals they should serve or to conclusions from presupposed premises. Such *teleological* or *deductive* models of argument lose themselves in an infinite regress, since the stated goals or presupposed premises themselves require grounding. Taking up transcendental-pragmatic conceptions, contemporary moral philosophy has shown that a final ethical grounding is also possible *reflexively*. Irrefragable assumptions are uncovered which everyone makes by entering the process of rational argumentation. It is a long path, however, with controversial steps along the way, from the formal insight into such irrefragable basic assumptions to anthropologically founded, material ethical norms. In the end, the conclusions of practical reason will be perspicuous only to those who can think along with the first and deepest act of reason, prior to all detailed for-and-against, namely, the recognition of an Unconditioned, removed from our own disposal.

It is pointless to deny the indisputable dependence of this recognition of reason on a fundamental orientation to reality, in which diverse biographical presuppositions, psychological dispositions, and in some cases a voluntary blindness can play a role. This recognition is something quite different from the paradoxical flight into a "nonjustifiable foundationless character" suggested by Wannenwetsch as a solution. From the viewpoint of Catholic moral theology, his pathosfull rejection of the task of rational grounding can be understood as an indication that the claim to validity of moral norms is independent of the sometimes poorly developed intellectual capacities of the individuals addressed. Nevertheless, it remains so that moral norms must *in principle* be capable of finding consent and thus not be a matter of an arbitrary positing, pure tradition, or authoritative decree, regardless of whether such heteronomous imposition presents itself in theological or other clothing.

For Catholic moral theology, the insistence that individual moral norms can be rationally grounded seems indispensable in light of the challenges which confront a Christian ethic in the pluralistic Western democracies. Only if the gospel of life finds an echo in human natural reason can its demands be persuasive for each individual. The natural rights of the person constitute the minimal claim which must be conceded to each person on the basis of their humanity, regardless of whether they are conscious of these rights or are able to claim them over against political society. When the church opposes torture and rape, discrimination and persecution, abortion and forced sterilization, and, with increasing determination, the death penalty, it is pursuing precisely these natural rights which each person possesses. It is claiming no special state protection for its own faith but rather the maintenance of these fundamental principles of justice that practical reason grasps with certainty and that can be denied from no perspective without contradiction.[1]

In that which concerns the *philosophical* insight into the personal quality of human life, the encyclical holds fast to the Christian tradi-

---

1. To ground such an assertion, Catholic theology usually appeals to the Thomist theory of practical reason and the *lex naturalis*. Today this is interpreted in a transcendental-philosophical sense, so that one asks after the irrefragable minimal conditions of moral freedom. By means of this reduction of the claim of natural law on the basis of the universal identity of human being, the transition is made to the subject-perspective of thought, already taken up by Thomas Aquinas but only brought to fruition in modern philosophy. As R. Saarinen shows in his contribution to this volume, the encyclical *Veritatis Splendor* takes no notice of this attempt to give a new transcendental-philosophical basis for the Thomist doctrine of natural law. It sees the indestructible "worth" of persons as grounded not in their moral character as subjects but in their participation as individuals in a universal human nature, to which all assertions about human worth primarily relate. On the possibility of a transcendental-philosophical reinterpretation of the Thomist theory of practical reason, see E. Schockenhoff, *Naturrecht und Menschenwürde: Universale Ethik in einer geschichtlichen Welt* (Mainz: Grünewald, 1996), pp. 181-97.

tion's anthropocentric understanding of the world over against all the temptations of a physiocentric approach. At the same time, on the basis of a biblical theology of creation, it places great emphasis on humanity's ecological responsibility for the whole of nature, which it refers to as "the environment in which he lives" (#42). The special and unique worth of human beings as persons is constituted by their ability to take responsibility for themselves, for their personal world, and for the nature that surrounds them. In the capacity of human persons to grasp in their own conscience the message that human life is inviolable and that nonhuman life is worthy of protection, the encyclical sees an important element for a philosophical definition of human being that should complement the classical determinations of insight and reason, free will and moral responsibility. Beyond this, it establishes life as something that precedes and surrounds the subject. This subject only becomes possible on such a natural foundation. Thus the precise sense of the biblical talk of the "gift" of life and its "sacredness" (#34, 40), often misinterpreted in Anglo-Saxon bioethics, is translated into the thought forms of the modern philosophy of freedom and nature.

As the rather reserved comments of the Protestant and Anglican conversation partners show, this form of speech, recently preferred by the magisterium of the Catholic church even within theological anthropology over the earlier *dominium*-theory, encounters the suspicion of a "vitalism in Christian dress" (Wannenwetsch) or of a "mysticism of nature" (O'Donovan).[2] The associations thus expressed point to an exposed flank of the formula of the sacredness or holiness of life, as does also its wide use in fundamentalist circles or in the language of contemporary civil religion. It can lead to material misunderstandings which, according to Catholic understanding, are clearly false. One can rightly speak of the sacredness of life only when one does not mean thereby a mystifying elevation of the natural phenomena of life. One must not repress the signs of mortality and the closeness of death, which cannot be wished away from natural human life (however they are to be theologically explained and brought into relation to God).

This intermingling of life and death, sin and holiness, joy and

2. See their contributions in this volume.

suffering, inseparable from a human standpoint, does not imply that it is theologically legitimate to view human life only in the half-light of its silhouette. At least from a Catholic perspective, it is possible to understand the "sacredness" or "holiness" intended for and promised to the person by God as an ontological quality which becomes the person's own, as something more than an externally appended attribute. The often overburdened distinction between a substantial and a relational ontology must not lead us to posit an irresolvable contradiction between complementary and equally legitimate thought forms, both of which have developed within the Christian context. Because Catholic theology thinks more in terms of the created structures of human existence, it interprets the creative call of God not simply as a constantly contemporary Word-event but rather as an abiding relation to persons, who receive this call internally and are determined by it *within* their creaturely being. The philosophical concept "substance" and the idea of a holiness that "inheres" in the human being here serve a theological assertion; they interpret the quality of the creative address by the "holy" God which is without analogy, different from every situation of human speech, and which permits persons to take up their creaturely existence. In this way of thinking, the holiness of the Creator is not conceived as a privileged attribute or an essential characteristic of the divine, but as a creative and abiding relation to persons, which qualifies their created being also as "holy." The formula of the "sacredness" of life does not, in the sense of some elemental naturalism or vitalism, refer to a characteristic of life independent of the "external" relation of this life to God. Rather, it refers to a consequence of the creature's ineffaceable createdness, which marks that the creature belongs to God.

Even if one grants that the broader biblical conception of holiness, uniting ontological, moral, and cultic elements, is less than precise from a philosophical point of view, against this background it is nevertheless clear that when the church took over this biblical conception into its language of proclamation, it had *no* intention of severing persons from the relationship to God which sustains them or of underwriting a human birthright independent of God. Talk of the sacredness of life is a reminder that persons receive their life as a gift. As gift, their own life and that of all others is not at their own disposal. Within the double relation described by the theology of creation, persons are constituted *in* their creaturely being *by* the external relationship to God which sustains them. The biblical semantics of holiness serves an original theological intention quite different from that of a traditional substantial anthropology. While the philosophical conception of substance derives the final nondisposability of persons from their self-givenness, by means of which every person possesses his or her existence (along a horizontal line) for his- or herself, the *dominium*-theory and the idea of holiness pursue the same goal in the opposite direction, by establishing that (along a vertical line) persons do not own themselves and that God has an abiding right over their lives.

For such an interpretation, the encyclical's normative background is the biblical idea of the holiness of God, not the civil-religious or natural-philosophical conceptions of holiness. This interpretation is supported by the broader context within which the theological foundation of the special worth of the human life is elaborated in *Evangelium Vitae*. In the style of a meditative exegesis of Scripture, the encyclical interprets the history of God with humanity beginning with the Exodus experience of the old covenant as a progressive history of discovery, within which occurs an ever deeper "perception of the meaning and value of life itself" (#31). This experience of the covenant people continues in the proclamation and actions of Jesus, his words and deeds, especially in his care for the poor and healing of the sick. The pope finds the high point of this biblical proclamation in the Johannine theology of life which in the person of Jesus Christ places before us the gospel of life in its highest reality as a historical *universale concretum* (#29) in relation to which the unique significance and irreplaceable value of every individual human life finds a final confirmation.

The worth of human life is grounded not only in its origin from God but also in the goal to which we are called: communion with the triune God. Our existence as children of God, granted in baptism, is here brought to completion. Already now participation in the divine life is opened up for humanity, like a seed sown in this earthly life which points beyond all limits of time (#34, 37-38). From a philosophical view, talk of "eternal" life is understood as a *qualitative* determination and as an assertion about the indestructible meaning of human life which establishes its unconditional and not merely quantitative worth. The argument is sometimes advanced by a utilitarian ethic that if human life has an infinite worth because of its determination towards participation in God's eternal life, then this eternal worth suffers no loss if life is artificially cut short. Such an argument grotesquely misunderstands the real philosophical intention of a biblical theology of life. It does not aim at making earthly life indifferent, its individual stages and phases subsumed in eternal significance. Rather, it emphasizes the special and unique worth of human life, valid for all its forms, conditions, and experiences and erased at no point along the line of its earthly extension.

2. The Prohibition of Killing, Abortion, and Euthanasia

The universal principle of the nondisposability of human life leads to three central assertions on the normative level of an ethic of life, which are solemnly emphasized in the encyclical: the unconditional validity of the prohibition of killing, as well as the exceptionless condemnation of abortion and active euthanasia. Although the pope appealed in relation to these assertions to his special teaching authority as successor of Peter and to his communion with all bishops, the formal magisterial qualification of these statements is not established beyond doubt in the encyclical (and thus they cannot be seen as infallible according to the dogmatic and canonical rules for the interpretation of magisterial pronouncements). Nevertheless, in view of their substance, they are hardly open to serious dissent among Catholic Christians. Thus, despite the unusual form in which the pope makes his assertions, he does not assert a new definition of the church's faith nor the proclamation of a moral dogma. He wishes rather to affirm a truth well anchored in the biblical and ecclesial tradition, continually taught, and about which a general consensus had reigned up to now within the Catholic Church — and, one may add, within the total Christian *oikumene*. This does not exclude that new accents may be made in grounding this truth, as occurs especially in connecting the prohibition of killing with the biblical idea of love.

The encyclical explains this connection, well known to the Reformation ethical tradition,[3] by making more precise the moral-theo-

3. In the Reformation churches, the prohibition of killing was from the beginning understood as an interpretation of the command of Christian love in view of the

logical distinction between *negative* prohibitions, which in a specialized philosophical description can be called unconditional duties of omission, and *positive* commands or duties of commission. Some negative moral prescriptions are unconditional and without exception, so that the inner immorality of such actions cannot be offset by any sort of good intentions or in themselves desirable consequences. Nevertheless, our possibility of realizing the good is dependent on many conditions, such as the degree of our moral strength, the concrete needs of other persons, and the occasions that present particular cases. The negative commands thus mark only a threshold in the sense of a beginning or necessary stage on the way to the freedom God's commands intend to teach the person. At the same time, they are an invitation to go beyond the minimum of the absolute prohibitions so that one can express a more objectively correct and appropriate yes to life, a yes that "will gradually embrace the entire horizon of the good" (#75, citing Matt. 5:48) over against manifold threats. The prohibition

---

physical life of the neighbor. In his *Small Catechism,* Martin Luther explains the fifth commandment: "We should fear and love God, and so we should not harm our neighbor's body, nor cause him any suffering, but help and befriend him in all his bodily needs" [1.12; *Weimarer Ausgabe* 30/1.386). This interpretation seems to place only the physical existence of the neighbor under God's protection. The repeated reference to the body underlines that for Luther it is here a matter of the maintenance of physical life. In his *Large Catechism,* Luther's interpretation of the fifth commandment moves beyond this defensive character and gives it a positive interpretation. With biblical texts such as the Sermon on the Mount or the pericope about the physical works of mercy (Matt. 25:31-46) in view, the prohibition of killing becomes a comprehensive command to give aid to the neighbor in need. Not just a deliberate bodily harm but the withdrawal of the love that maintains the neighbor's life is now seen as a violation of the fifth commandment. The commandment serves the defense and support of the neighbor; it is a protective commandment aimed at maintaining life in a comprehensive sense. In line with the principle that for the fulfillment of every *pro*scription there is a corresponding positive *pre*scription, Calvin also interprets the fifth commandment (by his count, the sixth) on two levels. Its immediate sense forbids any sort of injustice or violence toward our (innocent) neighbors. Beyond this, however, it pulls together the sense of all the commandments of the second table into a positive "summary" by asking what love for the neighbor in view of their bodily existence requires. "This summary is indeed no proscription, but a clear and explicit prescription: you should love your neighbor. Our command simply makes the specific application of this to the life of the neighbor" (*Auslegung der Heiligen Schrift* 2, no. 1 [Neukirchen: Neukirchener Verlag, 1901], pp. 616-17; cf. *Institutes* 2.8.39).

of killing is at once a negative barrier and a positive command in that it can be fulfilled according to its original intention only when it is understood in light of the more comprehensive biblical command of love as encompassing more than the immediate demands of justice. "The commandment 'You shall not kill' thus establishes the point of departure for the start of true freedom. It leads us to promote life actively, and to develop particular ways of thinking and acting which serve life. In this way we exercise our responsibility towards the persons entrusted to us and we show, in deeds and in truth, our gratitude to God for the great gift of life" (#76, citing Ps. 139:13-14).

In this development from the prohibition of killing to a comprehensive promotion of life in the spirit of love of neighbor is to be found not only a previously rather unusual reappropriation of a common ecumenical legacy of all Christian churches but also an important contribution to present bioethical discussions. This deeper grounding of the fifth commandment contradicts those philosophical conceptions of an ethic of life that see an ethic of mutual respect and an ethic of care, both requiring unconditionally only respect for individual autonomy, as complementary. The enlightened subjects of an open society then decide for whatever social solidarity corresponds to the values held by their own subgroup.[4] Over against such a view, the encyclical emphasizes: "The commandment 'You shall not kill,' even in its more positive aspects of respecting, loving and promoting human life, is binding on every individual human being" (#77). The concern here is not to draw a moral border — as Wannenwetsch presumes with reference to the moral distinction between acts evil in themselves, commanded acts, and supererogatory acts (cf. #86). Rather the unity of the ethical demand is emphasized.[5] The reference to the prophetic tradition of the biblical ethos and the reminder of the universal validity of the love command warn of the danger that a philosophical ethic,

4. On this bioethical standpoint, see H. T. Engelhardt, Jr., *The Foundations of Bioethics* (New York: Oxford University Press, 1986), pp. 74ff. Here the task of determining the precise extent of the principle of case is explicitly left to the decision of particular moral communities.

5. For the rejection of a too schematic contrast of commands and counsels, acts evil in themselves and works of supererogation, see also VS #16 and 17, where their shifting and reciprocal relations are described in the context of a more comprehensive exploration of the Sermon on the Mount.

by means of any overly sharp demarcation of concepts, can erode the idea of moral responsibility, divide ethics into distinct regions, and so lose sight of the unity of the moral subject.

3. The Valuation of Individual Normative Questions

The avoidance of a precise philosophical terminology and of the clarification of the moral-theological implications of individual normative questions brings with it difficulties which cannot be resolved with sufficient clarity on the basis of the text of the encyclical, despite its unambiguous sounding formulations. Even in the case of an unconditionally valid norm of natural law, such as the prohibition of killing, a practical power of judgment is required to apply it in specific situations. The theological depth attained by the biblical, salvation-historical, and christological grounding of the prohibition of killing is no substitute for a normative ethical involvement with the problems of practical application of universal assertions in concrete life. In the context of medical ethics, one must ask about the doctor's responsibility for unborn life: does the unconditional prohibition of every intentional and direct abortion, a prohibition the encyclical upholds (#58), also apply to a case of mortal danger in the strict sense? Thanks to the progress of modern medicine, such cases where life truly stands against life, where the life of the mother can only be saved at the cost of the life of the child, have become increasingly rare. This does not free a normative ethic from the necessity of inquiring about a morally correct or ethically defensible treatment of such a conflict. Most Catholic moral theologians today view such a medically indicated abortion as indirect killing as described by the classical doctrine of double effect and thus as a morally defensible alternative. Such a solution, seen as permissible by such magisterial pronouncements on the local level as the German moral catechism *Leben aus dem Glauben* (Living from Faith), goes beyond what is explicitly said in *Evangelium Vitae*, but, in contrast to earlier papal statements, is not explicitly excluded.[6]

This question at least shows that the limitation of the prohibition

6. Cf. *Katholischer Erwachsenen-Katechismus*, vol. 2, *Leben aus dem Glauben*, ed. German Bishops' Conference (Freiburg: Herder, 1995), p. 292.

of killing to "innocent" persons does not remove all the difficulties that can follow from the distinction between an unconditionally valid norm and its linguistic formulation. In addition to the classical exceptions (self-defense, capital punishment, the killing of a tyrant), others arise because the limited norm of not killing *innocent* persons is not yet appropriately defined. A mentally deranged, violent criminal is not usually seen as guilty, yet the police may shoot a deranged person on a rampage when the lives of other persons are at extreme risk. Similarly, it is permitted under the conditions of the law of war to kill enemy soldiers although their mere membership in an opposed army in no way suffices to view them as individually "guilty."[7] Even if the encyclical gives a highly restricted formulation of the criteria under which killing is permitted in a just war, limited to the strict case of defense (#55), it cannot be thought that the unconditional formulation of the prohibition of killing the innocent intends to exclude categorically in the future the previously valid regulations that apply to the police's duty of protection or that apply under the conditions of the law of war. Context rather suggests that the encyclical wishes to meet arguments that would permit *new* exceptions to the prohibition in the presently controversial areas of the ethics of life, above all in relation to the termination of pregnancy and assisted suicide. These ethical arguments are often justified by the claim that traditional ethics and the moral teaching of the church have at least tolerated self-defense, capital punishment, the killing of a tyrant, and war. One then seeks to conclude that the inviolability of life is *relative,* not *absolute,* and can be offset in particular cases by other goods.

7. Contemporary moral theology seeks to avoid this difficulty by means of a distinction between combatants and noncombatants rather than between "guilty" and "innocent" assailants. A possible permissibility of killing within the context of a war is then justified, not through the ascription of a fictitious "guilt" to the opposing soldiers, but through the objective situation that their physical existence as combatants constitutes a present threat to one's own population. The distinction between combatants and noncombatants seeks not only to describe the conditions under which killing enemy soldiers is allowed but to provide for a restricted application of this criterion by setting alongside it the moral command to spare the civilian population.

4. The Significance of the Corporeality of Our Practical Existence

Such an argument undervalues the anthropological significance of the spiritual-physical unity of the human person. Since late German idealism and the phenomenology of our century, philosophical anthropology has worked out ever more sharply that the body and physical life are not "goods" external to human personal realization, standing in a purely instrumental relation to the person's authentic determination as a moral subject. The body is rather the irreducible means of expression in which human persons in all their acts, even in the highest self-realization of the spirit, are represented. Even in relation to the capacity of moral action, the human person must be seen as a physical-spiritual unity. All persons in their means of moral self-determination are present to themselves only in and through their own bodies. Respect for the personal worth of persons relates not only to their inner convictions or moral values but must also include the inviolability of their bodily existence. We respect other persons only when we accept them in the concrete form in which they encounter us, whether as healthy persons at the height of their personal attractions and professional accomplishments, or as ill, handicapped, dying, or even unborn persons in the extreme vulnerability of their physical existence. The fundamental principle of a humane ethic of life, according to which we owe the same respect to every form of human life from its beginning to its end, rests finally on the respect we give to every person within our democratic culture of freedom and self-determination.

In this sense, the body can be called the concrete limit of freedom. The anthropological principle that in physical life we respect the actualization of the freedom of other persons and their self-presentation is valid even in the extreme borderline cases of incurable illness and painful death. Whoever wishes to make persons responsible for their own allegedly "humane" death, appealing to individual self-determination, not only hands such persons over to their own anxieties, temptations to resignation, and moods of depression, but also to the demands of society. Over against the pressures that can fall on the incurably ill even before the onset of the last phase of dying, the prohibition of killing protects the freedom of the dying and their right to their own death. In line with the original sense of these words, this does not imply an artificial event brought about by human agents but rather a line drawn for all persons and thus not erasable by themselves or others. Against this background the ethical significance of the distinction between killing and letting die becomes understandable (#65). The doctor who stops a therapy that has become futile and lets a patient die does so in the knowledge that medical art is to serve the good of concrete persons, not the prolongation of life at any price. The doctor respects such patients in the vulnerability and neediness of their bodily existence by seeking to make such a death easier but also by respecting the final limit of death, which the dying also recognize for themselves.

In bearing a common powerlessness, we display a deeper human solidarity and a more decisive respect for the worth of the suffering person than can be shown in the escape of an artificially contrived death. The idea of active euthanasia unconsciously presupposes a dualism which remains captive to the paradigm of the modern medical system the excesses of which are allegedly being combated. The killing carried out by the doctor, destroying the patient's *physical life,* allegedly expresses respect for the patient's self-determination as a *person.* Only on the basis of this latent dualism and the attendant depersonalization of the medical killing (as an allegedly medically indicated measure) can the fiction be constructed that the personal relation to the dying patient is upheld and not broken off by killing. Only when suffering and dying persons are completely reduced to their physical existence can the otherwise contradictory thought become imaginable that we are liberating them from their unbearable suffering when we at the same time liberate them from life.[8] On a subordinate level, it remains also remarkable (and relevant also for a strictly consequence-oriented ethic) that the question of the prevention of abuses is not raised with sufficient seriousness, not to mention then satisfactorily answered. Within a society that accepted active euthanasia within its moral rules, only a few persons would really be given the alternative to a self-chosen death as a happy death at the appropriate time. The rule would become a planned death in harmony with the medical, material, and

8. See the penetrating analysis of Johannes Fischer, "Aktive und passive Sterbe-hilfe," *Zeitschrift für evangelische Ethik* 40 (1996): 110-27, esp. 118-19.

human resources of the society, to which the dying would be consigned under the banner of humanity and personal dignity.

The argumentation that interprets the assertion of the unconditional validity of the prohibition of killing as an emphatic overvaluation of life expressive of an alleged idiosyncratic religious opinion of the Judeo-Christian tradition misperceives more than just the corporeality of our practical being, an irreducible condition for the existence of every person.[9] It also overlooks the fact that in the classical exceptions to the prohibition, life stands against life. The situations of ethical conflict to which the thesis of the relative worth of life appeals are in fact true conflict situations only under the presupposition that the respective right to life of those involved is not a priori relativized. Moreover, this argumentation expresses an anachronistic outlook: should we seriously view active euthanasia or the killing of an unborn child as morally allowed simply because earlier generations viewed capital punishment as an indispensable means to protect society from capital criminals? Over against such superficial equations and the far-reaching consequences that are drawn from them, the encyclical's reminder of the unconditional validity of the prohibition of killing is very much to the moral-philosophical point. The examples cited show, however, how difficult it is to formulate this moral norm with the needed precision in order to avoid involuntarily subsuming under the norm cases one does not intend to prohibit.

5. The Invitation to Repentance and Reconciliation

Surprisingly, the encyclical in another respect differentiates precisely between the level of a fundamental moral principle and that of the concrete evaluation of particular cases. Maintaining the moral norms that reject killing the innocent, intentional abortion, or active euthanasia as morally unacceptable is not to be confused with morally judging the personal guilt of those who violate these prohibitions. The

9. Such an argumentation is put forward today especially by the Australian ethicist Peter Singer, *Praktische Ethik* (Stuttgart: Reclam, 1984), pp. 102-3, and his student Helga Kuhse, *The Sanctity of Life-Doctrine in Medicine* (Oxford: Oxford University Press, 1987), pp. 109-19.

encyclical deals in a very careful and differentiated way with the motives that might move a woman to abort her child. It recognizes that these subjective grounds are not always matters of egoistic convenience or lack of readiness to sacrifice, but that this decision is for the woman herself "often tragic and painful" (#58). Nevertheless, however serious the personal motives, for example, the mother's concern for her own health or for an adequate quality of life for children already born, these can never justify the planned destruction of a weak and needy person, for that is what the unborn child in the womb is.[10] In many cases of abortion, however, the primary guilt for the killing of the unborn child does not lie with the woman: "In the first place, the father of the child may be to blame, not only when he directly pressures the woman to have an abortion, but also when he directly encourages such a decision on her part by leaving her alone to face the problems of pregnancy" (#59).

The pope also names certain more anonymous factors that can give the final push to a decision against life: family surroundings as well as a widely shared social mentality of abortion linked to the "structure of sin" of an extreme individualism and a form of life oriented to one's own self-assertion. One sees here that a right to an abortion, claimed as an alleged protection of the moral self-determination of the woman concerned, often serves quite different ends in view of the actual pressures presented by the environment. Such a "right" would primarily protect the unstated demand to avoid the undesired consequence of one's own sexual behavior, the demand for an irresponsibility without consequences. Men have long claimed this for themselves; they now wish to concede this to women as a sign of equality and fairness.

A differentiated understanding of the concrete situations in which a conflicted pregnancy can lead to abortion is expressed in the word the pope addresses directly to women who have decided for the

10. A Catholic moral theologian can thus only agree with the reflections of B. Wannenwetsch when he rejects the theory of a "proportionalism of guilt" and the extension to every situation of moral conflict of Bonhoeffer's idea of a responsible acceptance of guilt. If the agent is unavoidably guilty, then not only is human freedom and responsibility paralyzed, but the alternative courses of action become indifferent — with the result that all decisions in the end appear morally legitimate if only one meets them with a sufficiently developed consciousness of guilt.

abortion of a child. He explicitly emphasizes what the church throughout its history has held fast: that the wrong of abortion finds forgiveness before God and that no woman need remain alone with her anxieties, self-doubts, and feelings of guilt. Human understanding, forgiveness, and reconciliation mean something quite different from an attitude of indifference to the wrong deed. The certainty of receiving forgiveness presupposes the insight into the wrongful character of the preceding act and the acceptance of one's own guilt; in fact, it makes these possible. Those who know themselves invited to reconciliation are empowered by the word of forgiveness spoken to them to face the truth of their own life history and to convert to a new outlook. The pope sees here a particularly authentic witness to the gospel of life:

> I would now like to say a special word to women who have had an abortion. The Church is aware of the many factors which may have influenced your decision, and she does not doubt that in many cases it was a painful and even shattering decision. The wound in your heart may not yet have healed. Certainly what happened was and remains terribly wrong. But do not give in to discouragement and do not lose hope. Try rather to understand what happened and face it honestly. If you have not already done so, give yourselves over with humility and trust to repentance. The Father of mercies is ready to give you his forgiveness and his peace in the Sacrament of Reconciliation. You will come to understand that nothing is definitively lost and you will also be able to ask forgiveness from your child, who is now living in the Lord. (#99)

The deepest ground why many persons evade the claim of moral norms or in their conscience can no longer understand them lies in the increasing loss to contemporary consciousness of a sense for the seriousness of guilt and for the reality of forgiveness. When the word of forgiveness is no longer heard, an unhealthy alibi-mechanism leads ineluctably to an exclusion of the claim of moral truth. The demand for justification before one's own conscience and before public judgment to which individuals are then exposed will not permit an unblinkered perception of one's own guilt and failure without deep anxiety and insecurity.

The insights of modern psychoanalysis into the long-term workings of the human soul teach well enough that the repression of a consciousness of guilt does not lead to an acceptable solution of a moral conflict. Without the possibility of forgiveness, knowledge of one's own guilt becomes unbearable. The deepest aporia of an ethic without guilt is that it entangles persons in the unhealthy demand for self-justification because it cannot speak the liberating word of forgiveness. The confession that one has fallen short of the moral demand and done wrong becomes psychologically impossible if it entails the loss of moral self-respect that must follow if the possibility of reconciliation is removed.

When guilt is not repressed but can be accepted, then the first step has already been taken toward a new, productive orientation of life. This becomes possible in the reception of forgiveness. The partial disappearance of this connection from the ethical consciousness of our time is perhaps the deepest reason why the moral message of Christianity is extensively experienced as a merciless and excessive demand rather than as a liberating gospel.

6. The Relation Between Moral Norm and State Law

On the basis of an understanding of natural law, it corresponds to a long tradition of Catholic teaching to point out the ethical basis on which modern democracy rests. The encyclical recognizes the precedence of democracy over all other forms of government, even while granting it only the instrumental value of peacefully attaining a person's existential life goals (#70). But this precedence does not follow from the principle of majority rule nor from that of conformity to constitutional law, but rather from the recognition of human rights, which are prior to the actions of the state and to the interactions of individuals. Already during the debate in Germany over fundamental values during the 1970s, the church emphasized that the democratic state must not interpret its constitutionally mandated neutrality over against differing worldviews as a mandate to withdraw from all moral conflicts in society. As the guarantor of a free and democratic legal order, it can neither understand itself as value-neutral nor view its impartiality as a position of strict equidistance from all the moral convictions at work in society. If the democratic state, faced with socially divergent convictions, no longer sees in the core areas of common life a sphere of rights not open to the intervention of shifting majorities, then in the long run it endangers the legitimacy which gives it a precedence over other forms of government.

Within political ethics, we are led to the conclusion that a hypothetical or really existing legal system of norms that does not meet fundamental criteria of justice no longer corresponds to the concept of a legal order. It is thus not surprising when the pope points to the dangers democracy faces from a widespread ethical relativism. Over against the temptation to confuse the civil virtue of democratic tolerance with an in-principle indifference to the claims of the moral law, he emphasizes that "the value of democracy stands or falls with the values which it embodies and promotes" (#70). As values underlying democratic government, the encyclical lists the worth of human persons, their inalienable rights, the solidarity of individual social groups, and the common good as the goal and criterion of political life.

The idea which stands in the background of the encyclical's exposition, that of a grounding of the legal order in objective values, was also widely addressed in German jurisprudence following the Second World War. Many then considered this grounding well suited to overcome legal positivism without needing to appeal to the idea of natural rights. The thesis that law must be understood as an ordering of values, that it finds its material basis in the moral and social values it realizes, today encounters strong objections, some of which the encyclical mentions (#68). Questions about the ontological and epistemological status of moral values remain extensively unsettled. Legal philosophical discussions are preoccupied above all with the practical impossibility of achieving a binding intersubjective consensus about the significance, normativity, and varying priority of individual values.[11]

The encyclical's exposition does not pursue the goal of justifying an objective hierarchy of values for the total complex of the legal order. It limits itself to emphasizing the governmental duty to protect the most

---

11. See G. Luf, "Zur Problematik des Wertbegriffs in der Rechtsphilosophie," in *Jus Humanitatis: FS A. Verdross,* ed. H. Miesler (Berlin: Duncker u. Homblot, 1980), pp. 127-46; E.-W. Böckenförde, "Zur Kritik der Wertbegründung des Rechts," in *Recht, Staat, Freiheit: Studien zur Rechtsphilosophie, Staatstheorie und Verfassungsgeschichte* (Frankfurt: Suhrkamp, 1991), pp. 67-91.

basic legal right to life. A democratic state must not make this right dependent on the subjective valuation human life enjoys in the eyes of specific groups or individuals. One can ask, however, whether this point might not have been better made if the encyclical had more strictly held to the natural-law conception of the natural rights of the human person which stake a claim over against the democratic state prior to any of its specific laws. Clearly, the encyclical uses the concepts "natural rights" and "moral values" in a broader sense than is usual in the legal-philosophical discussion. The suggestion of an objective grounding of law in values is better understood as a supplement to its grounding in natural law than as an alternative. Nevertheless, it is amazing that a magisterial document needlessly lays on itself the difficulties of a philo-sophical determination of the concept of value and of its relation to the idea of natural rights, issues long familiar to the church's social thought. Presumably, the basis for this procedure lies in the general linguistic usage of the public discussion as well as in the personal development of the present pope, whose ethical thought has been decisively stamped by the debate with the philosophy of value.

An understanding of the legal order which understands it as an order of values and which then measures the state only in terms of the moral values it realizes or, in particular areas, fails to realize, underestimates a further aspect decisive for the self-understanding of the modern state. Even when understood against a foundation and norm that is more than positivistic, the political-ethical legitimation of the free legal order does not lie *alone* in the public realization of a normative understanding of justice. Rather there are principles *internal* to the rule of law which are also of great ethical significance, such as the applicability of laws to all citizens, the obligation to make laws public, the prohibition of retroactivity, principles often only grasped in the mirror of an experience of arbitrary tyranny. It is not simply that a legal order loses its quality as a rule of law when specific laws contradict moral commands or no longer satisfy their requirements in a sufficient manner. Rather this occurs first when such a contra-diction or nonagreement with the moral order touches central areas of the common life of the society and so crosses a certain threshold at which the moral legitimacy of the entire legal system is called into question. The warning that disrespect for rights that are prior to the state by state violence or tolerance for such disrespect by social practice can have effects on other areas of law and undermine the entire legal order has a particular historical background: the conflict with National-Socialist tyranny. This line of argument is encountered already in the sermons against the Nazi euthanasia program by Bishop von Galen of Münster and reappears following the Second World War in the basis the jurist Gustav Radbruch gave for his rejection of legal positivism.[12]

John Paul II sees the Western democracies today exposed to a comparable danger if they do not effectively deal with the tendency toward a creeping disrespect for basic human rights, especially for the claim of persons to life and bodily integrity from the beginning to the end of their earthly existence. In view of the terrible experiences of our century, for which the pope has a special sensitivity because of his life history and which are for him more lively than they are for most of his superficial critics, one can hardly doubt the danger of such a development. But even those who share these concerns of the pope can only regret the dark tone and argumentative one-sidedness of his analysis. It is also a result of this century's experience of injustice that Christians affirm the secular rule of law for the sake of its guarantees of freedom, even if it does not agree with their demands in all the forms of its social reality. The persuasive power of these passages of the encyclical would have benefited from a more cautious treatment of the inner dilemma of the modern state and an encouraging word on the difficulties of political action in a society where moral convictions drift ever farther apart. Finally, as O'Donovan's carefully weighed analysis of church teachings on the problem of capital punishment makes clear, the encyclical at other places (cf. #27 and 56) gives a more positive view of the modern state, seen in the extensive humanization of legal punishment (and which leads one to hope for the total abolition of the death penalty).

7. A Prophetic Alert

As a document of church teaching, a papal encyclical such as *Evangelium Vitae* is not to be confused with a philosophical treatise, a

---

12. See G. Radbruch, *Rechtsphilosophie,* 8th ed. (Stuttgart: Koehler, 1973), p. 345.

handbook of moral theology, or a collection of case studies in medical ethics. The true worth of this encyclical is thus not to be sought in its particular argumentative analysis in the various fields of bioethical controversy. It lies rather in the prophetic power with which it exposes the life-contradicting tendencies that proceed from the spiritual vacuum of meaning and the moral crisis of orientation of our time. Various political, cultural, and ecclesial commentators thus quickly placed it among the significant church documents of the postconciliar phase. German bishop Walter Kasper hazarded the assessment that in retrospect one will see *Evangelium Vitae* as one of the most important and fundamental texts of the end of this century, one that focused the divided situation of our transitional period at the threshold of the third millennium.[13] The severe judgment of the text's unsparing diagnosis of our time's superficially plausible democratic culture is completed by the call for a new civilization of life in the encyclical's concluding fourth section. Its contours are roughly sketched for the specific areas of family, church, and society, and in relation to social and scientific institutions such as schools, hospitals, and universities.

The pope repeatedly emphasizes that a fundamental renewal will be impossible without a break with the fond illusions of late bourgeois individualism. Here he sees the true practical heresy and the great spiritual challenge for Christianity. He sees in the symptoms of meaninglessness and lack of orientation, failure of solidarity and growing incapacity for commitment, and rampant loneliness and spiritual anxiety the increasingly manifest unintended consequences of the modern history of freedom. The balance is being upset among the three great ideals of the French Revolution — Liberty, Equality, Fraternity — which originally embodied the demand of the Enlightenment for a comprehensive reformation of social life. While the antagonism between liberty and equality has often been noted in political theory, today a new contradiction appears that is more difficult to reconcile. The dominance of individual self-assertion makes the slogan of freedom the only primary value of social life. Without the idea of shared social responsibility or the knowledge that respect for life is first and foremost respect for the life of *others,* the ideal of

13. W. Kasper, "Ein prophetisches Wort in die Zeit: Anmerkungen zur Enzyklika 'Evangelium Vitae,'" *Internationale kirchliche Zeitschrift* 24 (1995): 187-92.

democratic freedom degenerates into an individualistic caricature. Even more, it consumes the capacity for lived solidarity and forces into the background respect for the radical equality of all. The actual style of life that dominates in most Western countries thus betrays the great moral ideals which once stood at the cradle of modern Europe.

The prophetic alternative picture of a new civilization of life and love that the encyclical presents thus aims at a fundamental renewal of the shared social life. It intends a new lifestyle that preserves the priority of being before having and of persons before dead matter and material things, and in which is found a new valuation of life in its vulnerability and neediness. "This renewed life-style involves a passing from indifference to concern for others, from rejection to acceptance of them. Other people are not rivals from whom we must defend ourselves, but brothers and sisters to be supported. They are to be loved for their own sakes, and they enrich us by their very presence" (#98).

8. The Civilization of Love and the Anticulture of Death

The encyclical speaks with urgent words about the many-sided dangers to which human life in our modern civilization is exposed. The structure of its four parts is repeatedly interrupted by a circular, repeating line of thought, which already on the encyclical's first pages allows the most important arguments to be heard before they are developed, like individual musical themes. For this purpose the encyclical from the beginning employs as a structuring element a contrast between the imperative civilization of love and a "culture of death" painted in dark colors that at times approach the apocalyptic. This consistently and gradually mounting drama imparts to the encyclical a conceptual and linguistic virtuosity which for long stretches makes one forget that this is a text of the magisterium. In the style of a prophetic critique of the times, it repeatedly indicts the destructive power of death, which since Cain's murder of his brother runs like a blood-red thread through the non-salvation history of humanity and which, in view of the degree of the destruction of life in this century, is today more evident than ever. Compared with the verbal force of the metaphors employed to describe the destructive violence of evil, the depiction of the opposed civilization of love, despite valuable hints — for example, the promotion of such new forms of human solidarity as voluntary organ donation, "adoption at a distance," or respect for the elderly (#86, 93, 94) — remains pale and schematic.

This decline of verbal drama, also observable in such a literary masterpiece as Dante's *Divina Comedia,* is not simply to be ascribed to a creative failure in the final redaction of the text. The encyclical here at any rate approaches the limits of what is possible in a magisterial document. Rather must one ask in a sober analysis of the encyclical's arguments, intellectual motifs, and linguistic means of expression whether the material content of the concept "culture of death" can really measure up to its linguistic connotative power. This phrase, on the semantic level rightly seen as the authentic contrast figure to the opening words of the encyclical, has in recent years been elevated in the church's proclamation to a keynote in the diagnosis of the times. Its unclear intellectual heritage is hardly noticed anymore. In favor of this originally American talk of a "culture of death" is the way it names the common roots and cultural interconnections that lie at the basis of the life-opposed tendencies of our time. Alongside these commonalities, however, there are important differences among such practices as artificial birth control, abortion, forced sterilization, test-tube insemination, and embryo research, which the encyclical in its differentiated consideration of birth control and abortion (#12-13) and in its all-too-short discussion of population growth (#16) expressly recognizes. The more fundamental question is whether the fearful, self-destructive power of evil is rightly called a "culture" of death. Can one seriously speak of an abortion *culture* (#13) without doing violence to the original sense of this word and its weight in the total philosophical and theological tradition?

From its etymological roots, the word *culture* has predominantly positive overtones: it comes from the Latin *colere,* meaning to cultivate or care for, and presupposes a high degree of lively organization and order, an application of human intelligence and reason, creative formation and human capacity.[14] In most modern languages, this word

14. See W. Perpeet, "Kultur, Kulturphilosophie," in *Historisches Wörterbuch der Philosophie,* vol. 4 (Basel: Schwabe, 1976), pp. 1309-19.

stands for the highest interior completion of human existence. Against this background, can one apply such a term as a description of the destructive, disintegrative force of death? To ask the question is already to answer it in the negative. American cultural anthropology speaks of "cultural patterns," meaning the total orientation which each culture realizes on its own level of development and within its own sphere of validity. But the totalitarian violence of death, pulling along all in its wake, cannot be compared with that. We should use the phrase "culture of death" sparingly, if at all, and in quotation marks, to remind us of the strange and inauthentic character of this form of speech. It would be conceptually sharper and linguistically more precise to speak of an "anticulture" of death and to preserve the positive term *culture* for the life-promoting impulses in our social reality, which we should discover ever anew. In this sense, at the point at which it introduces this concept, the encyclical speaks also of a "crisis of culture" (#11) and of a contemporary "anti-solidarity-culture" (#12).[15]

Some readers might see behind these reflections on the right use of words an exaggerated linguistic purism that shows too little understanding for the specific character of the church's language of proclamation. Theology performs a needed service to the faith of the church, however (or, as O'Donovan says, to its "prophets"), when it insists on the clarity of central terms and warns about obscure emphases. Overly broad concepts, resonating connotations, and too-general categorizations only veil the persuasive power of the material issues the church's teaching puts forward. It can then all too easily be overlooked that the common outlook of the Christian churches on the central questions of an ethic of life rests on consistent and valid arguments able to stand the test of moral-philosophical analysis.

---

15. Translator's note: This phrase literally translates *Anti-Solidaritätskultur,* the German of *Evangelium Vitae.* The English translation at this point reads "a culture which denies solidarity." The official Latin text (*Acta Apostolicae Sedis* 87 [1995]: 414) is closer to the English: *"culturam quandam adversus omnem hominum solidarietatem."*

History, Roots, and Innovations: A Response to the Engaging Protestants

JAMES F. KEENAN S.J.

MY RESPONSE TO these theologically rich essays is to try to situate the two encyclicals into a broader Catholic context. First, I suggest that the disappointment that Donfried and others expressed about *Veritatis Splendor* not developing a Scripture-based ethics is in part due to the encyclical's inability to free itself from the history of Catholic moral theology. Second, to the recurring Lutheran complaint that the same encyclical fails to recognize the absolute priority of faith in the life of sanctification, I add that some Roman Catholic moral theologians note that the roots of the moral life in charity are also overlooked. To illustrate this point, I contrast some theologians' writings with the encyclical's comments on the distinction between goodness and rightness. Finally, to O'Donovan's and Wannenwetsch's essays on *Evangelium Vitae* I describe the important contribution made by Pope John Paul on sanctity of life.

I. History

In his paper "The Use of Scripture in *Veritatis Splendor*," Karl Donfried expresses his disappointment in the encyclical because its first part suggests a forthcoming discipleship ethics based on a christological vision. Such a vision would respect "the freedom and dignity" of the disciple while still calling the disciple to a moral life. Clearly Donfried expects an ethics of interiority, an ethics that addresses the disciple at the depths of his or her vocation and offers a variety of expressions to guide character formation. Instead the encyclical turns not to the disciple's interior response but rather rushes to assert the need for "obedience to universal and unchanging moral norms." This perfunctory turn to norms for guiding external conduct prompts Donfried to offer the same final verdict of disappointment as William Spohn has: "The encyclical promises a Christonomous ethics of discipleship but it cannot deliver because it reduces morality to a matter of rules and principles."[1]

Why is it that the promising first part never delivers the vision that Donfried expects? Why does it seem, at least to Donfried, that the biblical writings in the encyclical simply "cloak" the "objective norms of morality . . . with the authority of Christ and the authority of the Old and New Testaments"? I would suggest that the magisterium's inability to develop a discipleship ethics of interiority in part stems from both the centrality of the external action in the history of Catholic moral theology and the long-standing separation between manuals for the moral life and manuals for the spiritual life. The absence of any development in the encyclical of a gospel-based ethics is due to the fact that Catholic morality has rarely reflected at length on the interior life. Where Protestants might find the development of a christological ethics from the Scriptures a natural move, the Catholic occupation with particular external actions has caused it to overlook those more personal dimensions of the moral life, like the formation of character, the setting of goals, and so on. To make this case, I present a brief historical survey of moral theology and then turn to the use of the Ten Commandments in the sixteenth century, where we can see the differences between the Catholics and the Reformers.

In *The Making of Moral Theology*, Jesuit ethicist John Mahoney demonstrates convincingly that the roots of Catholic moral theology are found in the practice of confessing sins.[2] To guide the confessor in determining the nature of sin and its suitable penance, "penitentials"

---

1. William Spohn, "Morality on the Way of Discipleship: The Use of Scripture in Veritatis Splendor," in *Veritatis Splendor: American Responses*, ed. Michael Allsopp and John O'Keefe (Kansas City: Sheed and Ward, 1995), pp. 83-105, at p. 102.

2. John Mahoney, *The Making of Moral Theology* (Oxford: Clarendon, 1987).

were reproduced throughout Europe from the sixth to the twelfth century.[3] In these penitentials, the general classifications of moral conduct were described in terms of particular external actions: the lie, the act of theft, the blasphemous word, the adultery, and so on. From these books, moral theology developed its primary interest in sin and identified sin as these particular external acts that corresponded to one of the seven deadly sins. Moral theology during these many centuries showed no sense of idealism or vision; it showed no concern for Christian identity nor for spirituality; and there was no developed concept of discipleship.[4] Judgment day alone was its central preoccupation, where persons' deeds in lieu of their hearts were scrutinized.

The growth of religious orders and their work of evangelization of the emerging towns was a hallmark of the thirteenth century. This period emphasized not the decay but the possible growth of the Christian. Ironically this movement was in part circumvented by the Fourth Lateran Council (1215), when Pope Innocent III imposed the Easter duty, making the turn to penance no longer a matter of spiritual election but ecclesiastical law. Henry Lea called this "the most important legislative act in the history of the Church."[5]

For the next three centuries, two types of moral instructions developed: the great *Summae theologiae* of high scholasticism and the confessional manuals, which were effectively sophisticated penitentials. Clearly, Thomas Aquinas's *Summa* represents the greatest achievement from this time. There he presented three parts, each representing a movement: God's movement toward us, our movement toward God, the two movements in the incarnation of Jesus

---

3. John T. McNeill and Helen M. Gamer, eds., *Medieval Handbooks of Penance* (New York: Columbia University Press, 1990).

4. Still, underlying these penitentials were many shared presuppositions. See the illuminating work by Hubertus Lutterbach, "Die Sexualtabus in den Bußbüchern," *Saeculum* 46 (1995): 216-48.

5. Henry Lea, *The History of Auricular Confession and Indulgences in the Latin Church* (Philadelphia: Lea Brothers, 1896), 1.230; see Kilian McDonnell, "The *Summae Confessorum* on the Integrity of Confession as Prolegomena for Luther and Trent," *Theological Studies* 54 (1993): 405-27; Thomas Tentler, *Sin and Confession on the Eve of the Reformation* (Princeton: Princeton University Press, 1977); Miriam Turrini, *La cosciènza e le lègge. Morale e diritto nei testi per la confessióne della prima Età moderna* (Bologna: Società editrice il Mulino, 1991).

Christ, both human and divine. Thomas directed the reader in pursuit of the end, which is union with God and is achieved through charity; he provided the virtues, the cardinal ones for the moral life and the theological ones for the spiritual life (together the seven virtues embody the end for all Christians); and he presented intentionality and not external deeds as the proper concern for determining moral living. Though other scholastics shared Thomas's concern with interiority, the virtues, and the integrated anthropological vision, by the fourteenth century moral reflection began again to focus not on who we are or who we ought to become, but on what we did wrong. While Thomas held that "all moral matter comes down to the virtues,"[6] those with a less integrated view of the person preferred simply to look at the confessional manuals that stretch from Innocent's edict until the Reformation. These confessional manuals are basically more systematized presentations of the penitential manuals, still considering external actions under the categories of the seven deadly sins.

Recent studies have shown that the moral reasoning of the sixteenth and seventeenth century was highly innovative in meeting the needs of the Europeans who through the explorations of the New World and trade with the East could no longer accept the older moral methods of the past. To answer those new and urgent needs, a new moral method rose quickly that looked not to existing principles but rather to cases. That new method of looking at cases was known as casuistry.[7] But regardless of the new method, the content of moral theology was the same: to determine which actions were forbidden

6. *Summa Theologiae,* 2.2. prologue, "Sic igitur tota materia morali ad considerationem virtutum reducta." On Thomas see Leonard Boyle, *The Setting of the "Summa Theologiae" of Saint Thomas* (Toronto: Pontifical Institute of Medieval Studies, 1982); James Keenan, *Goodness and Rightness in Thomas Aquinas' Summa Theologiae* (Washington, D.C.: Georgetown University Press, 1992); James Keenan, "Ten Reasons Why Thomas Aquinas Is Important for Ethics Today," *New Blackfriars* 75 (1994): 354-63; James Weisheipl, *Friar Thomas D'Aquino* (Washington, D.C.: Catholic University Press, 1983).

7. R. M. Henley, "Casuistry," in *Encyclopedia of Religion and Ethics,* ed. James Hastings (New York: Charles Scribner's Sons, 1928), 3:239-47; Albert Jonsen and Stephen Toulmin, *The Abuse of Casuistry: A History of Moral Reasoning* (Berkeley: University of California Press, 1988); James Keenan and Thomas Shannon, eds., *The Context for Casuistry* (Washington, D.C.: Georgetown University Press, 1995); Edmund Leites, ed., *Conscience and Casuistry in Early Modern Europe* (New York: Cambridge University Press, 1988).

and which ones were permitted. Moreover, from the eighteenth through the twentieth century that imaginative casuistry evolved into the rather unimaginative moral manuals of theology, which were textbooks, again for confessors.

A survey of the history of moral theology then shows that with few exceptions moral theology has been nearly exclusively concerned with sins, that is, with particular actions determined to be wrong. Mahoney is right then to make the claim that he does: the roots of moral theology are in its obsession with sin as external actions, but he also insists that, excepting Thomas, moral theologians have never done what they were always called to do, to recognize morality as a response to the Spirit's movements in our lives.[8]

Perhaps the reader doubts the singularity of the focus of Catholic moral theology. Then it helps to look at the preface of the first modern manual of moral theology to appear in English. There the English Jesuit Thomas Slater described Catholic moral theology as

> the product of centuries of labor bestowed by able and holy men on the practical problems of Christian ethics. Here, however, we must ask the reader to bear in mind that manuals of moral theology are technical works intended to help the confessor and the parish priest in the discharge of their duties. They are as technical as the text-books of the lawyer and the doctor. They are not intended for edification, nor do they hold up a high ideal of Christian perfection for the imitation of the faithful. They deal with what is of obligation under pain of sin; they are books of moral pathology. They are necessary for the Catholic priest to enable him to administer the sacrament of Penance and to fulfill his other duties; they are intended to serve this purpose, and they should not be censured for not being what they were never intended to be.

Slater did not want to deny that in other areas of church instruction the interior life is addressed. He added:

> Ascetical and mystical literature which treats of the higher spiritual life is very abundant in the Catholic Church, and it should be con-

---

8. Besides the important *Making of Moral Theology*, Mahoney's earlier *Seeking the Spirit* (London: Sheed and Ward, 1981) very powerfully makes this point.

sulted by those who desire to know the lofty ideals of life which the Catholic Church places before her children and encourages them to practice. Moral theology proposes to itself the much humbler but still necessary task of defining what is right and what wrong in all the practical relations of the Christian life. This all, but more especially priests, should know. The first step on the right road of conduct is to avoid evil.[9]

Slater's preface is an accurate description of the way Catholic moral theologians understood their competency over the past four centuries. This is supported by turning to the way the Ten Commandments were used for moral instruction in the sixteenth century. There we see how concretely the Protestant tendency to interiority differs from the Catholic interest in exterior action.

In the sixteenth century, in the place of the deadly sins, the Reformers established the Decalogue as the proper text for moral instruction.[10] The appeal of the Decalogue was strong. First, unlike the deadly sins, the Ten Commandments claimed divine sanction: they and not the sins enjoyed the biblical claim of expressing God's will. Second, they were a solid pedagogical tool that resisted any attempts at embellishment. Inasmuch as the seven deadly sins were no more than the names of seven vices, they afforded the medieval mentality the opportunity to compound and expand them by inventing newer sins that could be attributed to a particularly deadly vice. But the Ten Commandments were more than a name. They were at least propositional utterances with a specific text worthy of commentary. Third, unlike the seven deadly sins, they offered not only negative prohibitions but on occasion positive prescriptions. Finally, with the exception of pride, the deadly sins were primarily offensive to human life; the Commandments specified prescriptions and prohibitions regarding the divine as well as the human.

The Decalogue appeared in several important sixteenth-century texts. First Luther's *Large Catechism* (1529) dedicated nearly half of its

9. Thomas Slater, *A Manual of Moral Theology*, 2d ed. (New York: Benziger Brothers, 1908), 1:5-6.

10. John Bossy, "Moral Arithmetic: Seven Sins into Ten Commandments," *Conscience and Casuistry*, pp. 214-34. H. Leith Spencer contradicts those claims in *English Preaching in the Late Middle Ages* (Oxford: Clarendon, 1993).

one hundred and twenty pages to the Decalogue. Generally speaking in terms of prohibitions or prescriptions, Luther began his instruction of each commandment by following the specific form of the commandment but then turned to its corollary. Thus the commandment on killing began with an explanation of the prohibition but turned eventually to consider the failure to do good to one's neighbor. "God rightly calls all persons murderers who do not offer counsel and aid to men in need and in peril of body and life."[11] Moreover, his explanations focused not on particular actions that were in themselves right or wrong, but rather on dispositions or habitual stances, particularly in relationship to another. Thus the first application of the eighth commandment concerned "that everyone should help his neighbor maintain his rights."[12] But above all, it was the heart that dominated this treatment of the Decalogue. One sees this easily in his conclusion to the first commandment: "where the heart is right with God and this commandment is kept, fulfillment of all the others will follow of its own accord."[13]

These three features — matching prohibition and prescription, emphasizing habitual, relational conduct, and acting always from a charitable heart — were found in each of the ten expressions in the *Small Catechism* (1529), designed so that the head of the household could properly instruct family members. For instance, the description of the eighth commandment was simply: "We should fear and love God so that we do not deceitfully belie, betray, backbite, nor slander our neighbor, but apologize for him, speak well of him, and put the most charitable construction on all that he does."[14]

In his final edition of the *Institutes of the Christian Religion* (1559), Calvin treated the Decalogue at length. Here he balanced every prohibition with a positive injunction and again, like Luther, discussed habitual, relational ways of acting. Finally, while the sixth through the

---

11. Martin Luther, *The Large Catechism of Martin Luther* (Philadelphia: Fortress, 1959), p. 35.

12. Ibid., p. 44.

13. Ibid., p. 15.

14. Martin Luther, *Small Catechism* (Minneapolis: Augsburg, 1929), p. 83. He began each commandment's explanation with the same remark: "We should fear and love God so that. . . ."

ninth concerned licentious desires and intentions, the tenth concerned concupiscence, pure and simple. It began:

> The end of this precept is, that, since it is the will of God that our whole soul should be under the influence of love, every desire inconsistent with charity ought to be expelled from our minds. The sum, then, will be, that no thought should obtrude itself upon us, which would excite in our minds any desire that is noxious, and tends to the detriment of another. To which corresponds the affirmative precept, that all our conceptions, deliberations, resolutions, and undertakings, ought to be consistent with the benefit and advantage of our neighbors.[15]

The Catechism of the Council of Trent (1566) split most commandments into positive and negative "parts." Each commandment had an explication and then a specific application related to a variety of categories of sinful activity. Ironically, inasmuch as the *Catechism* was not for individual or family use but for the parish priest, the Decalogue basically replaced the seven deadly sins precisely in categorizing sinful activity. It advised at the outset:

> In the tribunal of penance the priest holds the place of a judge, and pronounces sentence according to the nature and gravity of the offence. Unless, therefore, he is desirous that his ignorance should prove an injury to himself and to others, he must bring with him to the discharge of his duty the greatest vigilance and the most practiced acquaintance with the interpretation of the law, in order to be able to pronounce, according to this divine rule, *on every act and omission.*[16]

As a result, the *Catechism* cataloged lengthy descriptions of wrong actions. Under the second commandment it devoted a paragraph-long description for each of the following sins: false oaths, unjust oaths, rash oaths, oaths by false gods, irreverent speech, neglect of prayer, and blasphemy. The eighth commandment likewise described false testimony in favor of a neighbor, falsehoods in lawsuits, false

15. John Calvin, *Institutes of the Christian Religion* (Grand Rapids: Eerdmans, 1949), 1.447. See Bossy, "Moral Arithmetic, p. 216.

16. *Catechism of the Council of Trent for Parish Priests* (New York: Herder, 1934), pp. 357-58. Emphasis added.

testimony out of court, detraction, flattery, lies of all kinds, and hypocrisy.[17]

Sometimes the *Catechism* distinguished an apparently prohibited action from a real prohibited action. Under the first commandment, for instance, were several paragraphs on "not forbidden" actions: veneration and invocation of angels, and of saints, representations of the divine persons and angels, images of Christ and the saints, and other sacred images. Likewise, the fifth commandment did not forbid the killing of animals, execution of criminals, killing in a just war, killing by accident, killing in self-defense. The purpose of the Decalogue in this catechism remains the same as other works of Catholic moral theology: to determine those wrong objects of activity that contaminate the soul.

Pastoral advice was also offered on how to avoid sinful actions. For instance, the sixth commandment described at length such aids as avoiding idleness, practicing temperance and custody of the eyes, avoiding improper dress and impure conversation, reading, and pictures, frequenting the sacraments, and practicing acts of mortification. None of these prescribed actions were for moral or spiritual betterment; they were simply prophylactic actions to keep us from sinful ones.

As a comparison of the different expositions of the Decalogue shows, the agenda of the confessional, that is, the need for the priest to judge specifically wrong acts, singularly and exclusively dominated Roman Catholic moral instruction. With few noteworthy exceptions,[18] Roman Catholic moral instruction, from the penitentials and confessional summas to the *Catechism*'s treatment of the Decalogue, the manuals of casuistry, and the more recent moral manuals, considered the moral life singularly under the question of what was sin and what was not. *Veritatis Splendor* follows in that history.

17. Ibid., p. 369.
18. See Boyle's essay, *The Setting of the "Summa Theologiae,"* which precisely argues that Thomas's *Summa Theologiae* was an intentional departure from the *summae confessorum* and was meant not for being taught in the academic world but for those preparing for ministry. Besides Thomas, Jean Gerson clearly tried to integrate the devotional and the moral. See Louis Pascoe, *Jean Gerson: Principles of Church Reform* (Leiden: Brill, 1973); D. Catherine Brown, *Pastor and Laity in the Theology of Jean Gerson* (New York: Cambridge University Press, 1987).

Roman Catholic moral theologians have been trying to develop a more integrated moral theology. That agenda has been endorsed in particular by the American Catholic moralist Norbert Rigali, who has insisted that moral theology be integrated into spirituality.[19] That latter field composed of devotional and ascetical manuals dealt with the order of charity observing vigilance and seeking perfection. These manuals were positively oriented, not sin-based; their point of departure was the subject called by Christ seeking to find from within herself (through grace) a way of responding to the Lord; their material content was not a catalog of discreet vicious actions, but rather good habits, dispositions, and relational activity, that is, virtues; their audience was the laity and they were written in the vernacular, rather than in Latin for the confessor. This theology provided a more suitable point of departure for a christological ethics. But as Slater insisted, moral theology has defined itself in distinction from spirituality.

Nonetheless, Servais Pinckaers and others encourage us to recognize the encyclical's attempts, at least in the first part, to lead us from the tradition's fixation on external actions to an ethics that starts with an interiority and moves into action.[20] But with Donfried we have to wait for that attempt to be realized, for as he noted well, the emphasis on an interior, integrated call to discipleship, so promising in the first part, is never developed in the subsequent parts.

19. Rigali's essays are numerous; a few salient ones are "The Unity of the Moral Order," *Chicago Studies* 8 (1969): 125-43; "Christian Ethics and Perfection," *Chicago Studies* 14 (1975): 227-40; "The Future of Christian Morality," *Chicago Studies* 20 (1981): 281-89; "The Unity of Moral and Pastoral Truth," *Chicago Studies* 25 (1986): 224-32. Recent writers on the topic include Dennis Billy and Donna Orsuto, eds., *Spirituality and Morality: Integrating Prayer and Action* (Mahwah: Paulist, 1996); James Keating, "The Good Life," *Church* 11, no. 2 (1995): 15-20; James Keenan, "Morality and Spirituality," *Church* 12, no. 3 (1996): 40-42; Mark O'Keefe, *Becoming Good, Becoming Holy: On the Relationship of Christian Ethics and Spirituality* (Mahwah: Paulist, 1995). See also James F. Keenan S.J., "Catholic Moral Theology, Ignatian Spirituality, and Virtue Ethics: Strange(r Than They Should Be) Bedfellows," *Supplement to the Way on Spirituality and Ethics* (Spring 1997).

20. Servais Pinckaers, "The New Law in *Veritatis Splendor,*" *Josephinum* 3 (1996): 47-64; Livio Melina, "Desire for Happiness and the Commandments in the First Chapter of *Veritatis Splendor,*" *The Thomist* 60 (1996): 341-59.

II. Roots

Reinhard Hütter's comments on "God's Law" in *Veritatis Splendor* find parallels in the distinction between goodness and rightness. This distinction runs through the encyclical, and while it is not treated directly by any contributor to this volume, it is still one that Lois Malcolm, Theodor Dieter, Bernd Wannenwetsch, and most especially Gilbert Meilaender have in mind. Though Hütter does not address the distinction, I hope that by discussing it I can highlight the importance of one basic concern: the divine initiative for salvation and the sufficient cause for sanctification that is usually stressed in terms of faith by the Reformers and in terms of charity by Catholics. Hütter's concern about the priority of faith (and he means this priority on a number of levels) parallels the concerns of those theologians who insist on the priority of moral goodness or what most moral theologians refer to as charity.

I need here to make three caveats. First, I equate goodness with charity, but charity is first an infused grace; it is a gift from God, freely given without merit. Moral goodness is when we respond to the gift of charity in us, which we respond to *after* having the gift. Subsequent to the gift, we seek or strive for greater union with God.

Second, the philosophical distinction between rightness and goodness is very different from the theological distinction. When philosophers talk about rightness, they generally refer to duty language. When they talk about goodness, they talk about virtues and use aretaic language.[21] But the theological distinction is not one of methods of determining moral conduct. Rather, just as the Reformers rightly talk about faith as saving and faith as the point of departure for leading the life of sanctification, so too Catholics talk about grace as the presence of God and charity alone as the sufficient and necessary condition for the life of sanctification.

Just as Hütter describes the relationship between faith and good works as being in only one direction, Catholics also believe that there is only one direction in understanding the relationship between char-

---

21. See for instance, William Frankena, "The Ethics of Love Conceived as an Ethics of Virtue," *The Journal of Religious Ethics* 1 (1973): 21-31; "Conversations with Carney and Hauerwas," *The Journal of Religious Ethics* 3 (1975): 45-62.

ity and good works. For moral theologians, goodness is simply that fundamental response to God's initiative; rightness is whether one's actions are done in accord with right reason or the law. The distinction is found in this volume in Dieter's description of Luther's distinction between the good conscience of a believer which is faith and the "Gewissen vor den Leuten."

Third, still, sometimes the word *good* is a homonym. This is especially problematic among theologians, especially neo-scholastics, who do not always think of good as somehow synonymous with charity or faith, but rather with completion or perfection. There it has a metaphysical meaning like being complete or full, as when we ask the scholastic question, is God good, that is, is God complete or perfect? This question asks whether there is anything in God lacking. But other times we talk about God as good meaning the extraordinary caring, loving God who freely saves us. Thus sometimes when the neo-scholastics use the term *good* it actually conforms with certain notions of rightness or conformity to perfection. A good deed may not mean a deed out of faith or a deed out of charity; it may mean a deed that conforms to the law or to right reason.

If we turn now to the distinction between goodness and rightness, we see that it appears in ordinary language. Imagine returning home and hearing the words, "He did it out of love." You know one thing, something terrible has occurred. "He did it out of love" is a phrase like "He meant well." It does not express whether or not an activity was right; in fact, it prepares us for the high probability that the activity was disastrous. It does express something else, however: the agent of the probably disastrous activity was first and foremost loving.

This first and foremost is found in most of our expressions dealing with phrases starting with "out of." Out of love, jealousy, compassion, insecurity, and so on, are all ways that we try to explain deep down what a person's motivation is. Often we are distinguishing that insight from any comment about what the action was. "He did that act of kindness out of insecurity" is like "It was out of love that she went against his wishes": both try to express two components, a person's motivation and a person's conduct, and we use ordinary phrases like "out of" to make this central distinction.

Curiously, the phrase "out of" appears to cross language frontiers. Thomas Aquinas, for instance, used it only when talking about charity.

Unlike the other virtues, only charity is expressed as antecedent to all the other virtues,[22] working formally,[23] as the source of all moral expression.[24] Thus Thomas described the object of charity as that which is loved out of charity, using the phrase *"ex caritate"* sixty-six times in the question in the *Summa Theologiae*[25] and forty-nine times in the parallel question in *De caritate*.[26] Thomas described no other virtue in such a way: for Thomas, "out of charity" defined the acting person as good.

German speakers too take to this primary expression. Kant used *aus Pflicht* to describe the good will, and after him Schüller described goodness as acting *aus der sittlichen Ureinsicht*.[27] Fuchs too turned to the primary movement in his fundamental option.[28] All commentators described moral goodness as primary and antecedent to all other self-movements.

22. *Summa Theologiae* 2.2.23.4 ad 2; *De caritate* 5 ad 3.

23. *Summa Theologiae* 2.2.23.2 ad 3.

24. On the importance of charity as formal, see Gerard Gilleman, *The Primacy of Charity in Moral Theology* (Westminster: Newman, 1959), p. 164; Conrad van Ouwerkerk, *Caritas et Ratio: Étude sur le double principe de la vie morale chrétienne d'après S. Thomas d'Aquin* (Nijmegen: Drukkerij Gebr. Janssen, 1956), p. 47; Klaus Riesenhuber, *Die Transzendenz der Freiheit zum Guten. Der Wille in der Anthropologie und Metaphysik des Thomas von Aquin* (Munich: Berchmanskolleg Verlag, 1971), pp. 112ff.

25. *Summa Theologiae* 2.2.25.

26. *De caritate* 7.

27. Bruno Schüller, *Die Begründung sittlicher Urteile* (Düsseldorf: Patmos, 1980), pp. 136, 304. Elsewhere he writes on the distinction, "The Debate on the Specific Character of Christian Ethics," in *Readings in Moral Theology No. 2: The Distinctiveness of Christian Ethics,* ed. C. Curran and R. McCormick (New York: Paulist, 1980), pp. 207-33; "Direct Killing/Indirect Killing," in *Readings in Moral Theology No. 1: Moral Norms and the Catholic Tradition,* ed. C. Curran and R. McCormick (New York: Paulist, 1979), pp. 138-57; "The Double Effect in Catholic Thought: A Reevaluation," in *Doing Evil to Achieve Good,* ed. R. McCormick and P. Ramsey (Chicago: Loyola University Press, 1978), pp. 165-92; "Gewissen und Schuld," in *Das Gewissen,* ed. Josef Fuchs (Düsseldorf: Patmos, 1979), pp. 34-55; "Neuere Beiträge zum Thema 'Begründung sittlicher Normen,'" in *Theologische Berichte 4,* ed. Franz Furger (Zurich: Benziger Verlag, 1974), pp. 109-81; *Wholly Human* (Washington, D.C.: Georgetown University Press, 1985).

28. Josef Fuchs, *Essere del Signore* (Rome: Gregorian University Press, 1981), 108ff. Also see his *Christian Ethics in a Secular Arena* (Washington, D.C.: Georgetown University Press, 1984); *Christian Morality: The Word Becomes Flesh* (Washington, D.C.: Georgetown University Press, 1987); and *Personal Responsibility and Christian Morality* (Washington, D.C.: Georgetown University Press, 1983).

In terms of a conceptual term distinguishing goodness from expressions of rightness, *motivation* is often used. Unlike *intention,* which describes an end that one seeks, *motivation* describes an end out of which one acts. The earlier scholastic distinction here is between the *terminus ad quem,* which we seek, and the *terminus a quo,* out of which we act. The expression "out of" precisely conveys one's motivation. Antecedent to all other expressions of human acting, it represents the quality of the *a quo,* not the *ad quem:* good motivations communicate moral goodness. Thus the term has already been adopted by some of the major Catholic moral theologians: Fuchs,[29] Demmer,[30] and Schüller.[31] It is used particularly to distinguish it from intention.

Goodness in the Christian tradition is expressed by love, the first movement. Whether one loves is alone the question of goodness.[32] Of course, John, Paul, and Augustine made this as clear as Jesus did: not only was love the sufficient cause of goodness but even to die for "the faith" (another homonym!) would not be an expression of goodness unless done out of love. Love is the first movement in all good people.

Let me note, in an aside, that in this schema sin is not wrongness but badness. Therefore sin is not really the choosing of the wrong or even the failure to choose the right. Antecedent to choice, sin is the failure to be bothered. Saint Ignatius made this point well in *The Spiritual Exercises.* In the colloquy with the crucified Jesus the exercitant is asked to consider three questions: "What have I done for Christ?" "What am I doing for Christ?" and "What ought I to do for Christ?" The questions are not between what right things ought one

29. Fuchs, *Essere del Signore,* pp. 198-99.

30. Klaus Demmer, *Deuten und Handeln* (Freiburg, Switzerland: Universitätsverlag, 1985), p. 175ff; "Erwägungen zum intrinsece malum," *Gregorianum* 68 (1987): 613-37. See also his "La competenza normativa del magistero ecclesiatico in morale," in *Fede Cristiana e Agire Morale,* ed K. Demmer and B. Schüller (Assisi: Cittadella Editrice, 1980), pp. 144-69; *Leben in Menschenhand* (Freiburg, Switzerland: Universitätsverlag, 1987); "Sittlich handeln als Zeugnis geben," *Gregorianum* 4 (1983): 453-85; "Sittlich handeln aus Erfahrung," *Gregorianum* 59 (1978): 661-90.

31. Schüller uses "Urgewissen" in "Gewissen und Schuld," p. 40; in *Die Begründung sittlicher Urteile,* he uses "sittliche Uralternative" (pp. 137-38), "sittliche Ureinsicht" (p. 136), and "Grundhaltung" (p. 300), among other expressions of goodness. Motivation appears in "Neuere Beiträge," p. 129.

32. Besides Gilleman and van Ouwerkerk above, see George Klubertanz, "Ethics and Theology," *The Modern Schoolman* 27 (1949): 29-39.

to do versus what wrong actions ought one to avoid. Rather, the questions concern whether one is bothering to respond to the movements of God in the first place. Is one bothered about Christ or not? That question is antecedent to the question of right living or acting.[33]

That primary movement is understood in context: goodness is descriptive of the individual insofar as he or she responds to the divine initiative. But that response must consider a person's ability. Thus Thomas held that charity is striving or loving as much as one is able.[34] Goodness therefore describes a person striving as much as he or she can for the right out of love. Badness is foremost the failure to express love by the failure to strive in the first place.[35]

Moreover, goodness cannot be separable from rightness.[36] A good person does not strive to be good but rather to live and act rightly. This link means that goodness requires an effort to find and execute conduct that conforms not to our wishes but rather to the rational standards of the moral community.

Often, however, a person strives for the right but does not actually attain it. Contemporary Catholic moral theologians note that for a person to be called good, his or her conduct does not need to be right; striving out of love for the right sufficiently describes a good person.[37]

33. I have developed three brief essays on this topic, "What Do Right and Wrong Have to Do with Good and Bad?" *Church* 11, no. 3 (1995): 43-45; "Sin," *Church* 11, no. 4 (1995): 43-45; "Doing and Not Doing: The Key to Goodness," *Church* 12, no. 1 (1996): 39-41.

34. "[C]aritas dicitur perfecta quando aliquis secundum totum suum posse diligit" (*Summa Theologiae* 2.2.24. 8c).

35. Prior to the writings of Schüller, Fuchs, and Demmer, I found the best expression of the distinction in Pierre Bayle's writings. See John Kilcullen, *Sincerity and Truth: Essays on Arnauld, Bayle, and Toleration* (Oxford: Clarendon, 1988), pp. 175ff.

36. Contrary to the charge of *Veritatis Splendor* (#67), which claims that theologians separate the two. See the responses, Josef Fuchs, "Good Acts and Good Persons," in *Considering "Veritatis Splendor,"* ed. John Wilkins (Cleveland: Pilgrim, 1994), pp. 21-26; Brian Johnstone, "Erroneous Conscience in *Veritatis Splendor* and the Theological Tradition," in *The Splendor of Accuracy,* ed. Joseph Selling and Jan Jans (Grand Rapids: Eerdmans, 1995), pp. 114-35.

37. Besides Schüller, Fuchs, and Demmer, see Louis Janssens, "Norms and Priorities in a Love Ethics," *Louvain Studies* 6 (1977): 207-38; "Ontic Good and Ontic Evil," *Louvain Studies* 12 (1987): 62-82; James Keenan, "Die erworbenen Tugenden als richtige (nicht gute) Lebensführung: ein genauerer Ausdruck ethischer Beschreibung," in *Ethische Theorie praktisch,* ed. Franz Furger (Münster: Aschendorff,

Thus they can say unanimously: "A wrong action can be called good when a person acts out of love but errs." This parallels, I think, much of what Meilaender brings up in his essay.

Some might wonder whether they are relativists, since they describe as good those people whose conduct at this particular moment is wrong. They would answer that they are not relativists; they would simply distinguish two dimensions of the moral life. A person is good if she is responding as much as she can to live rightly; her conduct is right if it attains what right reason requires. With just as much ease they could invert the statement and again unanimously answer, "If a person acts rightly but fails to act out of love (or faith) then the action would be right, but bad."

In sum, the distinction between goodness and rightness provides two descriptives for two different concerns regarding the moral life. Though distinctive, these descriptives are not separable. Though one can be right and bad, or wrong and good, goodness is descriptive of one who responds to Christ and subsequently strives for rightness. If goodness did not aim for rightness, then goodness would be nothing more than a solipsistic description.

These insights are not completely new. Since the pre-Socratics, we have distinguished between a person's motivation and a person's conduct. However, Democritus had only one description for the moral life (the "good" or the required); still, he argued that in order to call a person good, not only does the person have to do the good, the person has to want to do it as good.[38]

The distinction is applicable to any ethics or moral theology,[39] but two figures are important for this discussion: Kant and Aquinas. It is my belief that the papal encyclical uses the distinction as Kant would,

1991), pp. 19-35; "A New Distinction in Moral Theology: Being Good and Living Rightly," *Church* 5 (1989): 22-28; Richard McCormick, "Bishops as Teachers and Jesuits as Listeners," in *Studies in the Spirituality of Jesuits* 28 (1986); *Notes on Moral Theology, 1981 through 1984* (Lanham, Md.: University Press of America, 1984).

38. See Democritus, *Fragmenta moralia* no. 109 as cited in Stephen Toulmin, *An Examination of the Place of Reason in Ethics* (Cambridge: Cambridge University Press, 1958), p. 170.

39. Contrary to *Veritatis Splendor*'s claim (#65, 75) that it is used predominantly by proportionalists, see a list of persons observing the distinction in Schüller, *Die Begründung,* p. 140.

but not as Aquinas would, and therein it overlooks charity, just as it overlooks faith. Let me explain.

Kant from the beginning of the *Foundations of the Metaphysics of Morals* distinguished between actions done out of duty *(Handeln aus Pflicht)* and dutiful actions *(pflichtmäßiges Handeln)*. In attempting to describe the only thing which we can call "good," that is, the will, Kant argued that a dutiful act was only good if the act was done out of duty. For example, a state executioner who executes on account of his duty to execute is good and the action is good. But if the executioner performs the dutiful act out of some other motivation, then the action is not good, though it is dutiful. Interestingly, Kant did not consider whether an act not dutiful could be called good. Was an executioner who acted out of duty but botched the job still called good?

Kant had a *moral standard* to measure both the action and the person's will, but from different perspectives. In this way he was not unlike Democritus above. Democritus would call a person good who intends the good as such. This is virtually the same insight as Kant. For Democritus it is the good intended as such; for Kant, the dutiful intended as such. The dutiful is the singular reality; whether one actually does it and whether one acts out of it are the two different dimensions of the person that Kant distinguished.

For Thomas there were *two moral standards:* charity and prudence. Kant only looked for one standard, duty. Democritus only looked for one, what he called "the good or the required." But for Thomas there were two.

Charity and prudence have different functions. Charity measures whether we are responding to God by loving God as much as we can. Prudence measures whether an action has attained the mean or what right reason requires. Thus inasmuch as goodness strives for rightness, charity seeks to live prudently. In fact Thomas acknowledged these distinct measures and stated that actions must be measured by two rules, charity and prudence (2-2 27.6 ad 3).[40] On the one hand, we must ask whether one acts out of a striving for greater union with God; on the other hand, we must ask whether the reasonable mean

---

40. Cf. parallel passages in *In III Sent* d.27 q.3 a.3 ad 1, ad 2, and ad 4; *In Rom* 12.1 964; *De caritate* 2 ad 13.

has been attained.[41] These measures, I think, are not far from our contemporary concepts of moral goodness and rightness.

When *Veritatis Splendor* (#63) talks about erroneous conscience, it does basically the same thing that Kant did. It provides only one measure. This is like the old manualist distinction between objectively and subjectively good. "Good" in the old manualists' writings did not mean acting out of charity, but rather something like Kant's or Democritus's singular standard, the required. There they talked about what right reason or the natural law required. (That is what we in theology would call today rightness.) The question of subjectively "good," however, was simply whether someone meant the objectively "good" or not.

In a manner of speaking, in the old distinction the only questions referred to a singular standard: was it right and did you mean it? It never really asked whether someone was acting out of charity or out of faith. Charity was never considered, nor was faith!

Thus the passage from *Veritatis Splendor* (#63) shows singularly a preference for truth, unaware that there may be another moral measure:

> In any event, it is always from the truth that the dignity of conscience derives. In the case of the correct conscience, it is a question of the objective truth received by man; in the case of the erroneous conscience, it is a question of what man, mistakenly, subjectively considers to be true. It is never acceptable to confuse a "subjective" error about moral good with the "objective" truth rationally proposed to man in virtue of his end, or to make the moral value of an act performed with a true and correct conscience equivalent to the moral value of an act performed by following the judgment of an erroneous conscience. It is possible that the evil done as the result of invincible ignorance or of a non-culpable error of judgment may not be imputable to the agent; but even in this case it does not cease to be an evil, a disorder in relation to the truth about the good. Furthermore, a good act which is not recognized as such does not contribute to the moral growth of the person who performs it; it does not perfect him and it does not help to dispose him for the supreme good.

41. See Keenan, "Distinguishing Charity as Goodness and Prudence as Rightness: A Key to Thomas' *Pars Secunda*," *The Thomist* 56 (1992): 407-26; Keenan, *Goodness and Rightness in Thomas Aquinas' Summa Theologiae*; van Ouwerkerk, *Caritas et Ratio*, p. 22ff.

This paragraph clearly is associating the "good" with the one standard of right reason, the law, or prudence, that is, the truth. It means by a "good" act that it conforms to prudence, or to the required, or to right reason, or to the law. But the passage ignores the virtue of charity. Thus the writers wonder where moral theologians are deriving "good" when the action lacks the (presupposed) one moral standard that it requires. Clearly, the writers interpret the distinction through the manualist and Kantian traditions and not through Thomas's.[42] Were they familiar with Thomas's distinction they would have asked whether one was acting out of charity. If the agent were acting out of charity, then the action, though clearly wrong, would still be good and would "help to dispose him for the supreme good."[43]

In sum, by only looking for the true, *The Splendor of the Truth* overlooked the distinctive gift of charity, which is absolutely prior to the moral life. Likewise, in only looking for the true, *The Splendor of the Truth* overlooked the distinctive gift of faith. The writers did this by equating the good with the true without realizing that the good sometimes functions as a homonym. Moreover they did this by insisting on the *terminus ad quem* of moral living, which is the right or the true, without asking what the *terminus a quo* of moral living was.

Since Vatican II, theologians like Chenu, Congar, de Lubac, Lonergan, and Rahner have turned greater attention to the human person than to the human act. Their turn to the subject became the moralist's turn to conscience and charity, a turn particularly made possible by the pre–Vatican II writings of Lottin,[44] Carpentier,[45] and Gilleman, among others. Subsequent to their writings, moral theolo-

---

42. Herbert McCabe also criticizes the writers for being more neo-scholastic than Thomistic in "Manuals and Rule Books," in *Considering "Veritatis Splendor,"* pp. 61-68.

43. See James F. Keenan S.J., "Can a Wrong Action Be Good?: The Development of Theological Opinion on Erroneous Conscience," *Église et Theologie* 24 (1993): 205-21.

44. In particular Odon Lottin, "La valeur normative de la conscience morale," *Ephemerides Theologicae Lovanienses* 9 (1932): 409-32; Odon Lottin, *Psychologie et morale aux XIIe et XIIIe siècles* (Gembloux: Duculot, 1942-1954); Odon Lottin, *Morale fondamentale* (Tournai: Desclee et Cie, 1954).

45. René Carpentier, "Conscience," in *Dictionnaire de spiritualité ascétique et mystique* (Paris: Beauchesne, 1953), 2:1548-75.

gians began to reflect on the conscience, not for the purposes of evaluating whether already executed actions should be attributed to agents or not, but rather as the locus of where Christ enables and calls us to be moral.[46] Conscience engraced by Christ, not particular acts, became the object of moral reflection; that is the same concern I find in Hütter's presentation. This concern is not for the end that conscience must seek, that is, the truth, but rather the root out of which a good conscience acts and by which it is called good.

III. Innovations

If *Veritatis Splendor* fails to offer the development of an integrated moral theology, *Evangelium Vitae* proposes a major innovation in its understanding of the sanctity of life argument. Inasmuch as it offers something new, I think it advances the tradition considerably. To appreciate that development, let us first look at earlier statements for the preservation of life and then the pope's new argument.

In his manual of moral theology, Thomas Slater examined suicide while treating the fifth commandment and declared, "The reason why suicide is unlawful is because we have not the free disposal of our own lives. God is the author of life and death, and He has reserved the ownership of human life to Himself."[47] Slater's stance was repeated throughout modern times. For instance, at the beginning of his presentation on the fifth commandment, Henry Davis wrote forty years later about the duty to preserve life, "By Natural law, man enjoys the use not the dominion of his life. He neither gave it nor may he take it away. God only is the author of life."[48]

In *Casti Connubii* (1930) Pope Pius XI declared, "The life of each is equally sacred and no one has the power, not even the public authority,

46. Josef Fuchs: "the phenomenon of morality, which is, in fact, nothing other than the irreducible phenomenon of moral conscience." See "The Phenomenon of Conscience," in *Christian Morality: The Word Becomes Flesh,* p. 120. Cf. "Our Image of God and the Morality of Innerworldly Behavior," in the same volume, esp. pp. 47-48.

47. Slater, *Manual of Moral Theology,* 1:302.

48. Henry Davis, *Moral and Pastoral Theology II* (London: Sheed and Ward, 1945), p. 141.

to destroy it."[49] Commenting on this encyclical, the Australian moralist Augustine Regan added, "His successor Pius XII made many pronouncements and statements during his long pontificate. . . . He reiterates as a constant refrain that man is not the author, and consequently is never the master, of human life, which is entrusted to him as its administrator. Therefore, it is always wrong for him to dispose of it as though he were its owner. In particular it can never be justified to attack directly the life of any innocent human being."[50]

In more contemporary teachings the same argument is found. In the *Declaration on Euthanasia* (1980) we read that suicide, like murder, "is to be considered a rejection of God's sovereignty and loving plan."[51] Gerald Coleman sums up the tradition well, "Human persons, then, have only a right to the use of human life, not to dominion over human life. What makes killing forbidden is that it usurps a divine prerogative and violates divine rights."[52]

The position functioned then as nothing more than a divine injunction.[53] In this context the distinction between direct and indirect killing arose. Moralists needed to find what was permitted. Here the issue was not to find the right but rather the permitted, for the permitted in terms of killing was considered the exception to the general prohibition (Exod. 23:7: "The innocent and the just person thou shalt not put to death").[54] In this legalistic context, the moralists looked for what the law would permit and found that where a killing could be described as indirect, proportionate reasoning could be invoked.

We should not underestimate the legalistic context here. The "traditional" distinction between direct and indirect killing is not founded primarily on some reasoned ground for excluding all in-

49. Pope Pius XI, *Encyclical Letter on Christian Marriage* (Boston: St. Paul Editions, 1930), #64, p. 32.

50. Augustine Regan, *Thou Shalt Not Kill* (Dublin: Mercier, 1977), p. 29.

51. Sacred Congregation for the Doctrine of the Faith, "Declaration on Euthanasia," in *Vatican Council II: More Post Conciliar Documents,* ed. Austin Flannery (Northport, N.Y.: Costello, 1982), pp. 510-17, at p. 512.

52. Gerald Coleman, "Assisted Suicide: An Ethical Perspective," in *Euthanasia,* ed. Robert Baird and Stuart Rosenbaum (Buffalo: Prometheus, 1989), p. 108.

53. On divine command, see *Divine Commands and Morality,* ed. Paul Helm (Oxford: Oxford University Press, 1981).

54. See Slater, *Manual of Moral Theology,* 1:311.

stances of direct killing. Rather, the distinction is founded on advancing the indirect as permissible. Moral theologians "received" both a divine injunction and, subsequently, some papal teaching. In that context they refused to violate the divine prerogatives but sought legalistic solutions to particular moral dilemmas.

The effects of grounding the prohibition against killing in divine injunction language are especially problematic. Years ago Gerald Hughes noted that if the church were to meet the rising interest in death-dealing practices like euthanasia then the decision to stand against that tide needed to be based on more evidently reasoned grounds.[55] Moreover, Bruno Schüller argued that the "traditional" opposition to direct killing was nothing more than reiterating what needed to be proven: why God's will is against it.[56] In answer to these charges Benedict Ashley agreed on the need to turn to other arguments to "bolster this *argument from God's dominion*."[57]

Sanctity of life provided that support. But surprisingly it is a rather new expression. For instance, in the fifteen-volume collection of the *New Catholic Encyclopedia,* it had no entry.[58] It appeared as a modest afterthought in the later supplement.[59] It is not found in new theological dictionaries from the United States, England, or Germany: *The New Dictionary of Theology,*[60] *The Oxford Dictionary of the Christian Church,*[61] *The Theological Dictionary.*[62] It did not appear in the German

55. Gerald Hughes, "Killing and Letting Die," *The Month* 236 (February 1975): 42-45; James Keenan, "Töten oder Sterbenlassen," *Stimmen der Zeit* 201 (1983): 825-37.

56. Bruno Schüller, "The Double Effect in Catholic Thought," in *Doing Evil to Achieve Good,* ed. Richard McCormick and Paul Ramsey (Chicago: Loyola University Press, 1978), pp. 165-92.

57. See Benedict Ashley, "Dominion or Stewardship? Theological Reflections," in *Birth, Suffering, and Death: Catholic Reflections on the Edges of Life,* ed. Kevin W. Wildes (Boston: Kluwer Academic Pub., 1992), pp. 85-106.

58. *New Catholic Encyclopedia* (New York: McGraw-Hill, 1967).

59. *New Catholic Encyclopedia: Supplement, 1967-1978* (New York: McGraw-Hill, 1978), 16:400-401.

60. *New Dictionary of Theology,* ed. J. Komonchack (Wilmington: Michael Glazier, 1987).

61. *The Oxford Dictionary of the Christian Church,* ed. F. Cross (Oxford: Oxford University Press, 1974).

62. *Theological Dictionary,* ed. K. Rahner and H. Vorgrimler (New York: Herder and Herder, 1965).

The Concise Dictionary of Christian Ethics;[63] in Palazzini's Italian *Dictionary of Moral Theology* there was only "Life, Respect for: see Murder, Suicide."[64] Only the Anglican John Macquarrie, who edited two dictionaries, ran entries on the sanctity of life, in both *A Dictionary of Christian Ethics*[65] and *The Westminster Dictionary of Christian Ethics.*[66]

The phrase first appeared in papal writings in the encyclical *Mater et Magistra* (1961, #194). "All must regard the life of man as sacred, since from its inception, it requires the action of God the Creator. Those who depart from this plan of God not only offend His divine majesty and dishonor themselves and the human race, but they also weaken the inner fibre of the commonwealth."[67] This phrase became key in *Humanae Vitae* (1968). There Pope Paul VI used it to affirm the limited dominion that the human has over human life and human generativity. Thus in its early use in papal encyclicals the phrase only emphasized divine prerogatives.

Pope John Paul II's contribution then is not that he introduced the sanctity of life concept. What he did was to give it new meaning in the context of magisterial teaching.[68] In its original form, sanctity of life functioned as a euphemism for God's dominion; as Richard Gula rightly notes: "Closely related to the principles of sanctity and sovereignty is the divine law prohibiting killing as found in the fifth commandment."[69] In *Humanae Vitae,* for instance, life is sacred because its owner, God, willed it so; like other objects that God owned and sanctified (the marital bond, the temple), life could not be violated.[70]

63. *The Concise Dictionary of Christian Ethics,* ed. Bernhard Stöckle (New York: Seabury, 1979).

64. *Dictionary of Moral Theology,* ed. Palazzini (Westminster, Md.: Newman, 1962).

65. *A Dictionary of Christian Ethics,* ed. John Macquarrie (London: SCM, 1967).

66. *The Westminster Dictionary of Christian Ethics,* ed. J. Childress and J. Macquarrie (Philadelphia: Westminster, 1967).

67. Pope John XXIII, *Mater et Magistra,* in *Gospel of Peace and Justice,* ed. Joseph Gremillion (Maryknoll, N.Y.: Orbis, 1976), pp. 184-85.

68. Here I must note the incredible failure to acknowledge any contribution from the late Joseph Cardinal Bernardin. See his *Consistent Ethic of Life* (New York: Sheed and Ward, 1988). One wonders why, if Gueric of Igny could be cited in the encyclical, the concept's most articulate spokesperson was not.

69. Richard Gula, *Euthanasia* (New York: Paulist, 1994), p. 26.

70. See James F. Keenan S.J., "Sanctity of Life and Its Role in Contemporary Biomedical Discussion," in *Sanctity of Life and Menschenwürde: Ethical Conflicts in Modern*

The sacredness rested not necessarily in anything intrinsic to the bond, the temple, or life, but rather singularly on the claim of God, who is definitively extrinsic to bonds, temples, and human lives. Their sacral quality rested simply in the fact that they were divine possessions.

In Pope John Paul II's writings, the sanctity of life argument takes center stage. In 1987, in his apostolic exhortation *Christifideles Laici* (#38), the pope spoke at length about the inviolable right to life. He remarked, "The inviolability of the person, which is a reflection of the absolute inviolability of God, finds its primary and fundamental expression in the inviolability of human life."[71] Nowhere did the pope refer to God's dominion or prerogatives. Rather the argument was simply that we are in God's image; as God's person is inviolable so is God's image.

In *Donum Vitae,* the Congregation for the Doctrine of the Faith developed the passage from *Mater et Magistra.*

> From the moment of conception, the life of every human being is to be respected in an absolute way because man is the only creature on earth that God has "wished for himself" and the spiritual soul of each man is "immediately created by God"; his whole image bears the image of the Creator.

It continues:

> Human life is sacred because from its beginning it involves the "creative action of God" and it remains forever in a special relationship with the Creator, who is its sole end. God alone is Lord of life from its beginning until its end: no one can in any circumstance claim for himself the right directly to destroy an innocent human being.[72]

Medicine, ed. Kurt Bayertz (Boston: Kluwer Academics, 1996). See also Joseph Boyle, "Sanctity of Life and Suicide: Tensions and Developments Within Common Morality," in *Suicide and Euthanasia,* ed. Baruch Brody (Boston: Kluwer Academics, 1989), pp. 221-50. See also James F. Keenan S.J., "The Moral Argumentation of *Evangelium vitae,*" in *Evangelium Vitae,* ed. Kevin Wildes (Washington, D.C.: Georgetown University Press, forthcoming), and Boyle's response.

71. John Paul II, *Christifideles Laici,* in *Origins* 18.35 (1989): 579.

72. Congregation for the Doctrine of the Faith, introduction to *Instruction on the Respect for Human Life in Its Origin and on the Dignity of Procreation,* para. 5.

This latter section, which expanded the "Lord of life" position, is repeated later in *Evangelium Vitae* (#53) and becomes the singular text in the *Catechism* (#2258) to interpret the fifth commandment. The entire paragraph is the most extensive statement on both the sanctity of life and God as Lord of life prior to *Evangelium Vitae*. In it we see some of the key elements that later appear in the encyclical: that human life is singular; in God's image; uniquely created by God for a special relationship that is, in turn, the human's destiny; and, finally as source and end of human life God is Lord of life. While not at all abandoning the "Lord of life" argument, the author of this paragraph gives it newer meaning, not by emphasizing God's dominion or prerogatives but by highlighting the uniqueness of human life.

In the encyclical a certain tension between these two interests develops. On the one hand human life has something intrinsic to it that makes it in itself inviolable; on the other hand that which it has, it derives from God the Creator who is Lord of life. Thus, a new argument for preserving life, the intrinsic worth of the human, is used to "bolster" the "Lord of life" argument *and* as a result the "Lord of life" becomes less a declaration of God's sovereignty and prerogatives and more a description of the Creator. In *Evangelium Vitae* (#53) these two play in tandem: "God proclaims that he is absolute Lord of the life of man, who is formed in his image and likeness (cf. GN. 1:26-28). Human life is thus given a sacred and inviolable character, which reflects the inviolability of God." Here clearly human life has *in se* an inviolable character.

The inviolability of life is now never extrinsic to human nature as it was in the "traditional" position. Thus, "Life is indelibly marked by a truth of its own" (#48). The Vatican summary of the encyclical highlights this:

> The light of revelation, which reaches its fulness in Jesus Christ, confirms and completes all that human reason can grasp concerning the value of human life. Precious and fragile, full of promises and threatened by suffering and death, man's life bears within itself that seed of immortal life planted by the Creator in the human heart.

It adds:

At this point we come to the decisive question, Why is life a good? Why is it always a good? The answer is simple and clear: because it is a gift from the Creator, who breathed into man the divine breath, thus making the human person the image of God.[73]

The act by which God created the human is that which invests each human life with its inviolable character that now lies within the human, the image of God. The human is not to be killed therefore because of what the human is. This image of God is hardly extrinsic. Speaking of the Yahwist account of creation, the pope writes that we have within us that divine breath which draws us naturally to God (#35).

Throughout the text, but in particular in the second section, we see greatly expanded the grounds for the inviolable character of human life. This is not simply by invoking a sanctity of life position, for as we saw earlier all that language did was emphasize God's dominion. But in John Paul II's personalist writings something terribly distinctive about human life emerges and all people are invited to see within human life an indelible mark of its sacredness. The pope breathes life into the concept of sanctity of life. For the first time since the manualist era, we have reasoned argumentation that places the "God's dominion" position into the context of creation and leaves us looking at the human as having *in se* the dignity to claim inviolability.

In the light of this innovation, then, Oliver O'Donovan's question is I think resolved. The pope, having argued that human life is intrinsically good, has now made the option to practice capital punishment even more difficult to prove.

IV. Conclusion

In this collection of essays we have a variety of Protestant theologians grappling with the recent papal encyclicals. They bring to this engagement traditional concerns. But these concerns are not "traditional" in the sense of being old-fashioned or conservative. Rather, they are

73. "The Vatican's Summary of *Evangelium Vitae*," *Origins* 24.42 (1995): 729.

traditional in the sense of expressing the living faith of those who share the same gospel of Jesus Christ. It is that tradition that both the presenters and their respondents invoke as they engage the papal writings. And, as they do, they advance that tradition with the same hope and the same intentionality as Pope John Paul II does.

Contributors

Theodor Dieter, research professor at the Institute for Ecumenical Research at Strasbourg (France), is a member of the Evangelical Lutheran Church of Württemberg (Germany). He has a major study forthcoming on *The Young Luther and Aristotle*.

Karl P. Donfried, professor of New Testament and early Christianity and chair of the Department of Religion and Biblical Literature at Smith College, Massachusetts, is a member of the Evangelical Lutheran Church of America. Among his numerous books are *The Setting of Second Clement in Early Christianity* (Leiden: E. J. Brill, 1974), *The Dynamic Word: New Testament Insights for Contemporary Christians* (San Francisco: Harper & Row, 1981), and (with I. Howard Marshall) *The Theology of the Shorter Pauline Letters* (Cambridge: Cambridge University Press, 1993).

Jean Bethke Elshtain, Laura Spelman Rockefeller Professor of Social and Political Ethics at the University of Chicago, is a member of the Evangelical Lutheran Church of America. Her most recent books are *Democracy on Trial* (New York: Basic Books, 1993), *Women and War*, 2d ed. (Chicago: University of Chicago Press, 1995), and *Augustine and the Limits of Politics* (Notre Dame, Ind.: University of Notre Dame Press, 1996).

Reinhard Hütter, associate professor of Christian ethics and theology at the Lutheran School of Theology at Chicago, is a member of the Evangelical Lutheran Church of America and has published *Evan-*

289

gelische Ethik als kirchliches Zeugnis: Interpretationen zu Schlüsselfragen theologischer Ethik in der Gegenwart (Neukirchen-Vluyn: Neukirchener Verlag, 1993) and *Theologie als kirchliche Praktik: Zur Verhältnisbestimmung von Kirche, Lehre und Theologie* (Gütersloh: Gütersloher Verlagshaus, 1997).

James F. Keenan S.J., associate professor of moral theology at Weston Jesuit School of Theology, Cambridge, Massachusetts, is a Roman Catholic and has published *Goodness and Rightness in Thomas Aquinas' Summa Theologiae* (Washington, D.C.: Georgetown University Press, 1992), *The Context of Casuistry* (Washington, D.C.: Georgetown University Press, 1995), and *Virtues for Ordinary Christians* (Kansas City: Sheed and Ward, 1996).

Lois Malcolm, assistant professor of systematic theology at Luther Seminary in St. Paul, Minnesota, holds a Ph.D. from the University of Chicago and is a member of the Evangelical Lutheran Church of America. Her forthcoming book has the title *Divine Mystery and Human Freedom: A Study of Karl Barth and Karl Rahner.*

Gilbert Meilaender holds the Board of Directors Chair in Christian Ethics at Valparaiso University, Indiana, and is a member of the Lutheran Church-Missouri Synod. Among his numerous books are *Faith and Faithfulness: Basic Themes in Christian Ethics* (Notre Dame, Ind.: University of Notre Dame Press, 1991), *Body, Soul, and Bioethics* (Notre Dame, Ind.: University of Notre Dame Press, 1995), and *Bioethics: A Primer for Christians* (Grand Rapids: Eerdmans, 1996).

Oliver O'Donovan, the Regius Professor of Moral and Pastoral Theology, Oxford University, is a member of the Church of England. Among his numerous books are *The Problem of Self-Love in St. Augustine* (New Haven: Yale University Press, 1980), *Resurrection and Moral Order: An Outline for Evangelical Ethics* (Grand Rapids: Eerdmans, 1986), and *The Desire of the Nations: Rediscovering the Roots of Political Theology* (Cambridge: Cambridge University Press, 1996).

Risto Saarinen, research professor at the Institute for Ecumenical Research at Strasbourg (France), is a member of the Evangelical

Lutheran Church of Finland. He is the author of *Gottes Wirken auf uns: Die transzendentale Deutung des Gegenwart-Christi-Motivs in der Lutherforschung* (Stuttgart: F. Steiner Verlag Wiesbaden, 1989) and *Weakness of the Will in Medieval Thought: From Augustine to Buridan* (Leiden: E. J. Brill, 1994), and *Faith and Holiness: Lutheran-Orthodox Dialogue 1959-1994* (Göttingen: Vandenhoeck & Ruprecht, 1997).

Eberhard Schockenhoff, professor of moral theology at the University of Freiburg (Germany), is Roman Catholic. Among his numerous books are *Das umstrittene Gewissen: Eine theologische Grundlegung* (Mainz: Grünewald, 1990), *Ethik des Lebens: Ein theologischer Grundriß* (Mainz: Grünewald, 1993), and *Naturrecht und Menschenwürde: Universale Ethik in einer geschichtlichen Welt* (Mainz: Grünewald, 1996).

Bernd Wannenwetsch, university lecturer of Christian ethics at the University of Erlangen (Germany), is a member of the Evangelical Lutheran Church of Bavaria (Germany). He has published *Die Freiheit der Ehe: Das Zusammenleben von Frau und Mann in der Wahrnehmung evangelischer Ethik* (Neukirchen-Vluyn: Neukirchener Verlag, 1993) and *Gottesdienst als Lebensform: Ethik für Christenbürger* (Stuttgart: Kohlhammer, 1997).

Index